GUIDE TO THE VATICAN MUSEUMS AND CITY

MONUMENTI, MUSEI E GALLERIE PONTIFICIE

PONTIFICAL MONUMENTS, MUSEUMS AND GALLERIES

General Director: *Carlo Pietrangeli*
Secretary: *Edith Cicerchia*
Treasurer: *Francesco Riccardi*

Departments

Byzantine, Medieval and Modern Art: *Fabrizio Mancinelli*
Ethnological Collection: *Father Józef Penkowski*
Nineteenth-century and Contemporary Art: *Mario Ferrazza*
Etruscan-Italic Antiquities: *Francesco Buranelli*
Classical Antiquities: *Paolo Liverani*
Epigraphical Collections: *Ivan Di Stefano Manzella*
Tapestry Collections: *Anna Maria De Strobel*

Services

Library: *Patrizia Pignatti*
Photographic Archive: *Guido Cornini*
General Inventory: *Alessandra Uncini*
Special Projects: *Patricia Bonicatti*
Scientific Research Laboratory: *Nazzareno Gabrielli*
Restoration Laboratory: *Gianluigi Colalucci*
Publications and Merchandising: *Georgina Bernett*

International coordinator of the "Patrons and Friends of the Arts
in the Vatican Museums": *Walter Persegati*

VATICAN APOSTOLIC LIBRARY

Librarian and Archivist of H.R.C.: *H.E. Cardinal Antonio M. Javierre Ortas S.D.B.*
Prefect: *Father Leonard E. Boyle O.P.*
Secretary: *Mons. Paolo De Nicolò*
Curator of Prints and Engravings: *Alfredo Diotallevi*
Curator of Museums: *Giovanni Morello*
Curator of Medals Collection: *Giancarlo Alteri*

***

© Copyright 1986 by
Gestione Vendita Pubblicazioni Musei Vaticani, Città del Vaticano
Text: Pontifical Monuments, Museums and Galleries Administration
Translation: J. Zweng
Photographs: SCALA (except for p. 139, by Mario Carrieri, and back cover, by Quilici Archives, Rome)
Plans: SCALA
Editor: Francesco Papafava
Assistant editor: Karin Stephan
Layout: Fried Rosenstock
Colour separations: Studiolito, Florence
Production: SCALA Istituto Fotografico Editoriale, Florence
Type-set: Conti Tipocolor, Calenzano Florence, 1989

Cover: ceiling of the Sistine Chapel
Back cover: aerial view of the Vatican City

TIPOGRAFIA VATICANA

TABLE OF CONTENTS

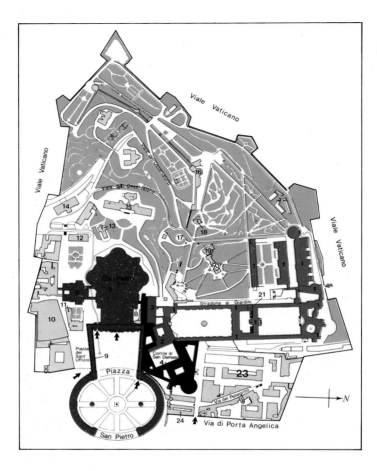

VATICAN CITY

➡ Entrance to the Vatican Museums

1 Vatican Museums
2 Medieval building of the Apostolic Palace, included in the visit to the Museums
3 Sistine Chapel
4 Buildings of the Apostolic Palace not open to the public

5 Entrance to Sacristy and Treasury
6 Sacristy and Treasury of St Peter's
7 Entrance to the Vatican Grottoes
8 Exit from the Vatican Grottoes and entrance to St Peter's dome
9 *Vatican Pilgrim and Tourist Information Bureau*
10 Papal Audience Hall
11 Teutonic College
12 Court House (Palazzo del Tribunale)
13 Church of St Stefano degli Abissini
14 Railway station
15 Government Palace
16 Offices of the Vatican Radio station
17 Bronze statue of St Peter
18 Fountain of the Eagle
19 Pontifical Academy of Sciences
20 "Casina" of Pius IV
21 Tower of the Winds
22 Fountain of the Sacrament
23 Northern area of the City with technical services
24 Barracks of the Swiss Guard

➡ MAIN ENTRANCES OF THE VATICAN CITY
from left to right:

Gate of the Holy Office
Arch of the Bells
(entrances to the Papal Audience Hall and to the City and Gardens)

Entrance to the Basilica of St Peter

Bronze Doors (Portone di Bronzo)
(entrance to the Apostolic Palace)

St Anne's Gate (Cancello di Sant'Anna)
(entrance to the northern area of the City)

▧ Vatican Museums

○─────○
Route of the regular bus service connecting the Vatican Museums with St Peter's Square (charge)

▦ Medieval building of the Apostolic Palace, included in the visit to the Museums

■ Buildings of the Apostolic Palace not open to the public

▨ St Peter's Square and Basilica

▨ Buildings in the gardens and city

▧ Vatican Gardens

Brief history of the Vatican

THE VATICAN REGION

The city of ancient Rome virtually stopped at the left bank of the Tiber. The right bank, until the beginning of the Imperial Age, was limited to ancillary wharves, a few small kilns, and small farms scattered among large areas of uncultivated land, parts of which were unhealthy fens.

Looking across the river from the city, an inhabitant of ancient Rome would have seen a flat strip of land, the *ager vaticanus*, running along the far bank, and, in the background, a range of hills, the *montes vaticani*, lying more or less parallel to the river. Both areas took their names from an ancient place-name derived from an Etruscan root, *vatico or vatica*. Strictly speaking, the *montes vaticani* were the hills to the north of Janiculum Hill, but the name was sometimes used to refer to Janiculum itself and even to the whole region. The very vagueness of the name indicates that the city had not yet expanded to include the district across the river, a fact also borne out by the sweeping name of *trans Tiberim* given to the 14th Augustan region, including the Vatican.

Towards the end of the Republican Age, the privileged classes began to build villas in the *trans Tiberim*. Agrippina, mother of the emperor Caligula (37-41 A.D.) laid out pleasant gardens on the land surrounding her villa. These gardens, together with those of the Domitian family, later formed the *horti Neronis*, the famous gardens of the emperor Nero (54-68 A.D.). Nero completed the circus which Gaius (Caligula) had begun, and embellished it with an obelisk brought from Egypt (the one now standing in St Peter's Square). The gardens also contained a *naumachia* (a stadium for naval contests) built by Augustus, and another one close to the hill; then there was a *gaianum* (a kind of hippodrome), created by Caligula. In short, the area was a large park devoted to sports and recreation. And among the cruelest spectacles that Nero was able to devise was the torture of numerous Christians, who were crucified and burnt in the circus (Tacitus, Annals, XV, 44).

Among Nero's victims was St Peter himself, who was buried a short distance from the place of his martyrdom. Constantine consecrated the memory of the apostle by building a basilica on the site in 324, during the papacy of Silvester I.

The city of Rome was literally degraded when Constantine transferred the capital of the Empire to Constantinople. Then came the sad times of the barbarian invasions: the Goths of Alaric (410), the Vandals of Genseric (445), and the terrible sieges laid by the Goths of Witigis (537-538) and Totila (545-546). As the old city withdrew further and further into itself, a new, thickly-populated quarter developed round the Vatican basilica. The inhabitants of this unfortified settlement may have counted on the relative immunity which the Christianized barbarians had so far granted the "holy place". In fact, it was invaders of another faith, the Saracens, who finally sacked St Peter's and St Paul's (in 846, during the papacy of Sergius II). As a result of this invasion, Pope Leo IV built strong defensive walls round the area surrounding the basilica, from Castel Sant'Angelo to the western foot of the Vatican hill. From that time on, the Vatican was referred to as a city (the "Leonine City").

THE RESIDENCE OF THE BISHOPS OF ROME

Originally, the official residence of the Bishops of Rome was not the Vatican, but the Lateran Palace, which once belonged to the Roman family of the Laterans, and was donated to the Roman Church. St Peter's was then an out-of-the-way basilica reserved for burials, as was St Paul's, on the Via Ostiensis. For the popes, the initial problem was merely one of finding temporary accomodation at the Vatican when they came to St Peter's for liturgical reasons. The first to build at the Vatican was Pope Symmachus, who, having been forced to abandon the Lateran for the duration of the Laurentian Schism (501-506), built two episcopal residences at the sides of the basilica. In 781 Charlemagne altered, for his own use, a palace standing to the north of the basilica. Eugene III built a "new palace", which Innocent III enlarged and enclosed within turreted walls.

Nicholas III was the first pope to adopt the Vatican as his permanent residence. For this reason he began, but did not complete, a fortified residence with angle towers, built round the present Court of the Pappagallo. He also built a new defensive wall, reinforced by battlements and towers, which probably extended to the north as far as the Mount of St Egidius, where two centuries later Innocent VIII was to build his Belvedere Palace.

The military character of these early buildings testifies to their use by the popes as an emergency refuge. The exile of Avignon (1305-77), and the Great Western Schism (1378-1417) signified a period of extreme neglect for all the edifices of Rome.

Recovery came during the papacy of Nicholas V, the humanist Tommaso Parentucelli. A new chapter was begun, in which the old concept of the Vatican as a fortified palace, as the papal seat *apud Sanctum Petrum*, was infused with the spirit of the early Renaissance.

THE VATICAN MUSEUMS

It was this spirit which inspired the creation of two of the most illustratious of the humanistic institutions of the Holy See: the Vatican Library and the Vatican Museums. Both were the out-come of a vision of Graeco-Roman culture as the perfect, almost timeless expression of human creativity at its highest levels—thought and art—, and as the precursor, at times almost the prefigurament, of Christianity, above all in the West. The Vatican Museums originated in the court of Innocent VIII's Belvedere Palace, which Julius II laid out in gardens and embellished with masterpieces of classical sculpture: the Apollo (consequently known as the "Apollo Belvedere"), the Venus Felix, the Laocoön, the Nile, the Tiber, and the Sleeping Ariadne. Other pieces of sculpture were used to decorate the Apostolic Palace itself (the Loggia of Raphael, for instance, in the time of Leo X).

The first reference to an art collection (or a "cabinet of rarities") in the Library, founded by Sixtus IV in 1475, goes back to the prefecture of Marcello Cervini, later Pope Marcellus II (1555).

The spirit of the Counter-Reformation (remember the austere St Pius V), with is moralistic rejection of the arts of antiquity, soon brought the growth of the Vatican collection to a standstill. However, the new emphasis on the defence of the Faith laid the rudimentary foundations for a study of the arts of antiquity that was both historical and archeological in approach, and no longer purely aesthetic.

The eighteenth century saw the first manifestations of the new approach. In 1756 Benedict XIV founded the Christian Museum of the Library "to increase", reads the inscription over the entrance, "the splendour of the City, and bear witness to the truth of religion through sacred Christian monuments". In 1767 Clement XIII founded the Profane Museum "to preserve the monuments of Roman antiquity".

Their responsibility for preserving a patrimony threatened by, among other things, the ever increasing exportation of antiquities, led the popes (Clement XIV, Pius VI, Pius VII) to set up the Pio-Clementine Museum

(1771-93), the Chiaramonti Museum and the Lapidary Gallery (1807-10), and the Braccio Nuovo (1822). The realization of the new museums involved renewed building activity, a sizable financial obligation (Monsignor Gian Angelo Braschi, Clement XIV's Treasurer General and successor—Pius VI—, used lottery proceeds to purchase antiquities) and the consultation of specialists (Johann Joachim Winckelmann, Commissioner of Antiquities of the Papal State 1763-68, and Antonio Canova, Inspector General of Antiquities and Fine Arts 1802-22). Of considerable importance to the preservation of antiquities was the realization of legislation, thanks also to the experience with the French under the Treaty of Tolentino, regarding archeological excavations, and trade in antiquities: the Pacca Edict of 1820, which regulated excavation and assured the right of first choice to public collections.

As a consequence of the intensive excavations carried out in Southern Etruria in the early 19th century, the enforcement of the law made a new museum "of Etruscan monuments" indispensable: the Gregorian Etruscan Museum was opened by Gregory XVI in 1837. The deciphering of hieroglyphics (by Jean-François Champollion, 1822) stimulated a similar interest in Egyptian antiquities: the Gregorian Egyptian Museum was opened in 1839.

New space for the classical antiquities that were continually coming to light in the Vatican State was found in the Lateran Palace, in the Gregorian Profane Museum, founded by Gregory XVI in 1844. A significant collection of Christian antiquities was established by Pius IX in 1854, two years after the creation of the Commission for Christian Archeology.

With the end of the Vatican State (1870), and the consequent reduction of its territorial jurisdiction, two lines of development presented themselves to the Vatican Museums. The first was to continue the critical study and exhibition of their traditional patrimony; the second to expand in a direction more expressly in keeping with the nature of the Church's mission in the world. The former led to the foundation of the Pinacoteca (Pius XI, 1932), in which the paintings taken away by Napoleon under the Treaty of Tolentino (1797), and returned after the Congress of Vienna (1815), were finally exhibited to the public; to the setting up of the Rooms of the Greek Originals (1960), outcome of a more precise identification of the specifically Greek characteristics of works formerly classified as Graeco-Roman (in 1988 the department was transferred to the Gregorian Profane Museum); and to the transfer to the Vatican, and subsequent exhibition of the Lateran collections: the Gregorian Profane and Pio Christian museums (1970), and the Missionary-Ethnological Museum (1973).

The second line of development led from the foundation of the Missionary-Ethnological Museum (Pius XI, 1926) to that of the Collection of Modern Religious Art (Paul VI, 1973). The Historical Museum (1973), in which old papal berlins, and arms and uniforms of the Vatican armed forces, disbanded in 1970, have now become history, may also be considered an indirect result of this new vision. The Museum was later (1985) divided into Historical Museum proper, housed in the Lateran, and the Carriage Museum.

3

THE CITY OF THE VATICAN

The great complex of the present papal apartments was built in 1589-1590 by Domenico Fontana during the reign of Sixtus V in the late Renaissance. During the Baroque age, Rome was radically transformed and the Basilica acquired its distinctive style. The Apostolic Palace, however, was not changed significantly. The Vatican was neglected because a new palace on the Quirinal hill, built by Gregory XIII, became the residence of subsequent popes who preferred it because of its healthier air.

During the papacy of Urban VIII, the work begun about a century earlier by Paul III was completed and the area of the Vatican was given a new set of walls, which were much larger and stronger than the earlier "Leonine" walls. Since then, these walls and the colonnade of St Peter's Square form the boundaries of the Vatican state.

The definitive return of the Popes to the Vatican, to the place where Peter, the first bishop of Rome, was killed and buried, only took place under Pius IX, after the unification of Italy and the capture of Rome in 1870.

As a result of these events, the territorial dominion of the Papacy came to an end. From the 8th century on, the papal dominions gradually grew to include the regions of Latium, Umbria, the Marches and Romagna, and guaranteed the independence of the popes. When Rome became the capital of the newly formed Italian State in 1870, the Pope withdrew to the Vatican, where his successors have lived ever since.

In order to guarantee the independence of the Papacy, it seemed necessary to reconstitute some form of temporal sovereignty. With the occupation of Rome, the Pope became a private citizen subject to Italian law. His juridical position as well as his freedom to perform his religious duties could have been modified by the laws of the Italian State. For this reason, in February 1929, the Lateran Pact was stipulated between the Italian State and the Holy See. This agreement recognized the sovereignty of the Pope over the area of St Peter's Basilica and Square and the surrounding territory within the Vatican walls, thus creating the Vatican City State. According to the terms of the Lateran Pact, this State is considered neutral territory. The spiritual significance and the art treasures of the Vatican State are protected by the Hague Convention (May 14, 1954), which provides for the protection of its cultural patrimony in the event of armed conflict. The State is thus recognized internationally for its moral, artistic and cultural patrimony, as worthy of respect and protection and as a heritage to all mankind.

The Pope, then, is both head of the Catholic Church and sovereign of the State. He carries out his primary ecclesiastical functions of teaching and pastoral activity through the organs of the Church, particularly the "Segreteria di Stato". Together with the Papacy, these organs constitute the Roman Curia (the central government of the Catholic Church). The Holy See has permanent representatives at the U.N. and in some of its organizations, such as UNESCO, FAO, UNIDO, WHO, ITU.

As far as the government of the Vatican City is concerned, the Pope exercizes legislative and executive powers by means of a Committee composed of a few cardinals. The Committee is renewed every five years. (Cardinals are nominated by the Pope and are his most important advisors. They also elect the new Pope when the Papal throne is vacant.) The Pontifical Commission is in charge of the various government offices which provide for the needs of the small State. The Vatican City has about nine hundred inhabitants (including two hundred women), and covers a surface of 44 hectares (1045 m. × 850 m.). It has a military organization (the Swiss Guard, consisting of about one hundred men, who protect the Pope's person and the main entrances to the City); a flag (yellow and white with St. Peter's keys under the triple crown); a national anthem (the Pontifical March by Charles Gounod); its own currency, postage stamps and car licence plate (SCV, today CV). It also has a post office and telegraph service, a radio station, a railway station and other services. The first radio transmitting station (1931) was located in the Vatican City, but the present more powerful station, built in 1957, is located about 25 km from Rome at Santa Maria di Galeria. Most of the 1300 employees of the Vatican government are non-resident.

In the Vatican City State, justice is administered by a judge, a Court of Assizes, a Court of Appeal, and a Supreme Court, which exercise their powers in the name of the Sovereign Pontiff.

The Vatican City State is recognized by the international community as a legal sovereign body, and it is a member of various international organizations (Universal Postal Union, International Telecommunications Union, International Union for the Protection of Literary and Artistic Works).

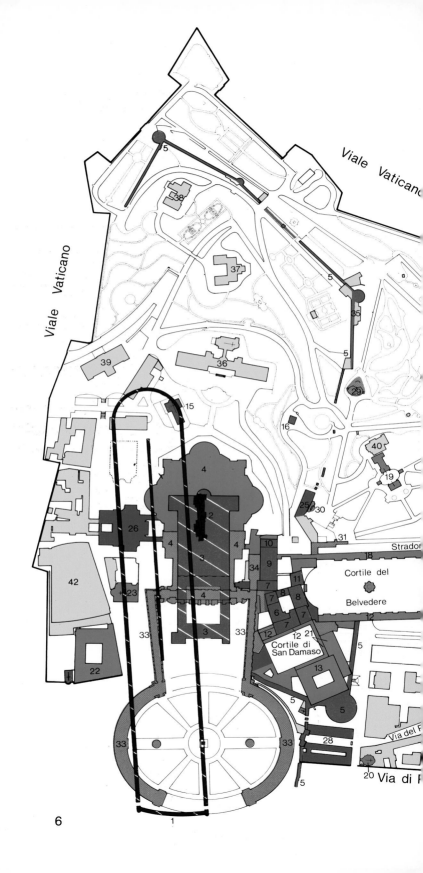

Viale Vaticano

Viale Vaticano

Stradon

Cortile del

Belvedere

Cortile di
San Damaso

Via del F

20 Via di F

6

HISTORICAL PLAN
OF THE VATICAN CITY

1 The circus of Nero and Caligula
2 Pre-Constantinian Necropolis
3 Constantinian Basilica
4 Present Basilica
5 Walls of Leo IV and Nicholas V

Development of the Apostolic Palace until the end
of the 16th century
6 Eugene III and Innocent III
7 Nicholas III
8 Nicholas V (see also 5)
9 Sixtus IV
10 Innocent VIII
11 Alexander VI
12 Julius II
13 Sixtus V

Buildings of major interest, not cited in the Introduction
14 Church of San Pellegrino
15 Church of Santo Stefano degli Abissini
16 House of the Gardener
17 Tower of Innocent VIII
18 Corridor of the west wing of the Court of the "Belvedere", built under Pius IV by Pirro Ligorio from a drawing by Bramante
19 "Casina" of Pius IV
20 Church of St. Anne
21 Loggias and Palace of Gregory XIII
22 Palace of the Holy Office (Palazzo del Sant'Uffizio)
23 Church of the Teutonic College
24 Museo Pio-Clementino
25 The Mint (Palazzo della Zecca)
26 Canonical Palace and Sacristy of St. Peter's
27 "Braccio Nuovo" of the Vatican Museums
28 Swiss Guard Barracks
29 Fountain of the Eagle
30 Fountain of the Sacrament
31 Building of Paul V and Fountain of the Mirrors
32 Fountain of the Galley
33 Colonnade of St. Peter's Square, by Bernini
34 Royal Stairway (Scala Regia), by Bernini
35 Villa of Leo XIII
36 Government Palace (Palazzo del Governatorato)
37 Ethiopian College
38 First Vatican radio station
39 Railway station
40 Pontifical Academy of Sciences
41 Vatican Pinacoteca
42 Papal Audience Hall
43 New wing of the Vatican Museums
44 Carriage Museum

Viale Vaticano

17

41 43

13 24

Cortile
della
Pigna   12

27   12   24

10

32 12

ini

ngelica

N

■ Classical Antiquity
■ Medieval
■ 16th century
▨ 17th century
■ 18th-19th centuries
□ 20th century

7

How to use this guide

PONTIFICAL MONUMENTS, MUSEUMS AND GALLERIES
including the Sistine Chapel

The text of this guide is divided into as many chapters as there are traditional sections of the Museums, each of which is described in the order in which it is visited.

References to areas of the Museums, or to works exhibited in these areas, are made as follows:

lower case letters indicate the main sections, each of which has a corresponding chapter in the guide (for instance: **f - Pio-Clementine Museum**);

Roman numerals indicate further subdivisions of the sections, each of which corresponds to a paragraph in the text (for instance: **VIII, OCTA-GONAL COURT** in the f - Pio-Clementine Museum);

Arabic numerals along the coloured edge of the pages refer to the single works described in the text; they are repeated on the relevant plan of the section to show the location of the works (for instance: the **Laocoön**, which is in the VIII, OCTAGONAL COURT in the f - Pio-Clementine Museum, is indicated by the number **5** on the edge of the page).

COLOURS

In this guide, various colour-keys are used to:

1. *Classify works and rooms according to periods or styles.* With few exceptions, distinct periods or styles of works correspond to the sections of the Museums. Each period or style is indicated by a colour, which is reproduced on the general plan of the Museums (pp. 24-25) and on the detailed plans in the text. The colours distinguish periods or styles of works as follows (see also p. 22):

▨ Oriental antiquities (Egypt and Assyria)

▨ classical antiquities (Graeco-Roman art)

▨ Etruscan-Italic antiquities (pre-Roman Italy)

▨ early Christian and medieval art (3rd-14th cent.)

▨ from the Renaissance (15th cent.) to the 19th century

▨ ethnology and history

▨ contemporary art (20th cent.)

2. *Distinguish 4 different itineraries for visitors,* and to indicate their routes within the Museums (see the "Illustrated scheme of the 4 suggested and indicated itineraries", pp. 16-21). The colours of this classification, with their relative capital letters, are reproduced in small squares at the top of the pages, to the side of the text.

THE ONE-WAY SYSTEM FOR VISITS

The Vatican Museums include structures of great historical and aesthetic interest, among which is the original medieval nucleus of the Apostolic Palace, renovated and decorated in the Renaissance (15th-16th cent.), as well as the galleries and museums proper. They make up a complex of imposing proportions, with more than 42,000 square metres at the disposal of the public, and more than seven kilometres of exhibitions. The various periods and types of buildings, the various uses for which the rooms were originally intended, and the great distances, as well as the large number of visitors, have made it necessary to adopt the *one-way system for visits*. This helps visitors to "find their way", though it does make it difficult to visit "freely" and selectively. Without this system, visitors would have to plan a personal itinerary before the visit so as not to continually retrace their steps.

THE 4 SUGGESTED AND INDICATED ITINERARIES

To help the visitor, the Museums Administration has designed 4 itineraries that take into account both the time available and personal preferences.

Visitors are advised to *choose one of the 4 itineraries* (see also the "illustrated scheme of the 4 suggested and indicated itineraries", pp. 16-21, and the table on p. 23) *before beginning the visit,* and to follow the route indicated, throughout the Museums, by the letter and colour key of the chosen itinerary.

The 4 itineraries are as follows:

A (violet).

Requires about an hour and a half.

This is the shortest itinerary from the entrance to the Sistine Chapel, and from the latter to the exit (which is the same entrance). It includes:

A selection of *classical art* (sculpture in the Gallery of the Candelabra, pp. 67-69); tapestries of the 16th and 17th centuries (Gallery of Tapestries, p. 70); *frescoes and decorations* (Gallery of Maps, p. 71); *Flemish tapestries and antique and medieval fabrics* (Apartment of St Pius V, p. 72) the *Sistine Chapel* (Michelangelo, Perugino, Botticelli, Ghirlandaio, Signorelli, etc., pp. 92-99); *minor arts* (enamel-work, jewelry, ivories, etc. in the exhibition galleries of the Vatican Library), and *ancient objects and instruments* (in the same galleries, pp. 100-104).

B (beige), and

C (green).

The first requires about 3 hours, the second about 3 and a half hours.

These are two alternative itineraries, not complete but selective, that allow visitors to see a large part of the Museums, choosing the sections that most interest them. The description follows:

B

To the sections of the shortest itinerary (A), the visitor adds:

Etruscan-Italic art (Gregorian Etruscan Museum, pp. 50-65); the *Roman frescoes* of the Room of the Aldobrandini Wedding (p. 101: X); the *masterpieces of the Pinacoteca* (paintings on wood and canvas, as well as frescoes and tapestries, by artists of nine centuries, pp. 104-112); *classical sculpture and Roman mosaics* (Gregorian Profane Museum, pp. 113-132), *early Christian art* (Pio Christian Museum, pp. 133-138), *ethnology* (Missionary-Ethnological Museum, pp. 139-152)— the last three museums are in the new wing of the Vatican Museums that was awarded a prize for its bold insertion into the historical Vatican complex; and *carriages of historical interest* (Carriage Museum, pp. 153-154).

C

As an alternative to itinerary B, the visitor adds the following to the sections included in the shortest itinerary (A):

The *mummies, objects and sculpture of the Gregorian Egyptian Museum* (pp. 29-32); the *classical art* of the Chiaramonti Museum (pp. 33-34), of the Pio-Clementine Museum (pp. 39-49) and of the Braccio Nuovo (pp. 35-37); the *frescoes by Raphael* (Stanze, pp. 74-78) and by *Fra Angelico* (Chapel of Nicholas V, pp. 83-84); *frescoes by Pinturicchio* (Borgia Apartment, pp. 85-89); the *Collection of Modern Religious Art* (in the Borgia Apartment and the galleries below the Sistine Chapel, pp. 90-91); and finally the *ancient illuminated codici* in the sumptuous Sistine Salon (p. 101: V) of the Vatican Library.

D (yellow).

Requires 5 hours or more.

This is the complete itinerary for those who wish to have only a general idea of the rooms and contents of all the Vatican Museums, leaving special interests for a later visit. This itinerary *includes all the sections* indicated in itineraries *A, B* and *C.*

THE CHOICE OF ITINERARY

Visitors can use either the descriptions contained in this guide, or the large notice-board near the entrance to help them to choose their itineraries. There are also notice-boards at several points along the 4 routes, in the Museums, to remind visitors of the contents of their itineraries.

On these notice-boards, the itineraries are described by means of photographs that symbolize the contents of each section of the Museums.—The same photographs appear at the beginning of each chapter of this guide, as each chapter corresponds to a section of the Museums.

Once again it is recommended that the *choice of itinerary be made at the beginning of the visit,* even though it is possible to make changes on the way.

The list of popes mentioned in the text, together with the dates of their respective papacies (p. 193), and the list of artists (pp. 195-196) facilitate the chronological reference to facts and works cited in the text.

Useful information for visitors

plan
p. IV

PONTIFICAL MONUMENTS, MUSEUMS AND GALLERIES
including the Sistine Chapel
(see also plan pp. 24-25)

The Vatican Museums are open with admission charge weekdays from 8.45 a.m. to 1.45 p.m. (8.45 a.m. to 4.45 p.m. during the Easter period, and from 1 July to 30 September, except on Saturdays when the hours remain 8.45 a.m. to 1.45 p.m.); no admittance in the last 45 minutes before closing time. Open also the last Sunday of every month (when admission is free), unless it falls on Easter, 29 June, Christmas or 26 December. The Museums are also closed on the following holidays: 1 and 6 January, 11 February, 19 March, Easter Monday, 1 May and Ascension Day, Corpus Christi Day, 29 June, 15-16 August, 1 November, and 8, 25 and 26 December.

Teleguides (in English, French, Italian, German and Spanish) prepared by the Museums Administration are transmitted continuously in the Sistine Chapel and Raphael Stanze. Listening devices are hired out at the entrance to the Raphael Stanze, and collected at the exit of the Sistine Chapel.

A self-service restaurant is open during museum hours.

There is a post office with writing-room.

There is a foreign currency exchange office.

There are three first aid stations.

The Museums are equipped with facilities for disabled visitors. Apply at the Information Office or at the ticket control counter. Wheelchairs are available, though it is advisable to reserve them (tel. 698.333.2).

A regular bus service connects the Museums with St Peter's Square (charge).

Exhibits and rooms may be photographed with hand cameras.

The use of tripods requires the permission of the Administration. The use of flash equipment is prohibited during museum hours.

Works and entire sections of the Vatican Museums are protected by a closed-circuit television system and by electronic alarm equipment. Visitors are therefore advised to respect areas marked off by transennae, ropes and the like, and to refrain at all times from touching exhibits.

As the tourist guides waiting inside the entrance to the Vatican Museums are not employees of the Museums, they are obliged to observe the charges posted in the entrance-hall.

PAPAL AUDIENCES

Public audiences are usually held on Wednesday at 11 a.m. in the Papal Audience Hall (10) (from November to February) and in the afternoon in St Peter's Square (March to October). Permission to attend can be obtained from the Prefecture of the Pontifical House, whose office is accessible through the Bronze Doors in St Peter's Square. The office is usually open on Tuesdays from 9 a.m. to 1 p.m., and on Wednesdays from 9 a.m. till shortly before the audience.

VATICAN CITY
(see also plan p. 160-161)

The following GUIDED TOURS are organized by the Vatican Pilgrim and Tourist Information Bureau (open every day except Sunday and important religious holidays from 8.30 a.m. to 6.30 p.m.) in St. Peter's Square (9):

Visit to the City and Gardens (2 hrs)

Buses depart at 10 a.m.: from March to October, every Friday; from November to February, every Tuesday, Thursday and Saturday.

Visit to the City and Gardens, including the Sistine Chapel (3 hrs)

Buses depart at 10 a.m.: from March to October only, every Monday and Thursday.

Visit to the City and Gardens, including St Peter's Basilica (3 hrs)

Buses leave at 10 a.m.: from March to October only, every Tuesday and Saturday.

Visitors are advised to buy tickets two days in advance. Buses leave from the Information Bureau (9).

ST. PETER'S BASILICA
(see also plan p. 173)

Entrance from St Peter's Square, every day from 7 a.m. to 6 p.m., in the summer to 7 p.m.; FREE ADMISSION. See above for guided tours.

Members of the "Peregrinatio ad Petri Sedem" (information booth in the atrium to the right of the entrance) provide a free guide service (in 24 languages) only to St. Peter's Basilica for the purpose of illustrating its spiritual as well as its historical and artistic significance.

Visit to the Dome

Entrance from the right side of the basilica (8), every day from 8 a.m. to 4.45 p.m., in the summer to 6.15 p.m. (lift available as far as the terrace); admission charge.

Treasury of St Peter's

In the Sacristy (6), entrance from the Basilica (5). Every day from 9 a.m. to 12.30 p.m., and from 3 p.m. to 4.30 p.m., in the summer to 6.30 p.m.; admission charge.

Vatican Grottoes

Below the aisles of the Basilica, entrance from the transept (7). Every day from 7 a.m. to 5.30 p.m., in the summer to 6 p.m.; free admission.

Pre-Constantinian Necropolis

Below the Vatican Grottoes. For permission to visit the Necropolis, write to the Reverenda Fabbrica di San Pietro, Ufficio Scavi (00120 Città del Vaticano), specifying names of visitors in group, languages spoken, address and telephone number in Rome, and length of stay.

GUIDE TO THE VATICAN MUSEUMS

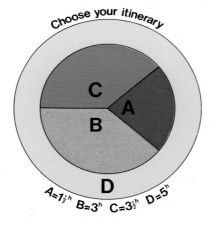

Chronological index to the history of the Museums

Julius II
1503 The pope places the statue of Apollo, subsequently known as the "Apollo Belvedere", in the inner court of the Belvedere Palace of Innocent VIII.
1506 14 January: discovery on Esquiline Hill of the marble Laocoön group.

Clement VII
1530 ca.: acquisition of the "Belvedere Torso", formerly in the Palazzo Colonna.

Clement XI
1700-21 First plan to gather ancient, pagan and Christian inscriptions, and to found a museum of Christian antiquities.

Clement XII
1730-40 Acquisition for the Vatican Library of precious manuscripts, 200 vases traditionally known as "Etruscan", and 328 ancient medals.

Benedict XIV
1740-58 Foundation of the Christian Museum of the Vatican Library (1756). First director: Francesco Vettori. Arrangement of the lapidary collection in the north end of the Bramante Corridor is begun as proposed by Giuseppe Bianchini. Ridolfino Venuti is nominated Commissioner of Roman Antiquities (1745).

Clement XIII
1764 Johann Joachim Winckelmann is appointed Commissioner of Roman Antiquities and *Scriptor* of the Library with the task of directing a future Vatican Museum of Classical Antiquities.
1767 Foundation of the Profane Museum of the Vatican Library.

Clement XIV
1770 Acquisition of the Mattei collection of classical antiquities.
1771-73 Building of the Clementine Museum. Architects: Alessandro Dori (died 1772) and Michelangelo Simonetti. Commissioner of Roman Antiquities: Giovanni Battista Visconti. Chief restorer: Gaspare Sibilla.
1774 Completion of the lapidary collection by Gaetano Marini.

Pius VI
1776-84 The Clementine Museum is enlarged with the construction of the Piano Museum and by acquisitions and excavations in numerous parts of the Pontifical State; in 1784 the Pio-Clementine Museum is nearly completed. Architect: Michelangelo Simonetti; Commissioner of Antiquities: Giambattista Visconti (died 1784), assisted by his son Ennio Quirino. Chief restorers: Gaspare Sibilla and Giovanni Pierantoni.
1785-88 Closing in of the Covered Loggia above the south wing of the Library and arrangement of the Gallery of the Candelabra. Architects: Michelangelo Simonetti (died 1787) and Giuseppe Camporese; Commissioner of Roman Antiquities: Filippo Aurelio Visconti; Chief restorer: Giovanni Pierantoni.
1790 Arrangement, in the present Gallery of Tapestries, of the first Vatican Pinacoteca.
1793 Completion of the Atrium of the Four Gates as entrance to the Pio-Clementine Museum. Architect: G. Camporese.
1797 The masterpieces of the Pio-Clementine Museum are taken to Paris on the basis of the Treaty of Tolentino.
1798-1800 During the Franco-Neapolitan occupation, the Profane Museum of the Library loses its collection of gems, coins and medals forever.

Pius VII
1800 Abbot Carlo Fea is appointed Commissioner of Antiquities.
1801 Acquisition of Antonio Canova's Perseus.
1802 A. Canova is appointed General Inspector of Fine Arts. Dispersion within the Vatican palaces of the first Pinacoteca. 2 October: Doria Pamphilj Edict on the protection of works of art.
1807-10 Canova arranges the Chiaramonti Museum. Amplification and definitive arrangement of the inscription collection in the Lapidary Gallery by Gaetano Marini. Foundation of a new numismatic collection (medals).
1814 The tapestries of the "Old" and "New" schools of Raphael are exhibited in the apartment of St Pius V.
1815 A series of Etruscan, Greek and Italiot vases is added to the Vatican Library.
1816 4 January and 11 August: return from Paris of the masterpieces of the Pio-Clementine Museum, thanks to the dictate of the Congress of Vienna (1815), and of the paintings taken from various places in the Vatican State. 21 February: foundation of the Pinacoteca (the pope decides to place the paintings returned from Paris in the Borgia Apartment).
1818 Acquisition of the Roman fresco known as "the Aldobrandini Wedding".
1820 The Vatican Library acquires the collection of Agostino Mariotti. 7 April: Pacca Edict, which regulates excavations and trade in antiquities.
1821 The Pinacoteca is transferred to the Apartment of Gregory XIII (the Bologna Room and adjacent ones).
1822 Opening of the Braccio Nuovo. Architect: Raffaele Stern (died 1820); work completed by Pasquale Belli.

Leo XII, Pius VIII, Gregory XVI
1827-36 Excavation and acquisition of antiquities from Etruria and Latium, and of Greek ceramics. Excavations by the Pontifical Government in association with Secondiano Campanari, at Vulci.

Gregory XVI
1831 The Pinacoteca is re-established in the present Gallery of Tapestries.
1835 2 June: discovery of the "Mars of Todi".
1836 Transfer of the Pinacoteca to the apartment of St Pius V.
1836-37 Excavation and acquisition of the contents of the "Regolini-Galassi" tomb at Caere.

14

1837 2 February: inauguration of the Gregorian Etruscan Museum.
Acquisition by the Library of a collection of paintings of the so-called "primitives".
1838 Arrangement of the Gallery of Tapestries and of the Room of Antique Frescoes in their present sites.
1839 2 February: inauguration of the Gregorian Egyptian Museum.
1844 14 May: inauguration of the Gregorian Profane Museum in the Lateran Palace and the Lateran Picture Gallery.

Pius IX
1852 Setting up of the Commission for Christian Archeology to supervise excavations and maintenance of the catacombs.
1853 The city of Rome donates to the pope the series of Roman frescoes with scenes from the Odyssey.
1854 Foundation of the Pio Christian Museum in the Lateran Palace.
1855-70 Excavations in Ostia; the antiquities found will be displayed in the last two rooms of the Lateran Profane Museum.
1857 The Pinacoteca returns to the apartment of Gregory XIII.

Leo XIII
1898 Acquisition of the Falcioni Collection of Etruscan-Roman antiquities.

Pius X
1906 The treasures of the Sancta Sanctorum are placed in the Christian Museum of the Vatican Library.
1909 19 March: inauguration of the Pinacoteca, after its various travels in the Vatican palaces, in its new site in the gallery below the Christian Museum of the Library. Transfer from the Library to the Pinacoteca of the Byzantine and so-called primitive (i.e. early Italian, 13th-15th cent.) paintings acquired by Gregory XVI and Pius IX, and of the picture gallery of the Lateran Palace.

Pius XI
1923 Definitive establishment of the restoration laboratories.
1925 Inauguration (19 February) of the new arrangement of the Gregorian Etruscan Museum. Missionary Exhibition in the Vatican: occasion for the founding (21 December 1926) of the Missionary-Ethnological Museum in the Lateran Palace.
1929 Institution of the Vatican City State.
1932 New entrance to the Vatican Museums from the Viale Vaticano. Architect: Giuseppe Momo. Sculptural decoration: Antonio Maraini. Inauguration (27 October) of the definitive seat of the Vatican Pinacoteca. Architect: Luca Beltrami.
1933 Creation of the Department of Scientific Research.
1935 Donation to the pope of the Benedetto Guglielmi Collection of vases and Greek and Etruscan bronzes.

Pius XII
1951 Donation to the pope of the Carlo Grassi Collection of Egyptian minor antiquities.
1955-60 The Gregorian Etruscan Museum extends to the whole upper floor of the restored Belvedere Palace of Innocent VIII, and to the Upper Hemicycle of Pirro Ligorio's "Nicchione".
1957-60 Restoration of the Laocoön: application of the original right arm, found in 1905 by Ludwig Pollak, by Filippo Magi.

John XXIII
1960 Opening of the Rooms of the Greek Originals.
1963 A new edifice is erected by the architectural studio of the brothers Fausto, Lucio and Vincenzo Passarelli, to house the three collections formerly exhibited in the Lateran Palace (Gregorian Profane Museum, Pio Christian Museum and Missionary-Ethnological Museum).

Paul VI
1965 Renovation and rearrangement of the Egyptian Museum is begun.
1967 Donation to the pope of the Teresa and Tommaso Astarita Collection of Etruscan, Italiot and Greek ceramics.
1970 Inauguration of the Gregorian Profane and Pio Christian Museums, formerly in the Lateran Palace, in the new building erected for this purpose designed by the Passarelli brothers.
1972-75 New placement of some works of the Pio-Clementine Museum to facilitate the flow of visitors. Installation of a diurnal televisionary control and telecommunications system. Substantial changes made to visitor services, with new post office, foreign exchange office, writing-room, first aid stations, cloak-room and refreshment vending machines. Building of a new stairway for the exit of tour groups from the Sistine Chapel to St Peter's Square.
1973 Inauguration of the Missionary-Ethnological Museum, formerly in the Lateran Palace. Inauguration of the Carriage Museum, and of the Collection of Modern Religious Art. New arrangement of the first three rooms (of the so-called Primitives) of the Pinacoteca.
1976 Re-opening of the first and second rooms of the Egyptian Museum, completely renovated.
1977 Renovation and rearrangement of the Room of the Greek Originals. Changes in the arrangement of the Rooms of Raphael of the Pinacoteca. The publication of a "Bulletin of the Vatican Museums" is begun. Setting up of selective itineraries for visitors, with routes indicated by a colour-key.

John Paul II
1979 New arrangement of the first three rooms of the Etruscan Museum.
1980 New arrangement of the Court of the Pigna. The base of Antoninus' Column is moved to the court of the Corazze. New arrangement of the Profane Epigraphical Collection from the Lateran.
1981 Beginning of restoration of frescoes by Michelangelo in the Sistine Chapel.
1982 Restructuring of the Restoration and Scientific Research Laboratories.
1984 New rooms of Byzantine icons and of the original models by Bernini in the Pinacoteca.
1985 Historical Museum transferred to the Lateran. Foundation of the Carriage Museum, formerly a section of the Historical Museum.
1987 Equipping of the itineraries for disabled visitors in wheelchairs.
1988 Acquisition of the second part of the Guglielmi Collection for the Gregorian Etruscan Museum. Transfer of the «Greek Originals» from the rooms named after them to the Gregorian Profane Museum.
1989 Restructuring of the first four rooms of the Gregorian Egyptian Museum. Completion of the restoration of the Sistine Chapel ceiling.

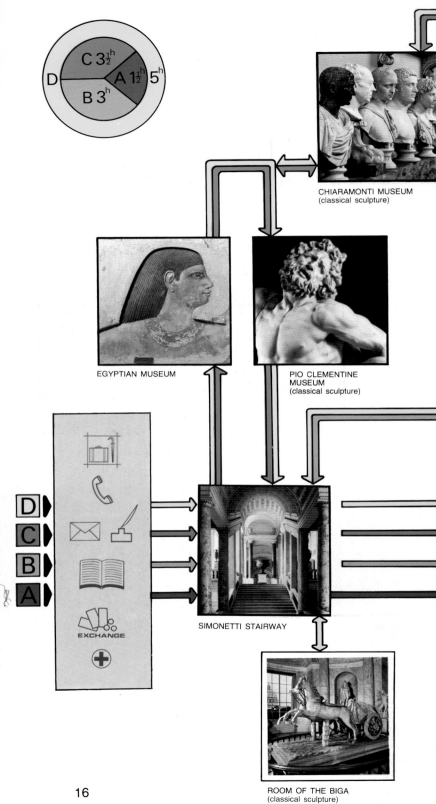

CHIARAMONTI MUSEUM
(classical sculpture)

EGYPTIAN MUSEUM

PIO CLEMENTINE
MUSEUM
(classical sculpture)

SIMONETTI STAIRWAY

ROOM OF THE BIGA
(classical sculpture)

EXCHANGE

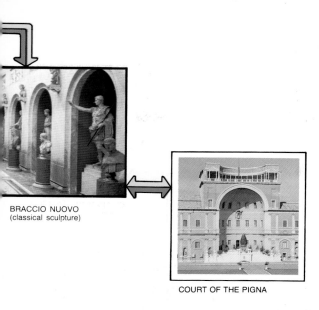

BRACCIO NUOVO
(classical sculpture)

COURT OF THE PIGNA

ETRUSCAN MUSEUM

VASE COLLECTION
(ETRUSCAN MUSEUM)

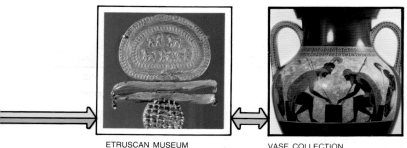

GALLERY OF THE
CANDELABRA
(classical sculpture)

GALLERY OF TAPESTRIES

GALLERY OF MAPS

ILLUSTRATED SCHEME OF THE 4 SUGGESTED AND INDICATED ITINERARIES

This scheme of the 4 itineraries corresponds to the one displayed on the large notice-boards at the beginning of the Museums, but is illustrated in greater detail. The extra illustrations not shown on the notice-boards are framed in white.

The interruption of the coloured lines indicates that the itineraries continue in that direction after the visit to other sections.

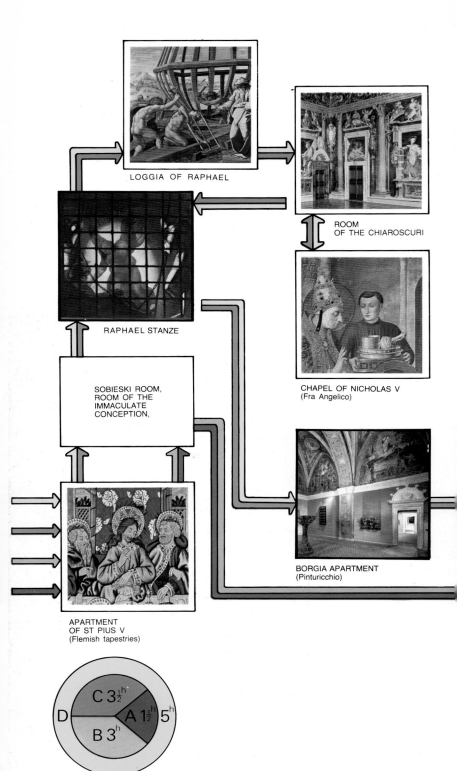

LOGGIA OF RAPHAEL

ROOM
OF THE CHIAROSCURI

RAPHAEL STANZE

SOBIESKI ROOM,
ROOM OF THE
IMMACULATE
CONCEPTION,

CHAPEL OF NICHOLAS V
(Fra Angelico)

BORGIA APARTMENT
(Pinturicchio)

APARTMENT
OF ST PIUS V
(Flemish tapestries)

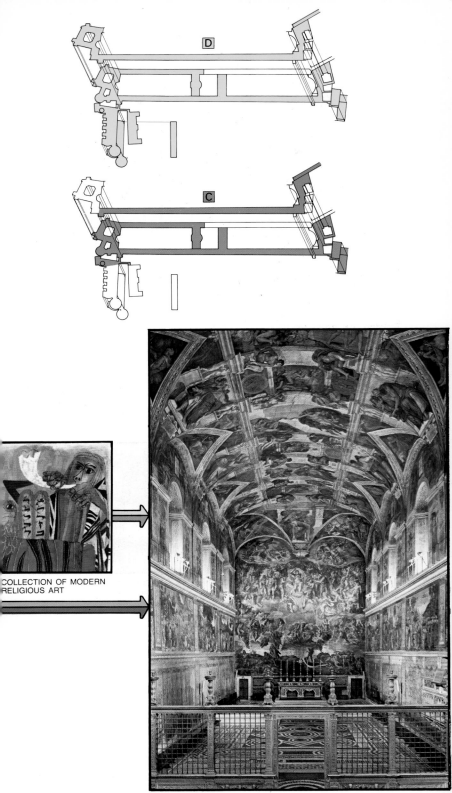

D

C

COLLECTION OF MODERN
RELIGIOUS ART

SISTINE CHAPEL

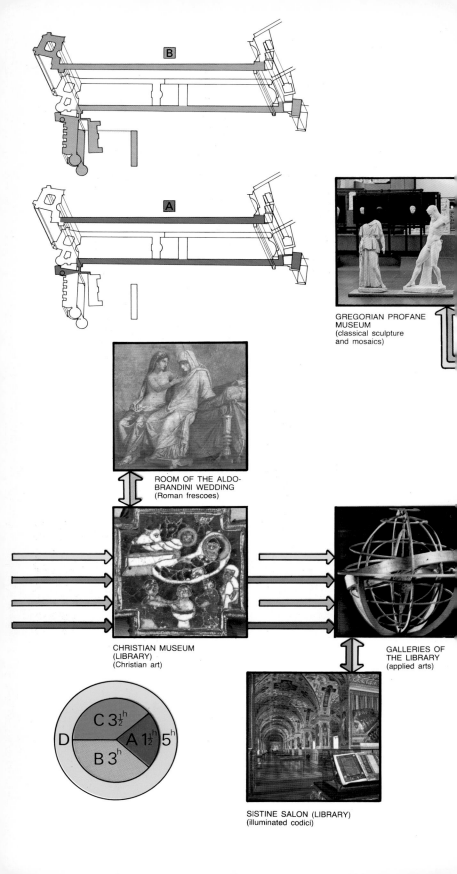

GREGORIAN PROFANE MUSEUM
(classical sculpture and mosaics)

ROOM OF THE ALDO-BRANDINI WEDDING
(Roman frescoes)

CHRISTIAN MUSEUM (LIBRARY)
(Christian art)

GALLERIES OF THE LIBRARY
(applied arts)

SISTINE SALON (LIBRARY)
(illuminated codici)

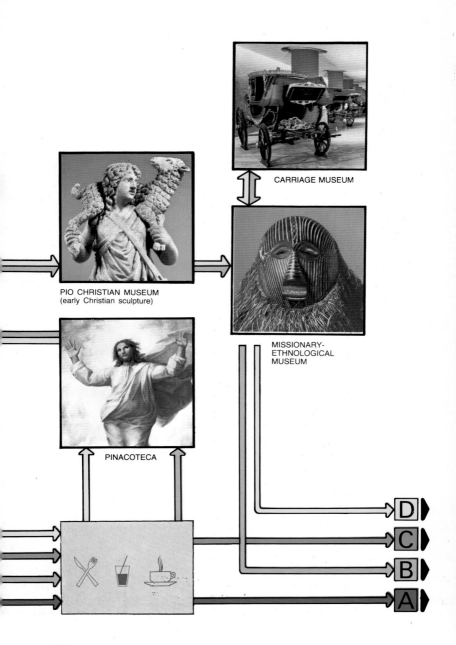

CARRIAGE MUSEUM

PIO CHRISTIAN MUSEUM
(early Christian sculpture)

MISSIONARY-
ETHNOLOGICAL
MUSEUM

PINACOTECA

D

C

B

A

Colour-key to the classification of works and rooms according to periods or styles

Oriental antiquities
(Egypt and Assyria)

classical antiquities
(Graeco-Roman art)

Etruscan-Italic
antiquities
(pre-Roman Italy)

early Christian
and medieval art
(3rd-14th cent.)

from the Renaissance
(15th cent.)
to the 19th century

ethnology and history

contemporary art
(20th cent.)

Symbols used in the guide and in the Museums

 Information Bureau of the Vatican Museums

 Tourist guides (not employed by the Museums)

 Teleguides available in English, Italian, French, German and Spanish

 Notice-boards illustrating the 4 itineraries suggested to visitors

∞ Lavatories

 Cloak-room

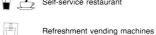 Self-service restaurant

 Refreshment vending machines

 Publications sales counters

 Writing-room

 Post office

 Telephones

 Foreign currency exchange office

 First aid stations

 Facilities for disabled visitors

 Lifts; lifts for disabled visitors

 Terminus of the regular bus service connecting the Museums with St Peter's Square (charge)

 Head custodian

 Closed-circuit television system linked to electronic alarm equipment

 Ticket office

 Booking-office for tourist guides

 Ticket control

 Visits allowed in *one direction only*

 Use of hand cameras is allowed

 The use of tripods requires the permission of the Museums Administration

 The use of flash equipment is prohibited during museum hours

 No admittance

No smoking

No talking

 No sitting

Periods or styles of works and rooms in the 4 suggested itineraries

	Itinerary A	Itinerary B	Itinerary C	Itinerary D
a - Egyptian Museum			■	■
b - Chiaramonti Museum			■	■
c - Lapidary Gallery			■ ■	■ ■
d - Braccio Nuovo			■	■
e - Court of the Pigna			■	■
f - Pio-Clementine Museum			■	■
g - Etruscan Museum		■		■
g - Vase Collection (Etruscan Museum)		■ ■		■ ■
h - Room of the Biga				■
h - Gallery of the Candelabra	■	■	■	■
i - Gallery of Tapestries	■	■	■	■
k - Gallery of Maps	■	■	■	■
l - Apartment of St Pius V	■	■	■	■
m - Sobieski Room, R. of the Immac. Conception.	■	■	■	■
n - Raphael Stanze, Chapel of Urban VIII			■	■
o - Loggia of Raphael			■	■
p - Room of the Chiaroscuri			■	■
q - Chapel of Nicholas V			■	■
r - Borgia Apartment			■	■
r - Collection of Modern Religious Art			■	■
s - Sistine Chapel	■	■	■	■
t - Vatican Library	■ ■ ■	■ ■ ■	■ ■ ■	■ ■ ■
u - Pinacoteca		■ ■		■ ■
v - Gregorian Profane Museum		■		■
w - Pio Christian Museum		■		■
x - Missionary-Ethnological Museum		■		■
y - Carriage Museum		■		■

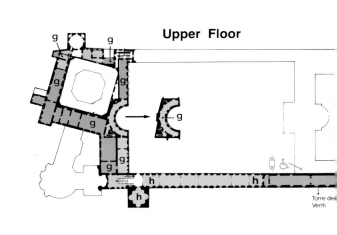

Upper Floor

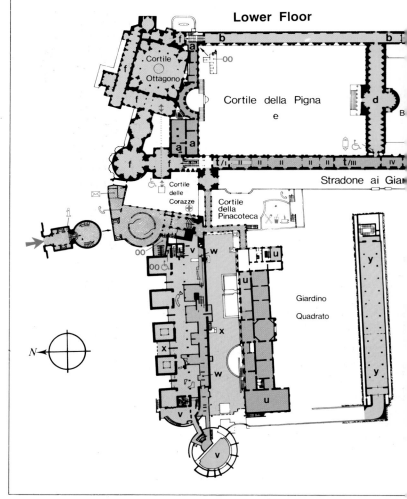

Lower Floor

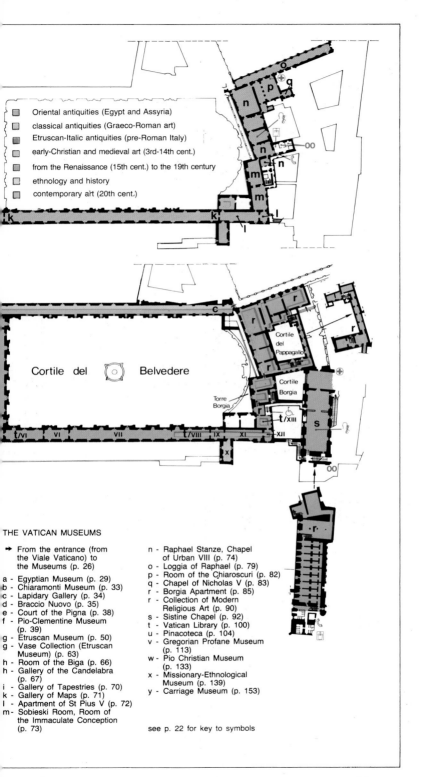

Oriental antiquities (Egypt and Assyria)

classical antiquities (Graeco-Roman art)

Etruscan-Italic antiquities (pre-Roman Italy)

early-Christian and medieval art (3rd-14th cent.)

from the Renaissance (15th cent.) to the 19th century

ethnology and history

contemporary art (20th cent.)

Cortile del Belvedere

Cortile del Pappagallo

Cortile Borgia

Torre Borgia

THE VATICAN MUSEUMS

→ From the entrance (from the Viale Vaticano) to the Museums (p. 26)

a - Egyptian Museum (p. 29)
b - Chiaramonti Museum (p. 33)
c - Lapidary Gallery (p. 34)
d - Braccio Nuovo (p. 35)
e - Court of the Pigna (p. 38)
f - Pio-Clementine Museum (p. 39)
g - Etruscan Museum (p. 50)
g - Vase Collection (Etruscan Museum) (p. 63)
h - Room of the Biga (p. 66)
h - Gallery of the Candelabra (p. 67)
i - Gallery of Tapestries (p. 70)
k - Gallery of Maps (p. 71)
l - Apartment of St Pius V (p. 72)
m - Sobieski Room, Room of the Immaculate Conception (p. 73)

n - Raphael Stanze, Chapel of Urban VIII (p. 74)
o - Loggia of Raphael (p. 79)
p - Room of the Chiaroscuri (p. 82)
q - Chapel of Nicholas V (p. 83)
r - Borgia Apartment (p. 85)
r - Collection of Modern Religious Art (p. 90)
s - Sistine Chapel (p. 92)
t - Vatican Library (p. 100)
u - Pinacoteca (p. 104)
v - Gregorian Profane Museum (p. 113)
w - Pio Christian Museum (p. 133)
x - Missionary-Ethnological Museum (p. 139)
y - Carriage Museum (p. 153)

see p. 22 for key to symbols

25

Ⓐ
Ⓑ
Ⓒ
Ⓓ

From the entrance to the museum collections

Spiral ramp; writing-room and post office; writing-room, telephones and sales counter; foreign currency exchange office

Entrance to the Vatican Museums is from the Viale Vaticano, in Italian territory, through the majestic portal in the 16th-century bastions forming the northernmost limit of the Vatican City. The portal is surmounted by two statues, one of Michelangelo, the other of Raphael, by Pietro Melandri. The statues support the coat-of-arms of Pius XI, the pope responsible for the creation of the two-storeyed structure, built in 1932 by Giuseppe Momo, permitting direct access to the Museums from the city of Rome.

1
2
The portal opens into an *atrium*, excavated in the slope of one of the hills of the Vatican area, and situated at the foot of the magnificent *spiral ramp* leading up to the floor of the Museums: there are also two lifts near by. The ramp was designed by Momo, and consists of two spirals, one for going up, the other for coming down. The bronze balustrade adorned with festoons in the classical style is by the sculptor Antonio Maraini.

3
At the top of the ramp is the *circular balcony*, decorated with valuable Roman mosaics dating from the 1st to the 3rd centuries. On the walls are numerous Roman busts. Here and in the immediate vicinity are the ticket office and various services at the disposal of visitors: a post office with a comfortable writing-room; telephones; two counters for the sale of publications regarding the Museums and the Vatican City (books, guides, maps, audiovisual material, slides, prints, postcards, greeting cards); a foreign currency exchange office; and a first aid station.

Nearby the circular balcony is the terminal of the regular bus service to and from St Peter's Square.

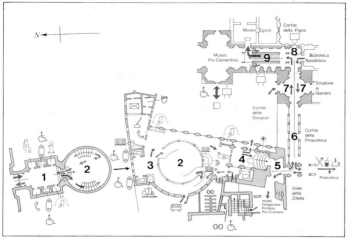

See p. 22 for key to symbols

From the circular balcony we enter a *passage*, at the beginning of
which is a bust by Enrico Quattrini of Pius XI, who commisioned the
building of the spacious new entrance. A plaque commemorates the
inauguration of the complex in 1932. The passage also houses various
Roman busts, and its walls are covered with lovely trapezoidal
mosaics. Off the passage is the room housing the lavatories, and,
beyond the ticket control, the cloak-room, where visitors should leave
bags, umbrellas and canes.

4

In the summer months, access to the Museums is to the left, through
the Court of the Corazze (cuirasses), where there are notice-boards
showing the 4 suggested itineraries for visitors, which are also indicated along the entire route. There are also numerous reproductions of
the Sistine Chapel frescoes, to enable tourist guides to explain them
before the visit.

In the center of the court is the base of Antoninus' Column. This
column of Egyptian granite, about 14.75 m. high, was erected shortly
after 161 A.C. at Montecitorio, in honour of the deified Antoninus Pius
by his sons Marcus Aurelius and Lucius Verus. It was discovered with
its base in 1703, but only the base remains today. On its sides, along
with the dedicatory inscription, are representations of the Apotheosis of
Antoninus and Faustina and of tournaments held on the occasion of
their funerals.

The Court of the Corazze leads into the *Atrium of the Four Gates* (Atrio
dei Quattro Cancelli).

7

When the weather does not permit access through the Court of the
Corazze, visitors proceed beyond the cloak-room, and up to the *vestibule*. Along the way are two more notice-boards illustrating the 4
suggested itineraries. The vestibule is also decorated with Roman
busts and mosaics. Among the latter are two large mosaics, one with
fruit and floral motifs (3rd cent. A.D.), the other with the four gods of
the winds (2nd cent. A.D.), from the Lateran Palace and the Raphael
Stanze respectively. On the right is the approach to the Gregorian
Profane, Pio Christian, Missionary-Ethnological, and Historical
museums, which the one-way system for visits places at the end of the
tour and therefore are described towards the end of this guide (see pp.
113-154).

5

To reach the Museums from this point, visitors must pass the Court of
the Pinacoteca, proceeding along the small *portico*—built in 1933 in

6

27

plan
←

Atrium of the Four Gates; Simonetti Stairway

the Quattrocento style—separating it from the Court of the Corazze. The portico, which runs along two sides (north and west) of the Court of the Pinacoteca, links the entrance with the Pinacoteca (see p. 104) and the self-service restaurant on one side, and the Atrium of the Four Gates on the other side.

7 The *Atrium of the Four Gates* is a monumental edifice built on a square plan, in the Neoclassical style, and is covered with a dome. It was built by Giuseppe Camporese in 1792-93, and was the former entrance to the Museums, approached from the avenue to the Vatican Gardens. On the inside, it is decorated with eight life-size statues arranged symmetrically in niches. These are idealized statues dating back to the Roman Imperial Age, 1st and 2nd centuries.

8 The atrium leads into the *Vestibule of the Four Gates.* (Beyond the vestibule, through a gate, is the Court of the Pigna (pine-cone) (see p. 38), named after the bronze pine-cone in the centre of the large niche. The "pigna" was once kept in the atrium of the Constantinian Basilica, replaced in the 16th century by the present basilica. The large niche, built by Pirro Ligorio during the papacy of Pius IV, is an elaboration of an exedra designed by Donato Bramante and modified by Michelangelo).

9 The VISIT TO THE MUSEUMS ACTUALLY BEGINS from the Vestibule of the Four Gates. We go up the first flight of the *Simonetti Stairway*, and find ourselves facing the Greek Cross Room, the first of the twelve rooms of the Pio-Clementine Museum, described further on (see p. 39). The splendid stairway is named after its architect, Michelangelo Simonetti, who built it and the Greek Cross Room in the 1780's, drawing his inspiration from Roman thermae (most of the columns supporting the barrel vault are from the environs of Rome).

On the right side of the landing is the entrance to the Egyptian Museum.

a - Egyptian Museum

Painted bas-relief dating from the Old Kingdom

Founded by Gregory XVI in 1839, the Egyptian Museum was arranged by Father L.M. Ungarelli, one of the first Italian Egyptologists. Rooms I and II still contain decorative motifs which imitate Egyptian architecture — cornices, columns and winged solar discs. In Room II note the hymn to Gregory XVI on the cornice, written in hieroglyphs and composed by Father Ungarelli to celebrate the foundation of the museum. Rooms III and IV still retain their original early 19th-century decoration, with the walls painted in imitation alabaster and various landscapes evoking Egypt painted by Giuseppe de Fabris. The collection is made up of Egyptian antiquities acquired by the Popes from the end of the 18th century, but especially of statues found in Rome (and nearby) brought from Egypt in Roman times; also on display are Egyptian-like objects produced in Italy in the 1st and 2nd centuries in imitation of Egyptian originals.

ROOM I   I

This room houses a collection of objects and monuments (stelae, statues and other items) with inscriptions, dating from the Old Kingdom to the Christian era.

Of particular interest:

Throne of a seated statue of Ramses II (19th dynasty; c. 1250 B.C.).   **1**

Two *stelae* and a *bas-relief* from the Old Kingdom (c. 2400 B.C.).   **2**

A large *stele* depicting some of the work undertaken in the temple of   **3**
Karnak by Queen Hatshepsut and her grandson Thutmose III (18th dynasty; c. 1400 B.C.).

A *scarab* commemorating the excavation undertaken by Amenophys III   **4**
(18th dynasty; c. 1350 B.C.) of an enormous lake near his Malgatta palace on the west bank of Thebes.

Statue of the high priest Udja-Hor-resne offering a naos, with its in-   **5**

29

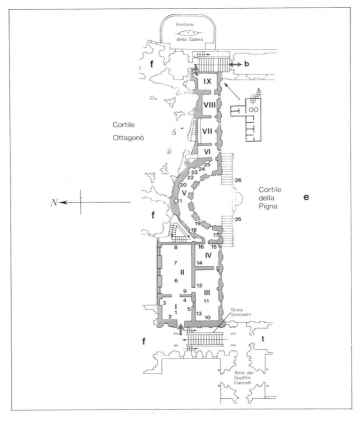

I

scriptions recalling the conquest of Egypt by the Persian king Cambyses in 525 B.C., some scenes of the conquest and the important role that Udja-Hor-resne played at critical moments.

ROOM II

Exhibited in this room are objects relating to the funerary cult of the Old Kingdom.

In the central show-case *painted sarcophagi*, most of them dating to the 21st dynasty (c. 1000 B.C.), *two mummies* and a collection of *canopic jars* in which the entrails extracted from dead bodies during mummification were conserved.

In the other show-cases more funerary equipment, including a beautiful collection of *ushabtis* (statuettes that were used to substitute the deceased in their humble labours in the afterlife).

On the way out, in the show-case near the door, we see two *funerary masks* of the Roman period (one in plaster, the other in gilt pasteboard) and a beautiful painted shroud of the 3rd century A.D. from Antinoupolis (Middle Egypt).

ROOM III

Here is a reconstruction of the most evocative part of the decoration of the Canopos Serapeum of Hadrian's Villa, the vast complex built near

30

Tivoli by the emperor Hadrian (117-138). This edifice, imbued with significance, symbolically represented Egypt submerged by the flood waters of the Nile and had a lavish decoration of statues from the Hadrianic era that were imitations of Egyptian statuary.

C
D

A *colossal bust of Isis-Demeter* was placed at the base of the monument where a waterfall gushed forth, symbolizing the impetuous flooding of the Nile.

10

The water (the Nile) then passed under a bridge where a group of statues represented the *cerimony of the awakening of Osiris-Apis*, that is, Serapis (a double bust on a lotus flower) symbolizing the eternal rebirth of the sun in its daily cycle. Gods inside the niches witnessed the scene: note that the two statues placed at the end of the bridge are turned slightly to «look» toward the centre.

11

Statues of Osiris-Antinous (representation in Egyptian dress of Antinous, Hadrian's favourite, deified after his drowning in the Nile in 130 A.D., during a journey of the emperor in Egypt) completed the scene.

12, 13

ROOM IV

IV

Statues and bas-reliefs in imitation of Egyptian originals carved in Italy in the Imperial age to decorate temples and holy places with Egyptian gods in Rome and its environs.

Note especially, besides the great Nile in black marble:

Fountain-statue of Apis, the genie of the flooding Nile (end of the 1st century B.C., or beginning of the 1st century A.D.); from its open mouth spouted a water that, after having passed through the body of the statue, was considered to be the water of the Nile that was necessary for various rituals; the statue undoubtedly comes from the Sallustian Gardens.

14

Statue of Anubis, mummification deity and guide of the dead, who here has retained a dog's head but is clothed in Roman dress and has the attributes of Hermes with whom he was identified (1st century A.D., from Anzio).

15

Statue of a baboon found in the Serapeum of Campus Martius in Rome. It is the "cacco" of the Church of S. Stefano del Cacco (from "macaco"-monkey). At the base of the statue are the names of the sculptors Ammonius and Phydias (on the right) and the text of the decree of 159 A.D. (on the left) which authorized its placing in the temple.

16

ROOM V (HEMICYCLE)

V

On display here is the collection of Egyptian statues, some of which come from Rome and its environs.

Note especially:

Head of King Mentuhotep from the 11th dynasty (c. 2100 B.C.).

17

Statue of the lion goddess Sekhmet (other examples are on the terrace of the hemicycle) from the temple of Mout at Karnak where two series of 365 statues of this deity, protectress of every day and night of the year, were found (age of Amenophis III, 18th dynasty, c. 1350 B.C.).

18

Fragment of a bas-relief from an Old Kingdom tomb (6th dynasty, c. 2250 B.C.).

19

A splendid *torso of King Nektanebos I*, from the 30th dynasty (378-361

20

plan
←

C **D** B.C.), one of the last native pharaohs; the torso was found at Nepi, near Rome.

21-24:21
23

22, 24

Group of *four colossal statues* comprising a statue of *Queen Tuia*, mother of Ramses II (19th dynasty, c. 1250 B.C.), a statue of *Ptolemy Philadelphus*, the Greek king of Egypt (283-246 B.C.), a statue of his sister *Arsinoes II* and *another* in imitation of the latter. The statues were found in Rome in the Sallustian Gardens, where they were undoubtedly put by the emperor Caligula (37-41 A.D.), whose insanity led him to pose as a pharaoh. Caligula, like Ramses II, was deeply attached to his mother Agrippina and, like Ptolemy Philadelphus, married and deified his sister, Drusilla, whose statue (a replica of the one of Arsinoes) was probably commissioned by him.

25

Beautiful *statue of a taurine god* (Late Period?) possibly found in Rome or nearby (Hadrian's Villa); it was in the collection of the engraver Piranesi before becoming part of the Papal collections.

VI, VII

ROOMS VI and VII

Exhibition of the collection of Carlo Grassi, donated to Pope Pius XII by Mrs. Nedda Grassi.
Room VI houses bronze objects from the Late Period (6th-5th centuries B.C.): sacred animals, gods, etc.
Room VII is dedicated to Graeco-Roman antiquities (bronzes, terracottas, etc.) from Alexandria and objects from Christian and Muslim Egypt.

VIII

ROOM VIII

In the show-case to the left a retrospective collection of vases and ceramics from the protodynastic era to the Roman period.
In the show-case to the right are objects from Mesopotamia (tablets with cuneiform inscriptions and cylindrical seals).

IX

ROOM IX

Assyrian reliefs donated to Pope Pius IX by Giovanni Benni, himself a native of Mosul, who with E. Botta took part in the excavations of Nineveh in 1842. The reliefs come from royal villas near Nineveh: the palace of Sargon II (722-705 B.C.) and Sennacherib (705-681 B.C.). For the most part they represent scenes of war, recurrent in Assyrian figurative art. Some of them bear visible traces of fire (the parts blackened by smoke or where the stone is transformed into a whitish lime, etc.), undoubtedly traces of the fire of Nineveh and the surrounding area which destroyed the Assyrian capital in 612 B.C., during the Babylonian conquest, and put an end to the supremacy of the Assyrian kingdom.

X

TERRACE OF THE HEMICYCLE (X)

Houses statues numerous of the lion goddess Sekhmet (cf. n. 18 in the Hemicycle) and three sarcophagi from the Late Period (6th-5th century B.C.).

26

At the bottom of the stairs and to the side of the fountain below the pine cone, *two lions in grey granite* from the reign of Nektanebos I (378-361 B.C.; cf. n. 20 in the Hemicycle) found in the temple of Isis and Serapis in the Campus Martius.

b - Chiaramonti Museum

Imperial Age portrait busts

Leaving the Egyptian Museum we come to a landing, situated at the end of the long corridor designed by Donato Bramante to link the Apostolic Palace (floor of the Borgia Apartment) with the Belvedere Palace, at that time the summer residence of the Pope. Looking right, in the direction of the Apostolic Palace, we can see through the Chiaramonti Museum and the Lapidary Gallery (see p. 33, 34), and as far as the first loggia of the Court of St Damasus.

The Chiaramonti Museum, named after its founder, Pius VII, has changed only slightly in appearance since it was first laid out by Antonio Canova.

Nearly a thousand pieces of ancient sculpture of every kind are exhibited: statues of gods, portrait statues, pagan altars, architectural ornaments, urns and sarcophagi. The paintings in the lunettes are by artists of the Academy of St Luke, commissioned by Canova to commemorate the impulse given to the fine arts by the pope. The "Museum Claramontanum Pioclementino adiectum", founded by Pius VII in the seventh year of his papacy, is celebrated in a lunette (bay XLI, on the left) painted by Luigi Agricola.

The walls on both sides are divided into bays, each of which is indicated by a Roman numeral.

I. *Sarcophagus of C. Junius Euhodus and of Metilia Acte*; the inscription dates it back to 161-170 A.D. Scenes from the myth of Alcestis, who was willing to die in place of her husband, Admetus. The heads of Admetus and Alcestis are portraits of the deceased. Inv. 1195.

1

II. Lower shelf: herma of *Hephaestus*, identified by the pilus (conical felt cap). Roman version of a famous statue of Hephaestus by Alcamenes, 430 B.C. Inv. 1211.

2

VII. Above, on the wall: *fragments of relief depicting Aglaurids and Horae*. Inv. 1284, 1285. Three *female figures dancing toward the left*, identifiable as the Aglaurid sisters, dispensers of nocturnal dew: Aglauros, Pandroso and Herse (Inv. 1284). *Figure moving towards the right*, identifiable, by means of other copies, as a Hora (Inv. 1285). Aglaurids and Horae are counterposed in the composition. Found together on Esquiline Hill. Neo-Attic copy of the time of Hadrian (2nd cent. A.D.) of a 4th-century B.C. model.

3, 4
3

4

33

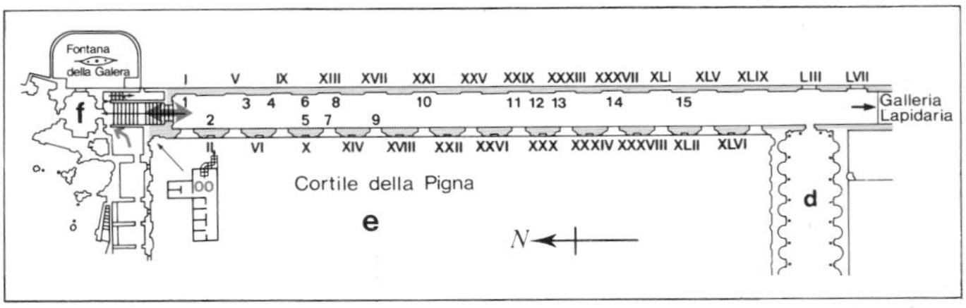

5 X. On the floor: *funeral monument of the miller P. Nonius Zethus*, block of marble with notches for cinerary urns. The reliefs at the sides of the inscription indicate that the deceased was a miller and flour merchant (1st cent. A.D.). Inv. 1343.

6 XI. Lower shelf: head of *Cicero* (106-43 B.C.), probably a Renaissance work. Inv. 1359.

7 XII. Above, against the wall: *funerary statue of Cornutus as Saturn.* The inscription reads: "Here am I, Cornutus, sorrowful, with my eight beloved children". The face is a portrait of Cornutus, but the figure—mantled, bearing a sickle in the right hand, surrounded by boys bearing fruit—is a typical representation of Saturn, Lord of the Golden Age. Late Roman Imperial Age (end of 3rd cent. A.D.). Inv. 1369.

8 XIII. Statue of *Ganymede with eagle.* Roman Imperial Age. Inv. 1376.

9 XVI. Colossal head of *Athene*, perhaps intended for a statue made of other material. The restored eyes re-create the vivacity of gaze characteristic of ancient works. The model of this Roman copy (of the time of Hadrian) is thought to be Phidias' Athena Promachos (5th cent. B.C.). Inv. 1434.

10 XXI. Statue of *Tiberius* (emperor 14-37 A.D.) seated. Statuary type frequently adopted in representations of Jupiter. Inv. 1511.

11 XXIX. Colossal head of *Augustus* (died 14 A.D.), from Veii, Inv.
12 1639.—Colossal head of *Tiberius* (emperor 14-37 A.D.), from Veii. Inv. 1642.

13 XXXI. Above, on the wall: relief with the *Three Graces.* This interpretation is probably based on one of the reliefs of the same subject on the Propylaea of the Athenian Acropolis, where a cult was devoted to the Graces. The original dates back to about 470 B.C., this copy to the late 1st century B.C. Inv. 1669.

14 XXXVII. Statue of *Hercules* leaning on his club, the lion skin over his left forearm. The original would appear to belong to the school of Lysippus (4th cent. B.C.). Inv. 1771.

15 XLIII. On the floor: statuette of *Ulysses*, part of a group representing the Cyclops episode; here the hero offers a drink to Polyphemus. Roman work (1st cent. A.D.) inspired by Greek models. Inv. 1901.

plan pp. 24-25

c - Lapidary Gallery

Beyond a gate at the end of the Chiaramonti Museum is the Lapidary Gallery. It may be visited by scholars on request. The collection, undoubtedly one of the richest and most important in the world, was conceived by Clement XI, begun by Benedict XIV, continued by Pius VI, and greatly enlarged by Pius VII. The inscriptions housed in this gallery number more than 3000. Christian inscriptions are displayed along the wall on the Court side, and pagan inscriptions along the opposite wall.

d - Braccio Nuovo

North wall

Visitors now enter the Braccio Nuovo ("new wing") from the Chiaramonti Museum.

Pius VII decided in 1806 to build this new wing, but it was not until 1817 (after the sculptures Napoleon "deported" to Paris were returned) that the scheme could be carried out. The wing was planned by the Roman architect Raffaele Stern; he died on 30 December 1820, and Pasquale Belli took over the job of supervising the construction. The wing was inaugurated in 1822. The reliefs above the niches are by Massimiliano Laboureur. The ancient mosaics (2nd cent. A.D.) in the floor are from excavations near Tor Marancia, on the Via Ardeatina (the representation of the adventures of Ulysses is especially noteworthy).

On the right:

Statue of *Silenus cradling the child Dionysus in his arms*. A Roman copy of a Greek original of about 300 B.C. Inv. 2292.

1

Statue of the *Augustus of Prima Porta*, wearing a lorica. Found in 1863 in Livia's Villa on the Via Flaminia, near Prima Porta, from which the statue takes its name. The portrait head identifies the figure as Augustus, who is represented in the attitude of the "adlocutio": his right arm is raised, and the fact that he is wearing armour suggests that he is addressing his soldiers. The relief decorations on the armour are of special interest. The central scene refers to an event that took place in 20 B.C.: a Parthian King (Phraates IV) returns the Roman insignias, lost by Crassus in 53 B.C., to Augustus' legate (Tiberius). The whole cosmos witnesses the peace-offering: above, Caelus in his swollen mantle, Sol on a quadriga, and, in front of him, personifications of Dawn and Dew; below, Tellus, the Roman earth goddess; at the sides, Apollo, holding a lyre, on a winged griffin, and Diana, holding a torch, on a stag. At the sides of the central scene are two seated female figures, personifications of provinces (Germania and Dalmatia?). The only decoration on the back of the armour is the rough outline of a "tropaeum". The weight-bearing leg is supported by the figure of Cupid riding a dolphin (an allusion to Venus, progenitress of the "gens Julia", to which Augustus belonged). The bare feet are in keeping with the heroic treatment of the subject (the position of the legs was taken from the Doryphorus). This is a copy, probably made for Livia after the death of Augustus (14 A.D.), of a bronze statue erected in honour of

2

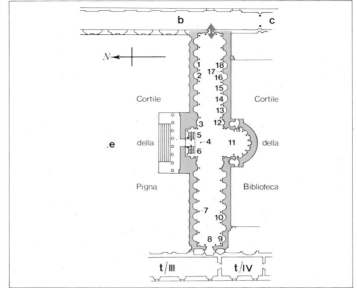

Augustus shortly after 20 B.C. The statue also constitutes the first official honouring of Tiberius, Livia's son from her first marriage, to Claudius Nero; as Augustus' step-son, Tiberius had now become his successor. (Cf. p. 120: III/15, and p. 122: III/25). Inv. 2290.

3 Togated statue of *Titus* (emperor 79-81 A.D.). The toga was the civilian dress of the Roman citizen, and the emperor is presented here as "primis inter pares". The richly carved drapery with "sinus", "balteus", and "umbo" is a characteristic of the Flavian period. Inv. 2282.

4 Head of *Julius Caesar* (assassinated 15 March 44 B.C.) on a bust not belonging to it. It has been so extensively reworked that nothing remains of the original surface. (Cf. p. 45: VI/10). Inv. 2309.

5, 6 Two *peacocks* in gilded bronze. During the Middle Ages these works stood in the first court of Constantine's Basilica of St Peter. They probably came from Hadrian's mausoleum (Castel Sant'Angelo. Symbol of astral immortality. Inv. 5117 and 5120.

7 Togated bust of *Pupienus* (emperor in 238 A.D.). Inv. 2265.

8 In front of the entrance of the Vatican Library: bust of *Pius VII*, founder of the Braccio Nuovo. By Antonio Canova. Inv. 2301.

On the other side of the gallery:

9 Statue of *Demosthenes*, Attic orator, enemy of the Macedonians (died 322 B.C.). Roman copy of a bronze original, by Polyeuktos, which stood in the Athenian Agora in 280 B.C. Inv. 2255.

10 Statue of a *wounded Amazon*, copy of a statue by Kresilas. The bronze original dates back to 430 B.C.; one of the Ephesian statues (cf. p. 44: V/10, copy after Phidias). Inv. 2252.

11 Colossus of the *Nile*, probably found in 1513 (Leo X) near the Church of Santa Maria Sopra Minerva (the area of the ancient temple of Isis and Serapis). The river god, identified by the sphinxes and crocodiles, is represented as a dispenser of blessings; the sixteen boys are thought to be an allusion to the number of cubits the level of the Nile rises when it floods, fertilizing the region which it crosses. The reliefs on the base represent life on the banks of the river. 1st-century A.D. Roman work, probably based on a Hellenistic original. Inv. 2300.

plan ←

Statue of *Julia*, daughter of the emperor Titus. Found in Lateran, together with the statue of Titus opposite (see above: 3). The hair-style is typical of the Flavian era; about 80 A.D. Inv. 2285.

12

Statue of the *Giustiniani Athene*, named after its first owner. Athene is identified by the helmet, shield and serpent. Roman version (2nd cent. A.D.) of a Greek bronze of the 4th century B.C. Inv. 2223.

13

Togated statue with a good portrait of the emperor *Claudius* (ruled 41-54 A.D.); the head and body do not belong together. Inv. 2221.

14

Statue of a *resting satyr*, a modest copy of one of the most admired works of antiquity, a statue unanimously attributed to Praxiteles. (Cf. copies p. 117: II/37-39, and p. 44: V/7). Inv. 2219.

15

Portrait head of *Lucius Vero* (died 169 A.D.) on a statue of an athlete. On stylistic grounds the latter is thought to be a copy of an original by Myron of the 5th century B.C. Inv. 2217.

16

Togated bust of *Philippus Arabicus* (emperor 244-249 A.D.). Inv. 2216.

17

Statue of the *Doryphorus* (spear-bearer), a Roman copy of a bronze original by Polyclitus of 440 B.C. The expression and attitude are simple and clear, yet conceived with supreme art. One leg carries the weight, while the other is relaxed; one arm is in action, while the other is at rest. Action and inaction alternate and merge in this figure, down to the smallest details. Tradition has it that Polyclitus created a model statue to exemplify the principles he set out in his theoretical work, the "Kanon". The original of the work before us could well be that statue, as it appears to summarize the art of Polyctitus. Inv. 2215.

18

To continue our tour of the Museums, we must now return to the entrance of the Chiaramonti Museum. From here we enter the Pio-Clementine Museum (p. 39).

e - Court of the Pigna

Court of the Pigna

The Court of the Pigna constitutes the northern end of the great Renaissance Belvedere Courtyard that extended from the Papal Palaces to Innocent VIII's 'palazzetto' and was subsequently divided into three parts with the construction of Sixtus V's Library and the Braccio Nuovo of Pius VII. The present courtyard, which takes its name from the enormous bronze pine cone set into the 'nicchione', is bounded on the south side by the Braccio Nuovo, on the east by the Chiaromonti Gallery, on the north by Innocent VIII's palazzetto and on the west by the galleries of the Apostolic Library.

In the centre of the 'nicchione':

Colossal bronze pine cone. Cast in the 1st or 2nd century by a certain *P(ublius) Cincius Salvius*, who left his name on the base, it was at one time situated in the Campus Martius, in the area that is still called 'Pigna', where it served as a fountain, water gushing from holes in the scales of the cone. Possibly towards the end of the 8th century it was moved to the entrance hall of the medieval St Peter's, in the centre of a fountain covered by an ornate baldachin, identified in Renaissance drawings. Finally, in 1608, during the construction of the present basilica, it was dismantled and placed where it is today. Inv. 5118.

Under the pine cone:

Capital from the baths of Alexander Severus (222-235 A.D.) with athletes and judges. Placed here as the base of the pine cone under Clement XI (1700-21). Inv. 5119.

At the sides:

Bronze copies of the Peacocks, recently moved to the Braccio Nuovo (p. 36: 5-6) for reasons of conservation.

In the middle of the eastern side:

Colossal head of Augustus. Found on the Aventine, in the 16th century it entered the Mattei collection. It remained at Villa Celimontana until 1801, when it was acquired for the Vatican Museums. It must have formed part of a colossal statue with the bare parts (head, arms and legs) made of marble and the rest of masonry and stucco. Inv. 5137.

38

The Laocoön group (by the Rhodes sculptors Hagesandros, Athanodoros and Polydoros, 1st cent. A.D.), detail

Pius VI provided a monumental entrance for the ancient museum of sculpture, the only one of its kind, in the form of the Atrium of Four Gates (see p. 28: 7). From there one went up the Simonetti stairway, entered the Greek Cross Room, and passed through to the Round Room, the Room of the Muses, the Room of the Animals, and thence to the ancient Court of the Belvedere Statues, the present Octagonal Court. In order to regulate the flow of "traffic", visitors are now required to follow the contrary route, i.e. from Room XII (Square Vestibule) to Room I (Greek Cross Room).

XII, SQUARE VESTIBULE

XII

This was the entrance-hall of the old Clementine Museum. In fact, the words MUSEUM CLEMENTINUM appear on the architrave, with "trompe-l'oeil" (illusionistic) arch, on the opposite wall. In front of the window is the bust of the founder of the museum, *Clement XIV*, who, with the purchase of the Fusconi and Mattei collections in 1770, determined the new arrangement of the museum in the Belvedere Palace.

1

In the niche in the left wall: *sarcophagus of Lucius Cornelius Scipio the Bearded* (consul in 298 B.C.), in grey tufa; from the Scipio Tomb on the Appian Way. The shape of the sarcophagus indicates a Greek-Hellenistic influence. The inscription, in archaic Latin verses, contains a eulogy of the deceased, and a description of his career and archievements. Inv. 1191.

2

We pass through the ROUND VESTIBULE, IX, and enter the

IX

X, CABINET OF THE APOXYOMENOS

X

The *Apoxyomenos*, Roman copy (1st cent. A.D.) of a bronze original, of about 320 B.C., by Lysippus; found in Trastevere in 1849. The athlete has just returned from the palestra; in his left hand he holds a

1

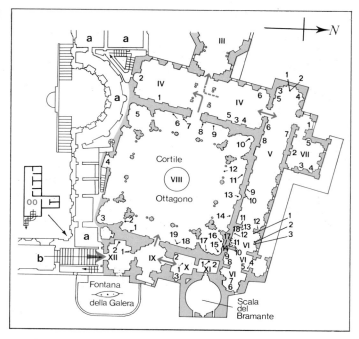

strigil, with which he cleans the dust and sweat from his right arm (the Greek word "apoxyein" means "to wipe off"). He gazes wearily into the distance. This is an image of a victor, not at the moment of glory, but "afterwards", when he is overcome by fatigue. Lysippus, who also made a statue of Alexander the Great, sought to portray men not as they are, but as they appear in the truth of each fleeting moment (Pliny, Nat, Hist., XXXIV, 65). Inv. 1185.

On the wall, right and left: inscriptions from the Scipio Tomb, on the Appian Way. Inv. 1149-55.—Shelf: portrait head, known as *Ennius*, with laurel wreath; from the Scipio Tomb. Inv. 1148.

On the opposite side, in the window-space: base with scenes from Trojan and Roman legends, the so-called *Casali altar*, gift of the Casali family to Pius VI. The inscription within the wreath of oak leaves, on the front, informs us that the monument was dedicated by Ti. Claudius Faventinus. Reliefs: front, Mars and Venus; back, legend of Romulus and Remus; sides, Trojan myths. The character and style of the figuration indicate a work of about 200 A.D. Inv. 1186.

XI, VESTIBULE

This small room gives access to the Bramante Stairway, built by Julius II in the early 16th century to provide an external entrance which could be ridden up on horseback to the palace. The spiral stairway is built within a square tower (it may be visited by request). In accordance with the principles of Vitruvius, the columns are of three types: Tuscan in the first part, Ionic in the second part, and Corinthian in the third part. At the base of the tower is the Fountain of the Galley, so named for the small lead galley (water spouts from its guns) placed there during the papacy of Clement IX. The fountain was made by Carlo Maderno for Paul V.

On the opposite wall: *relief representing an ancient warship*, the fore-end of a bireme of the late Republican Age. Inv. 31680.

Statue of the *Nile*, in gray marble. The river god is represented with his usual attributes, a sphinx and a crocodile, and with heads of wheat symbolizing fertility. The statue was extensively restored in the eighteenth century by G. Sibilla. Inv. 22838.

2

Above, on the wall: panels of a mosaic with circus and arena scenes.

We return to the Round Vestibule (IX), from which, on the right, we enter the Octagonal Court.

VIII, OCTAGONAL COURT

VIII

The internal court of the Belvedere Palace, originally square in shape and planted with orange trees, is the heart of the museum. It was here that Cardinal Giuliano della Rovere, who in 1503 became Pope Julius II, placed his ancient statues. His famous Apollo Belvedere was named after this palace. He also acquired other significant works such as the Laocoön group. In 1772 Clement XIV commissioned Michelangelo Simonetti to build the portico. In this way the court assumed its present octagonal shape. In the early 19th century Antonio Canova had the four corner-sections walled up; these dividing walls were pulled down in 1957.

On the left side of the portico, against the wall: *fragment of relief with subject from Roman history*, representing an attendant ("popa") leading a large bull; late Republican Age. Inv. 996.

1

In the centre, above the entrance: *frieze with Dionysian procession*: Bacchus and followers return from a banquet. Late Hellenistic work from Campania, 1st century B.C. Inv. 977.

2

Still to the left, proceeding clockwise:

CABINET OF THE APOLLO

The *Apollo Belvedere*, a Roman copy (c. 130-140 A.D.) in marble of a Greek bronze (c. 330-320 B.C.), probably by Leochares, which once stood in the Agora of Athens (Pausanias, 1, 3, 4). Julius II brought this statue, which was known as far back as the 14th century, from his palace near San Pietro in Vincoli to the Belvedere Court of the Statues. The hands, removed in 1924, were made by Giovanni Angelo da Montorsoli in 1532. The god, "he who strikes from afar", held a bow in his left hand, as a symbol of his role as avenger. In his right hand he presumably held an arrow, taken from his open quiver. The cloak draped over his shoulders and left arm emphasizes his radiant, youthful figure, the maximum expression of the nobility and purity of the Apollonian being. "Thus the gods dispose that poor mortals must live in anguish, but they themselves are not touched by pain", writes Homer (Illiad 6, 138 and 24, 525). Hölderlin remarked of this statue, "...the eyes observe with silent, eternal light". Johann Joachim Winckelmann wrote, "Of all the works of antiquity that have escaped destruction, the statue of Apollo represents the highest ideal of art". Inv. 1015.

3

On the south side of the Court, partial reconstruction of the "Fountain of the Tigris", arranged by Michelangelo on one of the corners of the Court itself.

Above is a *Reclining statue of a River God* (the so-called Tigris) of the 2nd cent. A.D. The head and several other parts have been restored. The statue has been in the Vatican since 1536.

4

Below: *Sarcophagus representing a battle between Greeks and Amazons* (about 160-170 A.D.), Inv. 896. During the Renaissance this served as the basin of the above mentioned fountain.

4

CABINET OF THE LAOCOÖN

The *Laocoön group*, in marble, was found on 14 January 1506 near the "Seven Halls" on the Esquiline Hill (Domus Aurea area). In his Natural History (XXXVI, 37), Pliny the Elder, who died in the eruption of Vesuvius in 79 A.D., wrote of this statue that it was the work of

5

plan
←
VIII

C
D
the Rhodes sculptors Hagesandros, Athanodoros and Polydoros, that it stood in the palace of the emperor Titus, and that it was to be preferred to all other depictions of a similar subject in painting or in bronze. When it was discovered, the statue was recognized from the ancient writer's description. Julius II purchased it on 23 March 1506, and had it brought here.

Laocoön, the priest of Apollo, and his two sons are locked in the coils of two serpents, on the steps of an altar. Laocoön's chest rises and swells as he vainly attempts to tear away the head of the serpent that is about to bite him on the hip. The other serpent has already sunk its fangs into the side of the younger son, who collapses in agony, while the elder son attempts to free himself from its coils. Virgil describes the episode in detail (Aeneid II, 199-233): the Trojan priest Laocoön had warned his compatriots against the wooden horse, left by the Greeks as "an offering to Athene", and had hurled his lance at it. This angered Athene, who sent serpents to kill Laocoön. Misinterpreting the omen, the Trojans ignored Laocoön's warning, and dragged the wooden horse into the city. Only Aeneas understood the true significance of the omen, and he and his family saved themselves by fleeing to Italy where Aeneas founded Lavinium, and his son Alba Longa. As far back as Caesar's time the legendary Trojan ancestry of the gens Julia had been used as a political argument. Augustus made the legend the keystone of his empire, using it to legitimize his claim to the throne. The Laocoön group, which Pliny saw in the imperial palace, was probably commissioned by the emperor in the first half of the first century A.D., and made by the Rhodes sculptors after a bronze original of the 2nd century B.C. The flexed right arm was discovered by Ludwig Pollak in 1905; it proved to belong to the figure of Laocoön, and was placed on the statue during the last restoration, in 1957-60. Since the significance of this sculpture is not limited to its merits as a work of art, but also includes its history, Montorsoli's old reconstruction has been preserved in a plaster cast, which can be seen from one of the windows of the Gregorian Profane Museum (see p. 129: IV/19).

6

Above, on the wall: *front of a sarcophagus with columns and three aedicules.* In the centre, the deceased; at the sides, she takes part in the teaching of philosophers. About 240 A.D. Inv. 871.

7, 8

At the sides of the exit are two *Molossi*, Roman copies (Imperial Age) of Hellenistic originals of the 3rd century B.C. Inv. 872-897.

9

On the wall: *Front of a columned sarcophagus* with representation of funeral edifice with open door (centre). About 250 A.D. Inv. 866.

CABINET OF THE HERMES

10

Statue of *Hermes* (once thought to be of Antinous). Roman copy from the time of Hadrian (once a Greek original in bronze (late classical period, 4th cent. B.C.), found near Castel Sant'Angelo. The lithesome posture, and travelling cloak thrown hastily over the left shoulder are sufficient in themselves to remind one of the messenger of the gods; definitively identified by means of other copies, some from tombs, in which the god served as "Psychopompos", guide of the dead to the underworld. Inv. 907.

11

Proceeding left: *sarcophagus with battle of Amazons*; in the centre, Achilles with headpiece, Penthesilea dying. 3rd century A.D. Inv. 933.

12

Opposite, in the passage leading to the court: two *fragments of a large bath-shaped sarcophagus*, with groups of fighting animals on both sides. 3rd century A.D. Inv. 922.

13

In the central niche, on the left: statue of *Venus Felix*, copy of the Aphrodite of Cnidos by Praxiteles (see p. 46: VII/2), with portrait head reminiscent of the young Faustina of about 170 A.D. According to the inscription on the plinth, the statue was dedicated to Venus Felix by Sallustia and Helpidus.

14

Proceeding left: *sarcophagus of a condottiere*. Here the theme of "clementia" (mercy shown by the victor to the vanquished) is represented as one of the great Roman virtues. About 180 A.D. Inv. 942.

CABINET OF CANOVA

VIII

When Napoleon took the most important works of the museum to Paris, Pius VII bought three of Antonio Canova's statues (made around 1800), and exhibited them here:

Perseus triumphant with the head of Medusa. Inv. 969.

15

The boxers *Kreugas and Damoxenos*. According to Pausanias (8, 40, 3-4), the two engaged in a boxing match at Nemea, the outcome of which was uncertain; Damoxenos consequently stabbed his opponent in the abdomen, and tore out his intestines. The referee disqualified Damoxenos, and declared the dead Kreugas the winner. Inv. 968, 970.

16, 17

On the entrance side: *Bacchic sarcophagus in the shape of a bath*; pairs of dancing satyrs and maenads, whit thyrsi. Mid-2nd century A.D. Inv. 987.

18

Above, on the wall: *relief from a very large sarcophagus*, with representation of a port. The heroized figure of the dead man appears in the centre, dominating the background. His wife, represented as Venus, sits in front of him. Both portrait heads are unfinished. Mid-3rd century A.D. Inv. 973.

19

Crossing the Octagonal Court, we return to the two Molossi flanking the passage to the next section.

IV, ROOM OF THE ANIMALS

IV

This room takes its name from the statues of animals exhibited here. Most of them have been so extensively and freely restored by Francesco Antonio Franzoni that they may be almost considered his own works.

In the floor, ancient mosaics. Passage floor: ornamental mosaic in black and white, with eagle and hare; 2nd century A.D. Right and left wings: groups of twelve panels, joined together with plaited ribbons, representing still-lifes. Early 4th century A.D.

South wing (to the left);

Marine centaur with nereids and cupids, a flat composition in which the external contour is emphasized. 1st century B.C. Inv. 464.

1

Statue of *Meleager*, hero of the Calydonian Boar-hunt, with dog and boar's head. Roman version (c. 150 A.D.) of a Greek original of the 4th century B.C., probably by Skopas. Inv. 490.

2

North wing (to the right):

Mithras group representing the killing of the primigenial bull (symbol of the procreative force) by the Persian god Mithras. As Creation begins with the bull's blood, the scorpion, serpent and dog (evil spirits) try to prevent the sacrifice. 2nd century A.D. (cf. p. 130: V/23) Inv. 437.

3

On the wall, two *panels of a mosaic with landscapes*, from Hadrian's Villa (cf. floor mosaics in the Room of the Masks, p. 46: VII). Inv. 421, 423.

4, 5

Crab in green porphyry, an extremely rare stone. Inv. 393.

6

V, GALLERY OF STATUES

V

This gallery was once an open loggia on the lower floor of Innocent VIII's Belvedere Palace, built by Jacopo da Pietrasanta from a plan by Antonio del Pollaiolo. Under Clement XIV it was changed into a sculpture gallery (1771) by Alessandro Dori. Under Pius VI, in 1776, the gallery was enlarged and joined to the Room of the Animals (which necessitated the pulling down of a chapel frescoed by Andrea Mantegna).

plan
←
V

1	**C** **D** Statue of *sleeping Ariadne* (once thought to be of Cleopatra). Ariadne, abandoned by Theseus, sleeps and awaits the divine appearance of Dionysus. A much admired copy of a Hellenistic original (2nd cent. B.C.). Inv. 548.

On the left, in front of the niche at the end of the gallery:

2 Serving as a base to the above: *sarcophagus depicting a struggle between giants with serpent-like legs, and gods* (the latter not shown). Late 2nd century A.D. Inv. 549.

3, 4 Two *ornamental candelabra* from Hadrian's Villa, 2nd century A.D. On the bases, figures of gods in relief: *Jupiter* (Zeus) with sceptre and thunderbolt; Juno (Hera) with sceptre; Mercury (Hermes) with ram. Inv. 547. *Mars* (Ares) with helmet and lance; Venus (Aphrodite) with flower; Minerva (Athene) with parade helmet, shield and serpent. Inv. 551.

Turning our backs to the Ariadne, on the right:

5 Statue of *Hermes "Ingenui"* (name inscribed on the base, indicating either the sculptor or the dedicator), 2nd-century Roman version of a Greek original of the 5th century B.C. Attributes: "kerykeion" (herald's staff), lyre, and wings in the hair, above the temples. Inv. 554.

6 *Eros of Centocelle* (on the Via Labicana). Identified from the marks on the back where wings were once attached. Roman copy of a Greek original (Peloponnesian school, early 4th cent. B.C. (cf. copies p. 116: I/23-25, and p. 36:15). Inv. 561.

7 On the left side of the gallery: statue of *resting satyr,* modest copy of the famous statue attributed to Praxiteles, 4th century B.C. (cf. copies p. 117: II/37-39, and p. 37:15). Inv. 561.

Back to the right side of the gallery:

8 *Head and torso of a triton* (water deity), Hellenistic period (2nd cent. B.C.). Inv. 765.

9 Statue of *Apollo "Sauroktonos"* ("he who kills the lizard"). Roman copy of a Greek original, in bronze, by Praxiteles, of about 350 B.C. From the Palatine. A charming work in which the god is shown blissfully absorbed in his innocent game, perhaps an allusion to Apollo's struggle with the monster Python, or to his healing powers. Inv. 750.

10 Statue of *wounded Amazon.* Copy of a bronze (the so-called Mattei Amazon) by Phidias of about 430 B.C., dedicated to Artemis of Ephesus. According to Pliny the Elder (Nat. Hist. XXXIV, 53), this work originated from a competition among artists. (Cf. p. 36:10). Inv. 748.

11 Seated portrait statue of *Posidippus*, famous Greek dramatist (died 250 B.C.), identified from the inscription on the base. Copy from an original of about 250 B.C. From Viminal Hill (found together with the next work, Inv. 588). The face has been extensively remodelled. Inv. 735.

12 On the other side of the passage: seated portrait statue, the so-called *Menander,* found together with the preceding work. Not yet satisfactorily identified. Head extensively remodelled. Inv. 588.

VI # VI, ROOM OF THE BUSTS

This room is divided into three sections (indicated by Roman numerals) by three arches, each of which rests on two columns of ancient yellow marble.

SECTION I

1 Left: portrait group (commonly known as *Cato and Portia*) of Gratidia M.L. Chrite and M. Gratidius Libanus, identified from an inscription no longer preserved. Busts of a Roman couple "dextrarum iunctio". From a tomb of the late 1st century B.C. Inv. 592.

Between the windows: *votive offerings* of the sick; rib-cage and open abdomen. Prayer for recovery, or thanksgiving for "grace received". Inv. 597, 599.

SECTION II

On the left, beyond the small room, lower shelf:

Head of the *child Caracalla* (the bust is modern), son of Septimius Severus, and his successor (211-217 A.D.); probably made shortly after 193 A.D. as a portrait of the future heir. Inv. 646. — **4**

Bust of a *boy dressed as commander-in-chief of the army* (distinguished by the "cingulum"), probably Diadumenianus (assassinated 218 A.D.), son of the emperor Macrinus. Inv. 648. — **5**

SECTION III

In the niche at the back: statue of *Jupiter Verospi* (named after the Verospi Palace, where it was formerly exhibited) on a throne; in his left hand is a sceptre (reconstruction), in his right a thunderbolt. 3rd century A.D., after the cult statue in the Temple of Capitoline Jupiter (a chryselephantine work—gold and ivory—by Apollonius, made after 85 B.C.). Inv. 671. — **6**

In front of the statue: *celestial globe* with stars and zodiac. Inv. 784. — **7**

SECTION II

Side opposite the window:

Lower shelf, on the left: head of *Menelaus* with parade helmet. Copy from the time of Hadrian of the celebrated group representing Menelaus with the body of Patroclus. 2nd century A.D. From Hadrian's Villa. Inv. 694. — **8**

Upper shelf, centre: basalt bust of *Serapis*, copy of the cult statue, by Bryaxis, in Alexandria (4th cent. B.C.). A syncretic deity embodying Osiris and Apis, Jupiter and Pluto. Inv. 689. — **9**

SECTION I

Side opposite the windows: portraits of Roman emperors.

Lower shelf, from left to right:

Head of *Julius Caesar* (assassinated 15 March 44 B.C.). Inv. 713. — **10**

Head of *Augustus* (died 14 A.D.) with crown of thorns, badge of the "Fratelli Arvali" religious fraternity. Inv. 715. — **11**

Head of *Titus* (emperor 71-81 A.D.). Inv. 721. — **12**

Bust of *Trajan* (emperor 98-117 A.D.). Inv. 724. — **13**

Upper shelf, from left to right:

Head of *Antoninus Pius* (emperor 138-161 A.D.) on a bust not belonging to it. From Hadrian's Villa. Inv. 703. — **14**

Bust of *Marcus Aurelius* (emperor 161-180 A.D.), from Hadrian's Villa. Inv. 704. — **15**

Bust of *Lucius Verus*, emperor together with Marcus Aurelius from 161 to 169 A.D. Inv. 705. — **16**

Bust of *Commodus* (emperor 176-192 A.D.). Inv. 706. — **17**

Bust of *Caracalla* (emperor 211-217 A.D.). Inv. 711. — **18**

plan
←
VII

VII, CABINET OF THE MASKS

The tower-like buttress from Innocent VIII's Belvedere Palace was included in the museum in 1780. The floor is decorated with four panels of an ancient mosaic with representations of masks, from which the room takes its name. Three of the panels depict theatrical masks, and the fourth an idyllic landscape with grazing animals, and a small sanctuary. They were found in 1779, together with the mosaics in the Room of the Animals (see p. 43: IV), in Hadrian's Villa near Tivoli, and date back to the 2nd century A.D.

The frame, ornamented with elements from the coat-of-arms of Pius VI, was made in the same period in which the mosaics were brought to this room. On the ceiling are mythological scenes painted by Domenico de Angelis: the Judgement of Paris, the Awakening of Ariadne, Diana and Endymion, Venus and Adonis.

1 In the vestibule, *bust of Pius VI*, who enlarged and completed the museum.

Starting from the right, and proceeding counter-clockwise:

2 Statue of the *crouching Venus*, Roman copy of a famous work by Doidalsas of Bithynia (3rd cent. B.C.). The goddess of love is shown crouching under a spout of water, intent on her bath. Inv. 815.

3 Statue of the *Venus of Cnidos*, Roman copy of the famous cult statue (sanctuary of Cnidos) carved by Praxiteles in the mid-4th century B.C. This work was famous in its day (Pliny, Nat. Hist. XXXVI, 20), and is known to us through copies, though none of these attains the high artistic standard of the original. This is the first example of a cult statue in which the goddess of love appears in the nude. Serene and imperturbable, her clothes draped on the bath, she seems unconscious of the presence of any onlooker. Inv. 812.

4 *Group of the Three Graces*, a 2nd-century A.D. Roman copy of a late Hellenistic work, whose charm consists of the interplay of variation and repetition. Inv. 810.

5 Statue of *satyr* in red marble; from Hadrian's Villa. 2nd century A.D. Inv. 801.

To reach the Room of the Muses, we now return to the Room of the Animals, and go through the door on the right (opposite the door leading to the Octagonal Court).

plan
→
III

III, ROOM OF THE MUSES

This room was built by Michelangelo Simonetti in about 1780. The ceiling frescoes, the work of Tommaso Conca, depict Apollo, the Muses and poets, forming a thematic link with the statues exhibited here (see below).

1 The *Belvedere Torso* (neo-Attic, 1st cent. B.C.) was placed in this room in 1973. The muscular figure in seated on an animal skin spread over a rock, on which are inscribed the words "made by Apollonius, Athenian, son of Nesto". The remaining fragments of the animal's head can be seen on the left thigh. According to the traditional interpretation, this is a lion's head, and consequently the figure that of Hercules, though the names of Marsyas, Skyron, Poliphemus and Philoctetes have also been suggested. Found in the 15th century, the statue was first kept in the Colonna Palace, and then moved to the Belvedere garden during the papacy of Clement VII. It was much admired by Renaissance artists, especially Michelangelo. Inv. 1192.

Against the walls are seven statues of Muses, and one of Apollo, their leader; found near Tivoli in 1774, in the so-called Villa of Cassius, 2nd century A.D.

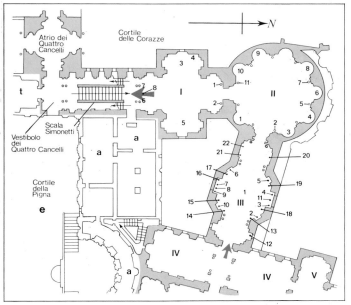

III

On the right side of the room: *Melpomene* (tragedy), Inv. 299; *Thalia* (comedy), Inv. 295; *Clio* (history, epic), Inv. 291; *Polyhymnia* (mime, song), Inv. 287.

2, 3
4, 5

On the left side of the room: *Erato* (hymns, love songs), Inv. 317; *Calliope* (heroic song, elegy), Inv. 312; *Apollo Citharedos*, "master" of the Muses, Inv. 310; *Terpsichore* (dance), inv. 308.

6
7, 8
9

From other sites: *Euterpe* (flutes, tragic choir), Inv. 303; *Urania* (astronomy), Inv. 293.

10,11

The room also contains ,Roman copies of portraits of famous Greeks. To the right of the entrance:

Less than life-size bust of *Sophocles*. On the lower edge, traces of the inscription bearing the name. Discovered in 1777, in the garden of the Conservatory of the Mendicants (near Constantine's basilica). The inscription on this portrait made it possible to identify the statue from Terracina exhibited in the Gregorian Profane Museum (cf. p. 117: II/43). Inv. 322.

12

Head of *Epicurus* (died 270 B.C.) on a modern herma; philosopher, founder of the Epicurean school. Inv. 301.

13

Opposite:

Head of *Euripides* (died 406 B.C.), from an original of about 330 B.C. Inv. 302.

14

Herma of *Plato* (died 347 B.C.). The inscription "Zenon" may be modern. Inv. 305.

15

Socrates (condemned to death 399 B.C.); from the Quintili Villa on the Appian Way. Identified from the Silenus-like features, as described by Alcibiades in Plato's "Symposium". Inv. 314.

16

Homer (2nd half of the 8th cent. B.C.), *Epimenides type*. Identified from the blidness of the subject represented. Copy of a Greek work of about 460 B.C. Inv. 315.

17

C
D

The following portrait hermae of famous Greek poets, philosophers and orators (Roman copies of Greek works) are from the same Roman Villa where the statues of the Muses and Apollo were found.

On the right side of the room:

18   *Aischines* (died 314 B.C.), famous Attic orator, adversary of Demosthenes; identified from the inscription. Inv. 297.

19   *Antisthenes* (died c. 365 B.C.), founder of the Cynic philosophical school; identified from the inscription. Inv. 288.

20   *Pericles* (died 429 B.C.) with Corinthian helmet of the commander-in-chief of the army ("strageos"); identified from the inscription. Copy of a work by Kresilas (c. 430 B.C.). Inv. 269.

Opposite:

21   *Periander* (7th-6th cent. B.C.), son of Cypselus, tyrant of Corinth; identified by the inscribed motto, "Practice is all". Inv. 276.

22   *Bias* (6th cent. B.C.), one of the Seven Sages, contemporary of Croesus; identified by the inscribed motto, "The greater part of mankind is wicked". Inv. 279.

II, ROUND ROOM

This round, domed room (external diameter of dome about 21,6 m, height about 22 m), a Pantheon-inspired masterpiece by Michelangelo Simonetti, was built in about 1780. The floor is decorated with ancient mosaics from Otricoli: scenes of battle between Greeks and centaurs; marine animals with nereids and tritons. In the centre of the room, a large monolithic basin in porphyry, 13 m in circumference, from the Domus Aurea.

1   In the niche to the left of the entrance: togated statue of the *Genius of Augustus*; a fold of the toga covers the head for the sacrificial act; in the left hand, a cornucopia (right arm with patera is restored). Inv. 259.

To the right of the entrance, proceeding counter-clockwise:

2   Colossal head of *Jupiter of Otricoli*, a Roman version of a well-known Greek representation of Zeus of the 4th century B.C. Inv. 257.

3   Colossus of *Antinous* (cf. below: 7) with attributes of the Dionysius-Osiris cult: ivy wreath, band, mystic cist (near the left foot), and pine-cone on the head (perhaps better identified as "Uraeus"). Inv. 256.

4   Statue of a goddess, restored as *Demeter*, Roman copy of a Greek work of about 420 B.C. (school of Phidias). Inv. 254.

5   Colossal head of *Hadrian* (emperor 117-138 A.D.), from his mausoleum (Castel Sant'Angelo). Inv. 253.

6   Colossus of *Hercules* in gilded bronze, late 2nd century A.D. Discovered in 1864 near the Theatre of Pompey, where it had been carefully buried. The stone slabs that covered its grave were inscribed with the words "Fulgor Conditum Summanium", indicating that the statue was struck by lightning, and buried on the spot. Attributes of Hercules: club, lion skin, and apples of the Hesperides. Inv. 252.

7   Colossal bust of *Antinous*, a young favourite of Hadrian; after his death (he drowned in the Nile in 130 A.D.) he was deified by the emperor. From Hadrian's Villa. Inv. 251.

8   Statue of a goddess, the so-called *Hera Barberini*; Roman version of a late 5th-century Greek work attributed to Agorakritos, pupil of Phidias. Inv. 249.

C
D

II

State of *Claudius* dressed as Jupiter; from Lanuvium. C. 50 A.D. Inv. 243.

9

Statue of *Juno Sospita*, an Italic divinity of Lanuvium. Probably a cult statue of the 2nd century A.D. Inv. 241.

10

Colossal portrait of *Plotina* (died 122 A.D.), wife of Trajan. The size of the portrait suggests that it was made on the occasion of her deification (129 A.D.). Inv. 240.

11

I, GREEK CROSS ROOM

I

The name of this room comes from its design in the form of a Greek cross, i.e. a cross with four equal arms. The room was built by Simonetti in about 1780, during the papacy of Pius VI, as the entrance-hall of the MUSEUM PIUM, which appears in large letters on the architrave above the portal leading to the Round Room.

The passage is flanked by two *Egyptian-style statues*, architectural supports ("telamones") modelled along the lines of the Pharaoh or Osiris type. From Hadrian's Villa. Red granite, 2nd century A.D. Inv. 196, 197.

1, 2

In the floor, centre: mosaic with bust of Athene, from Tusculum, 3rd century A.D., in a sumptuous 18th-century frame.

Right wing:

Sarcophagus of Constance, daughter of Constantine; porphyry, 350-360 A.D. From Santa Costanza on the Via Nomentana. The relief depicts cupids harvesting grapes; on the long sides, two peacocks; a ram and a cupid with garland (Dionysian tradition). Inv. 237.

3

Statue of *Augustus* (ruled 31 B.C.-14 A.D.), *from Otricoli*, based on the "Diomedes" model of 5th-century B.C. Greek sculpture. Inv. 181.

4

Left wing: *sarcophagus of St Helen*, mother of Constantine; porphyry, early 4th century A.D. From the Tomb of St Helen on the Via Labicana (Tor Pignattara). Victorius Roman cavaliers, and prostrate, enchained barbarians. Extensively restored, especially the heads and portrait busts in the upper corners. Presumably not made for Helen, but for her husband, Constantinus Chlorus. Inv. 238.

5

At the sides of the exit: two *reclining sphinxes* in reddish-grey granite. Roman Imperial Age (1st-3rd cent. A.D.). Inv. 236, 239.

6, 7

In the floor, between the sphinxes: *coloured mosaic with a basket of flowers*, modern copy of a 2nd-century A.D. original from the Appian Way, now in the vestibule leading to the Gregorian Profane and Pio Christian museums (see p. 113).

8

To reach the Gregorian Etruscan Museum from here, we proceed through the exit (between the two sphinxes), and up the next flight of the Simonetti Stairway.

Gold fibula (2nd half of the 7th cent. B.C.)

This museum was founded by Gregory XVI, and inaugurated 2 February 1837. Most of the artefacts on display came from private excavations carried out in necropolises of Southern Etruria (now part of Latium) by permission of the Vatican State. They were purchased by the Camerlengate, on the proposal of the General Consultative Commission for Antiquities and Fine Arts, and on the basis of the right of pre-emption guaranteed to public collections by the Pacca Edict of 1820. After the end of the Vatican State, and of its jurisdiction over Southern Etruria, the museum grew only sporadically, though the additions made were significant ones, such as the Falcioni Collection, purchased in 1898, Benedetto Guglielmi's donation to Pius XI in 1935, and Mario Astarita's donation to Paul VI in 1967.

A large collection of Greek and Italiot (Greek-colonized southern Italy) vases (see p. 63), and a smaller one of Roman antiquities (Antiquarium Romanum) from Rome and Latium (see p. 60) form an integral part of the museum. The vases of the first collection are of great importance to the history of ancient ceramics, though their original archeological context has been long destroyed (by the manner in which 18th- and 19th-century excavations were conducted). They are exhibited apart, in the rooms looking on to the Court of the Pigna (these

rooms are parallel to, and intercommunicate with certain sections of
the Etruscan Museum proper). For this reason, those who wish to visit
the Vase Collection after having visited the Etruscan Museum must
retrace their steps and enter the hemicycle after the Room of the
Bronzes, proceeding contrary to the chronological and typological
sequence of the exhibits, i.e. from Room XII to Room X.

On occasion, visitors may be required to follow an itinerary different
from that described in this guide.

The central rooms of the Etruscan Museum (Rooms V-IX) occupy the
first floor of the Belvedere Palace; Rooms I-IV and those housing the
Vase Collection (X-XIV) are in the building annexed to it by Pius IV.

I, ROOM OF THE SARCOPHAGI

Monuments of various kinds (sarcophagi, urns, free-standing sculpture,
reliefs, cippi, inscriptions, etc.), places of origin (Chiusi, Vulci, Cerveteri, Orte, Palestrina, etc.), and periods (6th-1st cent. B.C.) are
gathered here. Their only common denominator is the material of
which they are made, the modest local stone—varieties of tufa, or
travertine, and sandstone—preferred by Etruscan sculptors and stone-
cutters for the ease with which it can be cut. Its aesthetic shortcomings
were concealed by the heavy use of stucco-work and polychromy, now
almost completely lost. Within this typically 18th-century arrangement
of artefacts by material, others are soon evident: quality and state of
preservation (sarcophagi and sculpture), mythological content (sarcophagus reliefs), and epigraphical interest (inscriptions).

The description begins with the group of sarcophagi in the centre of
the room.

In front of the entrance: *sarcophagus in "nenfro"* (local variety of tufa)
with scenes of the Atridae saga on the front, and scenes of the Theban
saga on the back. The lid, which does not belong to the sarcophagus,
represents the deceased reclining (though the position of the limbs is
that of a standing figure), holding a scroll. From Tarquinia, 2nd century
B.C. Inv. 14561.

Proceeding clockwise, we come to:

Limestone sarcophagus with polychrome relief. The figure on the lid,
which is decorated at both ends in roof fashion, is a representation of
the deceased; the two decorated sides of the coffin depict a funeral
procession. Attic-influenced Etruscan work (late 5th cent. B.C.). Found
together with three other sarcophagi made of the same stone, in a
chamber tomb, the walls of which were originally painted. From Cerveteri. Inv. 14949.

Nenfro sarcophagus "of the magistrate". On the front, the last voyage
of the deceased, who appears on the biga (charriot), preceded by two
togated figures bearing "fasces". The inscription on the upper list gives
the name, the "cursus honorum", and the age of the dead man, and
directions pertaining to inhumation rites. The lid does not belong to the
sarcophagus. From Tuscania, 3rd century B.C. Inv. 14950.

Nenfro sarcophagus with representations of the slaying of the Niobids
on the front; left side, battle of the Centaurs; right side, Achilles with
the body of Hector. From a large dynastic tomb at Tuscania; found
together with another 26 sarcophagi (2nd cent. B.C.). Same manufacture as Inv. 14561 (see above: 1). Inv. 14947.

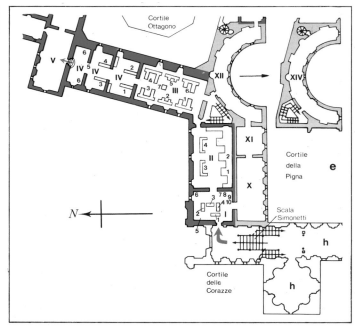

I

On each side of the window:

5

Left: *"bilingual" stele from Todi.* Rectangular sepulchral slab in travertine, bearing on both faces a text in Latin and Gallic (written in a special alphabet derived from Etruscan). It mentions the building of the tomb of a certain Ategnatos, son of Drutos, by his younger brother, Coisis. From Todi, 2nd half of the 2nd century B.C. Inv. 14958.

6

Right: sandstone statuette of a female figure. The bare breast suggests that the figure is a representation of a "Lasa" (Etruscan female demon, in this case of the underworld), rather than of the dead woman. This statuette, from a tomb near Chiusi, is one of the most charming creations of Greek-inspired Etruscan sculpture; even the unpretentious stone underlines the delicacy and submissiveness of the waiting girl. 3rd/2and century B.C. Inv. 14951.

In the corner opposite the window:

7, 8

Left: two *nenfro busts of horses.* From the entrance to a tomb at Vulci. The theme of the tomb as the home of the deceased here gives way to that of the funeral ceremony and the voyage to the underworld. 4th/3rd century B.C. Inv. 14953, 14954.

9, 10

Right: two *lions in nenfro,* from a Vulci tomb, where they were placed to guard the entrance, an act revealing the belief in the continued existence of the deceased within the tomb. Late 6th century B.C. Inv. 14955, 14956.

II

II, ROOM OF THE REGOLINI-GALASSI TOMB

The frieze: between stucco caryatids, frescoes depicting scenes from the life of Moses by Federico Barocci and Federico Zuccari (1563).

The artefacts exhibited here form the nucleus of the Gregorian collection, and were found in 1836-37 during the excavation of the necropolis of the Sorbo, south of Cerveteri, by General Vincenzo Galassi and the

archpriest of Cerveteri, Alessandro Regolini. To this material, which
comes from nine tombs built within four neighbouring tumuli (mounds),
were added artefacts found by Giovanni Pinza in 1906 in the Giulimondi Tomb, during a topographical survey of the necropolis.

B
D

The richest collection comes from the oldest and central tomb (the
Regolini-Galassi Tomb, named after its discoverers), and is exhibited in
the *large show-case* along the wall opposite the windows. The two
smaller show-cases in front of the windows contain finds from the
peripheral tombs, as well as finds from the excavations mentioned above.

1, 2
3, 4

Show-case A

The main tomb, which as a whole can be dated back to the mid-7th
century B.C., provides some of the most complete information so far
come to light on the mature "Oriental" phase of Etruscan civilization.
During this period, Etruscan cities, especially the coastal cities, among
which Cerveteri was prominent, were large and well-appointed, and
displayed an artistic expression of high monumentality. The material
found in this tomb testifies to their extensive trade contacts with Ae-
gean and eastern Mediterranean areas, and to the influence these
areas had on Etruscan art, and provides a picture of a complex society
capable of concentrating around itself the resources of considerable
parts of the inland, filtering them through its highly specialized artisan
and merchant classes.

The tomb, which can be visited at Cerveteri, is partly hewn out of the
living rock (tufa), and partly constructed of squarehewn stone; it has a
projecting ashlar false vault, which was covered with a mound of earth.
It consists of a sloping passageway, a long central cell, an end cell
(separated from the central cell by a partitian made of blocks of tufa),
and, near the partitian, two symmetrical, oval side cells completely
hewn out of tufa.

The objects exhibited here are laid out according to the approximate
position in which they were found in the tomb, a longitudinal section of
which is shown at the large show-case. The sequence of the exhibits is
counter-clockwise, and begins on the right as we enter.

We know that the tomb had two occupants: a woman of noble birth, in
the end cell (objects nos. 1-226), and a man of equally high rank, in
the central cell (nos. 234-327); the funerary furnishings of the latter
extended to the small cell on the left. There is less certainty about the
presence of a third occupant, a man, cremated, in the right cell (nos.
227-233).

To the woman belong the *bronze remains of a throne* (no. 217), and
the series of jewels and precious ornaments, some of which were
woven into the cloth of her garments. Of special interest is the enormous gold fibula (no. 1) with a foliated bow and a disc catchplate. It is
a parade piece, jointed at the back to make it less cumbersome, a
lavishly decorated version of the simple fibula known in Italy as far
back as the Bronze Age. The free-standing ducks on the bow consist
of two embossed pieces welded together; the lions on the disc are also
embossed, and were made from a separate plate. Details and
ornamental friezes of fine granulation.—The centre-piece of the woven
decoration (see gold fragments nos. 49-65) was undoubtedly the large
plate (a breastplate?), no. 28, whose concentric pattern was inscribed
with a punch.

1

The man lay on a *bed* (no. 236), a rare example in bronze of a type
more commonly made of stone. The "braked" funeral cart (no. 237)
was probably built to the same size. Note the remains of studded iron
rims on the latter.—Although it was found in the right cell, the biga (no.
227) appears to have belonged to the man in the central cell, who was
probably a warrior of high rank (see also the series of parade shields,
nos. 243-250).

2

B
D

The various vessels found in the tomb appear to have played a precise role in the funeral ritual. The presence of both local and foreign materials, and decorative motifs is significant. The silver jug with gold-plated handle (no. 165) is from Cyprus, and is a form often imitated in the local bucchero (typical, shiny black pottery produced in Etruria from about the 7th to the 5th century B.C.). The silver gilt cups decorated with Egyptian-style motifs (nos. 321-324) are from Cyprus or, according to a recent theory, Cumae. The small silver amphora with engraved double spiral (no. 164) is an outstanding example of a local form. The conical proto-Corinthian cups (kotyle), no. 370 et seq. have local counterparts in clay (no. 349) and silver (nos. 158-162).

Among the most important pieces in the whole Gregorian collection is the pyriform ink-pot (no. 327) in "bucchero" (a local clay), with inscribed alphabet on the base, and graffito syllabary on the sides. Writing, which here is used to decorate the very symbol of the art, was introduced to Etruria in the late 8th century B.C., by way of the Greek colonies in southern Italy.

3

Show-case B:

Finds from the Giulimondi Tomb, on the Via Braccianese, about 50 metres from the Regolini-Galassi Tomb, excavated by Giovanni Pinza in 1906. It was a chamber tomb with a doublesloped ceiling and a longitudinal canal at the top, and two beds along the walls. The furnishings, not all of which can be definitely assigned to one or the other of the occupants, are comprised of a series of small, spiral patterned amphorae in bucchero and various clay mixtures (nos. 458-466: cf. no. 164 in the Regolini-Galassi Tomb), and of proto-Corinthian ceramics. Among the latter are two globular "aryballoi" (perfume jars - nos. 513-514), a small "Thapsos type" cup (no. 515), and various ovoid aryballoi (nos. 508-512). Taken as a whole, the contents of this tomb, which may date back to the first quarter of the 7th century B.C., are probably the oldest of the collection.

4

Show-case C:

Finds from the Calabresi Tomb. Worth noting here are the spendid bucchero vessels, among which are a "kantharos" (a kind of chalice, no. 413), with ribbon handle and conical base bearing a long, spiral inscription, and an ampulla (no. 400) with two busts of horses, and handle in the form of a charioteer (c. 625 B.C.). The show-case also houses a red-earth cinerary urn with a rich orientalizing decoration. This kind of urn is commonly called "house-shaped" on account of its parallelepid form and because in some cases the gabled cover is decorated with reliefs that allude to the roof of a building. This example is called Calabresi after its discoverer, who found it in 1869 in the Banditaccia Necropolis at Cerveteri.

III

III, ROOM OF THE BRONZES

The frieze: between stucco caryatids, frescoes depicting scenes of the Old Testament by Santi di Tito and Pomarancio (1564).

In this room are all the bronzes, statues and votive offerings received from early 19th-century excavations. The exhibits are in chronological order except for certain objects grouped together by type (helmets, candelabra, mirrors, cists and a few others) and those few objects that are certain to belong together.

1

Note in *show-case A*, left of the entrance:

Ossuaries of the biconical type. In these two vases, the ancient form of the biconical ossuary made of the Villanovan clay mixture (cf. p. 59, VII/1, 2) has been influenced by Greek ceramics. 7th century B.C. Inv. 12865, 12862.

Spheroidal amphora on a high base (Inv. 12630), and chair made of tubular elements in bronze plate (Inv. 12631). It is not certain that the two pieces belong together. The development of the cinerary urn towards anthropomorphic forms, both in the body (here the vertical position of the ribbon handles is suggestive of human arms) and in the lid (missing from this piece, but undoubtedly in the rough form of a human head, perhaps in terracotta), is typical of the Chiusi region. The cinerary urn would be placed on a chair or, more commonly, a throne with a circular back, inside a large dolium, or jar, together, with other funerary objects, and buried. 7th century B.C.

Hands in bronze plate, decorated with small gold studs: they were made from a single sheet of bronze, closed at the wrists, and slightly folded over at the edges of the long fingers. The few comparisons that can be made would indicate Vulci as the place of origin. They appear to have a certain conceptual affinity with the bronze masks found on some Canopic vases from Chiusi, and in general with early Etruscan experiments in sculpting the human figure in bronze, which consisted of the joining together of separate pieces made of embossed bronze plate. 7th century B.C. Inv. 11930, 11931.

Tripod belonging to a series, probably made at Vulci; note-worthy for its imaginative detail, among other things. From Vulci, late 6th century B.C. Inv. 12110.

Eleven "bosses" with heads of lions and of Acheloos (a mythological figure, later a river god with the horns and ears of a bull). The original function of this unique class of objects is uncertain. They have been variously interpreted as shield bosses, as ceiling decorations (of houses or tombs having similar architectural features), and, the most likely explanation, as funeral bed ornaments having a magical, protective function. The examples exhibited here are from a chamber tomb in the necropolis of Mount Quaglieri, Tarquinia, and are splendid examples of Etruscan bronzework of the late 6th century B.C. In their economy of style, precision of line, and wonderfully stylized details (Inv. 12625 in particular) they bear a strong affinity with the terracotta masterpieces of Veii. Inv. 12461-12463, 12622-12629.

Show-case B: 2

Bronze statuettes of seated boys. Although most "ex voto" temple offerings were made of terracotta, some, such as these, were made of more expensive materials. Identified as offerings from the inscriptions, inscribed before the statues were cast. Inv. 12107 from Lake Trasimeno, Inv. 12108 from Tarquinia, 2nd/1st century B.C.

Statuette of a haruspex (Etruscan priest who examined animal viscera to interpret the will of the gods). Identified by the tall felt or skin hat, which was tied under the chin to prevent it from falling off (an ill omen) during the ceremony. From a tomb on the Tiber, 4th century B.C. Inv. 12040.

An old haruspex examines the liver of an animal. Etruscan fantasy has assigned him a pair of wings and the name of Chalchas, the most famous Greek soothsayer. From Vulci, early 4th century B.C. Inv. 12240.

Show-case C: 3

Worth noting among the headpieces exhibited here is Inv. 12304, with embossed cap representing the hair and ears of a silenus. It comes from Atella, and is certain to be an Italiot work, 4th century B.C.

Show-case D: 4

The bronze mirrors decorated on the back represent a particularly significant class of Etruscan handiwork. They were produced between the 6th and 3rd century B.C., with the 4th century having been a period

B
D
of particular development. The following scene is well worth noting:

Eos (Aurora) abducts the young hunter Cephalus. Silver-damascened ivy branch, a rare relief technique. From Vulci, c. 470 B.C. Inv. 12241.

Oval cist (box for woman's toilette articles). The cast handle is of local inspiration, while the embossed decoration (depicting a battle of Amazons) on the body reveals a clear Hellenistic influence. From Vulci, 3rd/2nd century B.C. Inv. 12259, 12260.

5

Show-case E:

There is a very fine collection of candelabra, the largest of which is 1.5 metres high (Inv. 12411), of the well-known type produced at Vulci. The cymae are decorated with isolated figures, or with small cast bronze groups, some of a mythological nature, others drawn from the world of the dance or the palestra. Most of the examples exhibited here date from the mid-5th century (Inv. 12407) to the 4th century B.C.

6

Show-case F:

The rich series of bronze articles (craters on high, cast bases, situlae, "oinochoai", paterae, etc.) are from a chamber tomb near Bolsena, and date back to about the mid-4th century B.C. The word "suθina" ("tomb" or "funerary") appears on many of the vases, indicating their role as tomb furnishings. The occupant of the tomb is known from the inscriptions on the situla Inv. 12806, and on the patera Inv. 12787: "Larisal Harenies suθina" ("Tomb [furnishings or gift] of Laris Harenie").

7

The "*Mars of Todi*" stands in the centre of the room. Cast in several parts, it is one of the few large Italiot bronzes that have survived. It represents a young warrior leaning on a lance with his left hand, and offering a libation with the cup held in his outstretched right hand. Interesting also for the Umbrian inscription ("Ahal Trutitis dunum dede") on one of the front fringes of his armour. The work reflects Greek influences of the second half of the 5th century B.C. From Todi, where it was found buried between four slabs of travertine. Late 5th century B.C. Inv. 13886.

IV

ROOM IV

The frieze: remains of the decoration of the time of Pius IV depicting mythological and allegorical scenes.

SECTION I

1

Show-cases A, B, C:

"Villanovan" material found in the necropolis discovered towards the middle of the last century at Villanova near Bologna. The biconical urn is the most typical product of the cultural phase found in Etruria in the Iron Age. The distinctive feature of these urns, in addition to their biconical shape, are the single handle (wherever there was a pre-existing second handle it was deliberately broken off) and the incised and impressed geometric decoration. The bronze pieces are mainly "leech shaped" fibulae with long catchs and incised decorations on the back of the swollen bodies. Worthy of note are two examples with bodies made of alternating discs of bronze and amber and disc shaped catch with incised geometric ornaments. The material is mainly from Vulci, 9th/8th century B.C.

Show-case D:

B
D

Material from Iron Age tombs, excavated in 1816-17 between Marino and Castel Gandolfo. The "hut" urn (see inv. 15407) known (as was the "Villanovan" urn) also to the cremators of Etruria, is a characteristic product of Iron Age Latium, as are the vases decorated with "mesh" patterns (see Inv. 15404) and the so-called calefattoi (see Inv. 15401, 15405). 9th/8th century B.C.

SECTION II

Show-case E:

3

On display here are clay mixture vases of the 8th and 7th centuries B.C. from Etruria and Agro Falisco. Worthy of interest in the centre of the show-case are two vases: on the top shelf a large jug (Oinochoe) decorated with engravings depicting a horse, three stags and a long snake in the imitations of the animals decorating Corinthian ceramics of the oriental style age of Etruscan civilization; on the bottom shelf: a black polished clay mixture stamnos, decorated with the excision technique in which the cavities have been filled with a red colouring so as to give life and polychromy to the composition as a whole. Between the handles are human figures between two quadrupeds (horses?), probably identifiable with the motif "Signore dei Cavalli" of common use in the Faliscan circles of the 7th century B.C.

Show-case F:

4

Here are various kinds of bucchero vessels (typical Etruscan ceramics). Worthy of note are the oldest examples (late 7th century B.C.) decorated with little dotted fans, and the later ones decorated in relief.

SECTION III

Show-case G:

5

Funerary monument with dying Adonis. The young hunter of mythology lies on a bed, mortally wounded. This carefully executed scene may allude to the cause of death of the subject; at all events, the Adonis myth was a favorite in Etruscan representations of death and the under-world from the 4th century on. The intersecting clay partitions inside the monument show that it was not an urn. The holes in the surface were made to assure thorough ventilation of the clay during the firing. From Tuscania, 2nd/1st century B.C. Inv. 14147.

This room contains alabaster and limestone *cinerary urns* from Volterra, Chiusi, Perugia, etc. Worth noting is the:

6

Volterra-type urn in veined alabaster. The lid, unfinished as there was not enough material, shows the couple reclining at a banquet. The decorations on the body of the urn depict Oenomaus, king of Pisa in Elis, dying at the end of the chariot race he organized as a competition for the hand of his daughter Hippodameia; the race was won, unfairly, by Pelops, son of Tantalus. An Etruscan version of angry Furies appears in the centre and at the sides. From Orte, 2nd century B.C. Inv. 13887.

V, GUGLIELMI ROOM

As is indicated on the plaque above the entrance, Pius XI set aside this room to house the collection donated by Benedetto Guglielmi in 1935. The room is divined into three sections: painted ceramics from Greece (*show-cases B, C, D, K*) and Etruria (*show-case E*), bronzes (*show-case A*), jewelry (*show-case G*), and bucchero (*show-case F*).

1-5
6-8

plan
V →

B
D Of the last, note the small earthen pot to the left on the central shelf of the show-case. It has graffito decorations and an inscription reading "mi Ramuthas Kansinai", in which the vessel, speaking in the first person, identifies itself as the property of one Ramutha Kansinai. Late 7th century B.C.

All the material exhibited here comes from the necropolises of ancient Vulci (near Montalto di Castro).

VI

VI, JEWELRY ROOM

Rooms VI, VII, VIII and IX are the third floor of the Palazzetto of Innocent VIII, presumably planned by Antonio del Pollaiolo and built by Jacopo da Pietrasanta between 1484 and 1487.

1

Show-case A:

In the centre: two earrings (?) in gold, rock crystal and hard stone. Only one other example of this type of jewelry is known. From Vulci, late 6th century B.C. No. 20.

Bottom shelf: a series of gold, and silver gilt rings with engraved and embossed elliptical settings. From Vulci, 4th century B.C. Nos. 30-31.

2

Show-case B:

Top shelf: amber objects, including some pendants. Note the horse-head (late 5th cent. B.C.), and the head of a silenus carrying a wineskin on his shoulders (c. 500 B.C.) Nos 4-7.

Middle shelf: cylindrical earrings. From Vulci, 6th century B.C. Nos. 17-27.

At the back of the show-case is a series of rings with scarab-shaped settings and, on the underside, engravings resembling seals. The fashion of Egyptian-style rings lasted from the 6th to the 5th century B.C. The lovely pair (nos. 44-45) in the centre of the shelf date back to the early 5th century. From Vulci.

3

Show-case C:

Shown here is a kind of locket, called a "bulla" by the Romans, designed to contain an amulet.

The bulla worn by the youth of the statuette no. 10 is of the same type as above, and was cast from a real jewel. 4th century B.C.

4

Show-case D:

A type of earring common in Etruria (see the head, no. 32, and the mirror, no. 27) is shown here in its various phases of development. The final horseshoe shape was already known in the 4th century B.C. From Vulci.

5, 6

Show-cases E and F:

These show-cases contain funerary diadems in gold foil, 4th/2nd century B.C.

To the right of show-case E some of the 4th century B.C. materials found in a tomb in Vulci in 1835, reconstructed according to 19th century sources. These include two diadems, a pair of earrings, a necklace and three large gold bullae showing Zeus and Athena on a chariot and Aphrodite between Adonis and Eros.

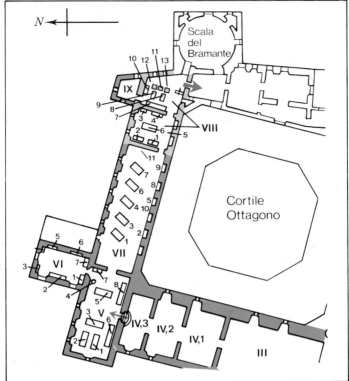

VI
7

Show-case G:

In the centre: Roman jewelry in gold; note the large, shiny bulla from Ostia, 1st/2nd century A.D.

VII, ROOM OF THE TERRACOTTAS

VII

1

Show-case A:

A "chest" urn with human head protruding from the lid. The lid is suggestive of the custom of burying corpses in tree trunks, a practice especially common in inland areas of Southern Etruria. Found in 1838 at Orte, where this unique class of urns appears to have flourished. 7th/6th century B.C. Inv. 14145, 14141.

Bust of a winged horse, once a high relief ornament on the pediment of a temple. The animal is shown as it takes flight, its forelegs extended towards the sky. Attic-inspired Etruscan work from Cerveteri, early 5th century B.C. Inv. 14130.

Show-case D:

2

Material found in a tomb discovered in 1901 at San Benedetto, near Castiglion del Lago. The relics consist of four terracotta urns (Inv. 16254, 16255, 16256, 16257), a large pointed amphora, a smaller amphora (Inv. 16259), and a jug ("lagynos", Inv. 16260), a mirror (Inv. 16262), an armlet (Inv. 16265), a tile bearing a now almost illegible inscription, an earthen pot, a "distaff" vase for balsam and a small jug.

plan
⟵
VII

B
D

The inscriptions painted on the urns cite four members of the Ceicna family; one branch of the same "gens", under the Romanized name of Caecina, was one of the most prominent families of the Volterran aristocracy. Second half of the 2nd century B.C.

4-9

Show-cases E, G, H, I, L:

A large collection of votive offerings from temples in the ancient city of Caere (Cerveteri) is exhibited here. It consists of small reproductions of cult images, and of several representations of various parts of the human body (offered according to the divine favour desired or received), especially heads and half-heads, offered by the faithful as a sign of their piety. Most of these are common representations made **6** from standard moulds, though some have been varied slightly (*show-case G*, a head with blonde hair, and a head with dark hair, both from **4** the same mould; *show-case E*, a head with a bearded face, and one **6** with a clean-shaven face. Inv. 13854, 13852). There are only a few original portrait statues (see the bust of a woman. Inv. 14107, *show-* **4** *case G*, and the male statue, of which only the head remains, Inv. 13847, *show-case E*). Most date from the 3rd to the 1st century B.C.

On the right over the wall show-cases:

10

Four slabs with floral decorations and human heads. Acanthus flower motifs frame male heads (Dionysus?) and female heads (Ariadne? Maenads?). The slabs were once attached to the horizontal beams of a temple. Free-hand work. The present exhibition shows them to be the result of a 19th-century reassembly of fragments belonging to several slabs, the number of which is uncertain. At present attributed to Cerveteri, though evidence is insufficient. 4th century B.C. Inv. 14129.

On the wall at the end of the room:

11

Terracotta *pediment reliefs* from Tivoli (late 4th-3rd cent. B.C.) found in 1835 during road work at the foot of the Ponte Gregoriano on the Aniene. The subject of the scene may be deduced from the acanthus tree beside figure no. 4, from which hangs one of the hind legs of an empty sheepskin. This detail recalls the iconography of the Golden Fleece, and confirms beyond all doubt that the central theme of this monument is the quest of the Argonauts. The figures decorated the pediment of a temple, as their size and pronounced forward inclination—which made them clearly visible from below—demonstrate. The reconstruction is intended merely to suggest one way in which the reliefs might have been arranged originally.

At this point we come to two separate collections which have been inserted into the Etruscan Museum area: the Antiquarium Romanum, and the Greek, Italiot and Etruscan vases (the latter are being rearranged). The Antiquarium Romanum and the Vase Collection form an integral part of the museum, and owe their presence here to the traditional intermingling of Etruscan with Greek and Roman works.

VIII

VIII, ANTIQUARIUM ROMANUM

These rooms contain works (mainly Roman, and of the minor arts) of various periods that were once with the Etruscan collection.

SECTION I

1-4,7

Show-cases B, C, G, F, and *show-case H* of the adjoining room:

A collection of architectural ornaments in terracotta, from Rome and Latium, dating from the 1st century B.C. to the 2nd century A.D. (the "Campana Reliefs", named after the famous mid-19th century collector and archeologist G.P. Campana).

Between show-cases A and E, on the wall:

B
D

Reliefs depicting three of the labours of Hercules; the killing of the Nemean Lion, the Hydra of Lerna, the killing of the Cretan Bull. These form part of the frequently depicted Twelve labours performed by Hercules for King Eurystheus of Tiryns, on the orders of the Pithia, as an act of expiation after he had murdered his own children in a fit of madness. From Rome, 2nd century A.D. Inv. 14163, 14160, 14177.

5

Show-case D:

6

Top shelf, left: ivory doll with jointed limbs, originally dressed in cloth interwoven with gold. From a sarcophagus (evidently that of a little girl) found in Rome near the Basilica of St Sebastian. 2nd/4th century A.D. Inv. 12224.

Bottom shelf: small vases in silver and silver-plated bronze. The inscriptions on two of the vases indicate that they were dedicated to Apollo by ancient visitors to the still-existing Baths of Vicarello, near Bracciano. The fact that they were found in a cleft of the rock near the fount suggests that these thermal springs were the "Aquae Apollinares" mentioned in itineraries and maps of late antiquity. 2nd/3rd century A.D. Inv. 12131-32, 12134, 12137-38, 12143, 12148.

SECTION II

Show-case I:

8

Bottom Shelf:

"Megara" cup, a turned vase with moulded decorations on the outside; a type common in central and eastern Mediterranean areas during the Hellenistic period. From Vulci, 2nd century B.C. Inv. 15459.

Italic vases in the "Megara" style, signed C. Popilius and Lappius. From Vulci, 1st century B.C. Inv. 15461-63, 14411.

In the same *show-case* (I), and in *show-case K:*

8, 9

Several clay lamps. Most date from the 1st to the 4th century A.D.; the oldest (e.g. Inv. 14359, *show-case K*, bottom shelf) are of the late Hellenistic period (1st cent. B.C.). Both pagan and Christian examples are included.

9

Show-cases L and M:

10, 11

Among the artefacts exhibited here are those made of transparent polychrome glass. Some (*show-case L*, second shelf on the left) are from Etruscan tombs, and date from the 6th-5th century B.C; others (*show-case M*) are Roman works of the 1st-2nd century A.D. An unusual piece is the cup, Inv. 14637 (*show-case M*, top shelf on the right), in cast rather than blown glass, whose form recalls that of the Megara cups mentioned above (2nd cent. B.C.).

10
11

11

The Bramante staircase built in 1512 at the time of Julius II as access to the Palazzetto Belvedere is seen beyond an iron gate.

SECTION III

Bust from a portrait statue in bronze; cloak over the left shoulder (most of which has been restored) and extended left forearm (it probably covered the lower part of the body); right arm raised (it probably rested

12

plan
←
VIII

B
D

on a "hasta", or lance). The partial nudity of the statue suggests that it is an idealized portrait statue (possibly of Marius or Sulla, neither of whom have so far been recognized in other portraits). 1st century B.C. Inv. 15055.

13

Bronze portrait head with laurel wreath, probably of Trebonianus Gallus, Roman emperor from 251 to 253 A.D. Inv. 15032.

IX

IX, FALCIONI ROOM

The frieze is part of the decoration of the time of Julius III (1550-1555), executed by Daniele da Volterra and his pupils.

Exhibited here is the Falcioni Collection, purchased by Leo XIII in 1898, consisting of Etruscan and Roman artefacts, most of which are from the Viterbo area.

Here the contents of the show-cases reflect the characteristics of private collections, in which are assembled indiscriminately or without logical criteria archeological finds such as: the most ancient clay mixture vases of the proto-Villanovan age and of the 8th century B.C., bucchero vessels, artifacts in bronze (vases, statuettes, candelabra and cists) gold and votive objects up to the latest Roman period, such as common ceramics, lamps, weaving weights and terracotta seals.

ASTARITA ROOM
(second donation)

This small room contains various material from the collection donated by Mario Astarita to Paul VI.

In the show-case on the left are various examples of Roman glasswork: bottles, jugs, pitchers, and bowls.

In the show-case on the right are terracotta votive offerings (heads and statuettes), polychrome antefixes and cymae from Magna Graecia, red-figure pottery of the 4th cent. B.C., black enamel pottery, and a fine example of Samnite amour in bronze laminate.

g – Vase Collection
(Etruscan Museum, Rooms X-XIV)

Black figure amphora, by the potter and painter Exekias (Attic work, c. 530 B.C.), with Achilles and Ajax playing morra, detail.

Visitors coming to the Vase Collection by way of the Etruscan Museum proper must retrace their steps to the Hemicycle and begin the visit proceeding contrariwise to the chronological and topological sequence of the exhibits. In this case the following descriptions should be read in reverse order.

The Greek vases, whose presence alongside Etruscan antiquities is justified by the fact that a great many of them were found in Etruscan necropolises, are exhibited in an area apart from, and parallel to the main area.

X, ROOM OF THE SUN-DIAL

X

The name refers to a small room, today part of this large hall, of the Apartment of Cardinal F. S. de Zelada, Secretary of State under Pius VI, who lived in these rooms until 1801, before they were allocated to the Museums. The room received its name from the astronomical instruments it contained. These included a sun-dial. Together they formed the Cardinal's observatory. The vases exhibited here are the oldest of the collection (except for those of the Regolini-Galassi group), and consist mainly of Greek and Etruscan black figure ceramics.

Show-case B (top shelf, left): the olpe (pyriform jug with high flaring rim), Inv. 16334, is decorated with Oriental-style bands depicting series of panthers, bulls, deer, herons and sphinxes; the ivory-coloured background is studded with rosettes formed by a circle of points round a central point. Made in Corinth in about 630/615 B.C. by a ceramist who owes to this exemplar (and to the number assigned to it in Carlo Albizzati's publication, "Vasi antichi dipinti del Vaticano") the title of "Painter of the Vatican 73".

1

Show-case D (bottom shelf, right): Cerveterian hydria. It belongs to a class comprised of about fifty examples produced almost exclusively at Cerveteri. It is the product of a school certain to have also made temple

2

paintings, one certain to have been founded by an Ionian Greek master who emigrated to Cerveteri, working there during the second half of the 6th century B.C. The vase portrays Heracles about to slay the giant shepherd Alkyoneus in his sleep. Inv. 16521.

Show-case E (top shelf, left): Pontic amphora. An entire class of vases owes its name, and its original assignation to an Ionian Greek colony on the Black Sea coast, to the Scythian costume of the archers represented on the shoulder of this vase. However, the class is now unanimously attributed to a Vulci workshop active in about 550-525 B.C., a period when Etruscan art was profoundly influenced by that of Greece and Asia Minor. Inv. 14960.

Show-case G (bottom shelf): Laconian cup with Prometheus and Atlas (or Sisyphus and Tityos). It is attributed to Sparta, and dates back to about the mid-6th century B.C. The best examples of black figure ceramics of this centre are characterized by the large internal medallion divided into two segments, one intended for the main scene, the other to serve as "base", and the ornate exterior with its typical long, horizontal palmettes, and cross and pomegranate festoons. Inv. 16592.

XI, ASTARITA ROOM
(first donation)

The frieze: scenes of the Old Testament, allegorical figures and scenes by Orlando Parentini (reign of Pius IV). This room contains the ceramics collection donated by Mario Astarita to Paul VI in 1967.

All the exhibits are of great interest. Worthy of special attention in *show-case A,* on the bottom shelf, is a Corinthian hydria (A 653), in *show-case E* miniature-like cups of Tleson (A 345, A 693) and of Sakonides (A 4). The most important nucleus of the collection is definitely the Attic red-figure ceramics, highlighted in *show-case D* by outstanding examples of the ceramist decorator Oltos and the potter Kachrylion (A 46, A 47, A 142, 1 248, A 262, A 280, A 298, A 299, A 301, A 306, A 492, A 632, A 701, A 763), of the Douris Painter (*show-case H:* A 48, A 131-139, A 265, A 760) and by the stamnos of the Kleophrades Painter (*show-case G,* bottom shelf). In *show-case I:* large late-Corinthian crater. The front side portrays the mission of Odysseus and Menelaus to obtain the return of Helen. The scene goes back to a famous epic tradition which was probably widespread in both poetry and painting (560 B.C.). Inv. A 565.

XII, HEMICYCLE

On the walls frescoes by an anonymous artist (1780) illustrating works executed at the time of Pius VI.

Show-case A (top shelf, left): Attic black figure wine jug, a late work of a prolific vase-painter known as the Painter of Amasis, one of the last and most skilful to use the black figure technique. The lavish use of added colours is one of the devices employed by the painter to force the limits of the austere two-colour technique. C. 525 B.C. Inv. 17771.

Show-case E: Cups with both red and black figure decoration. In about 530 B.C., Attic vase-painters began to abandon the technique of "black figures" painted on the natural ground of the vase, in favour of that of "red figures" painted in reserve on a black ground. This change was to lead to a significant evolution in the art of vase-painting. In the early phase, painters sometimes employed both techniques simultaneously, as is the case with the "kylikes" (cups), Inv. 16584 and 16515, whose interiors are ornamented with black figures, and exteriors with red figures. C. 520 B.C.

Show-case F: Attic black figure amphora, one of the masterpieces of Attic ceramics, signed by the potter and painter Exekias. On the front, Achilles and Ajax have laid down their arms, and are playing morra.

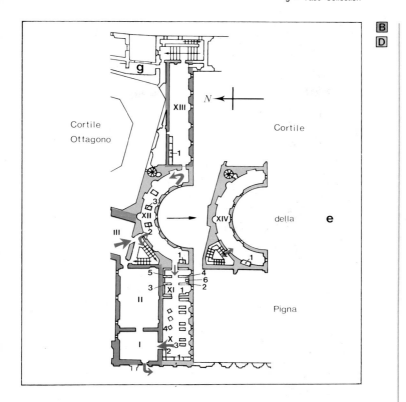

XIII, ROOM OF THE ITALIOT VASES

This room is being completely rearranged

This room contains red figure vases and painted black vases produced in Magna Graecia (southern Italy) and Etruria. Most of the red figure vases date from the mid-5th century to the early 3rd century B.C.; the painted black vases date back to the 1st century B.C.

Show-case U (middle shelf): crater of Assteas (U 19). Most Italiot potters drew the inspiration for their vase decorations from the theatre. Here, one of the greatest vase-painters of Campania, active about 350-325 B.C., has depicted a scene in which the grotesque hair-styles of the actors identify it as a burlesque of mythology; Zeus woos Alcmene, wife of Amphitryon, under the eyes of Hermes. Inv. 17106.

XIV, UPPER HEMICYCLE

This room can be visited by scholars on request.

Show-case B (in the middle): hydria with Apollo on a tripod. Long considered one of the loveliest vases in the Vatican collection, this hydria is the work of the "Painter of Berlin", one of the best vase-painters active in Athens in about 480 B.C., distinguished by his compositional preference for isolated figures on a shiny ground. Here Apollo is portrayed as sitting on the Delphic tripod as he flies over the sea. Inv. 16568.

XIII

1

XIV

1

65

View of the room

This domed room is situated above the Atrium of the Four Gates. It was begun in 1786 by Giuseppe Camporese, and finished only in 1794. Four niches between pilasters and four arched bays form the walls of the small rotunda. The dome is decorated with octagonal lacunars. The biga, from which the room takes its name, is illuminated by the opening in the ceiling.

1

In the centre: *body of a biga*, completed for exhibition in the museum by Francesco Antonio Franzoni (wheels, shaft, horses). It used to be in the Church of San Marco, where it served as a bishops throne. Its form recalls that of an ancient triumphal chariot; the relief decorations (laurel branches) recall certain representations of the chariots of the gods (Ceres, Triptolemus). Roman, 1st century A.D. Inv. 2368.

On the right, starting from the entrance:

2

Statue of *Dionysus "Sardanapallos"* (ancient inscription on the hem of the cloak folded diagonally across the chest). An excellent Roman copy (1st cent. A.D.) of a Greek original of the circle of Praxiteles (late 4th cent. B.C.). Inv. 2363.

3-7

Five *children's sarcophagi* with depictions of cupids competing in cart-races at the circus. The race is undoubtedly a symbol of the struggle for survival, the circus is life itself, the finishing-post the goal of life.

3, 4
5-7

Made in the 2nd-3rd century A.D.: *Inv. 2364*, c. 140 A.D.; *Inv. 2356*, c. 160 A.D.; *Inv. 2351*, c. 170 A.D.; *Inv. 2348*, c. 190 A.D.; *Inv. 2358* (opposite), c. 100 years later.

8

Statue of a *discobolus preparing to throw the discus*. The attitude of the young athlete expresses his total concentration (head restored). The vigorous forms and balanced forces suggest a model of the Polyclitus school, probably by Naukydes. A good Roman copy of the 1st century A.D. Inv. 2349.

9

Statue of a *discobolus throwing the discus*. The inclination of the head (reconstructed), the twisting of the chest, the movement of the left leg, and the stretching of the arms express the athlete's concentration with unprecedented vivacity. A copy from the time of Hadrian (2nd cent. A.D.)—as is demonstrated by the tree-shaped support—of a bronze original by Myron of about 460 B.C. (the inscription on the tree trunk is modern). From Hadrian's Villa. Inv. 2346.

h - Gallery of the Candelabra

View of the gallery

Originally (1761) an open loggia, under Pius VI it was closed in by Simonetti and Camporese, and divided into six sections by a range of arches carried on columns and pilasters. The gallery was named after the candelabra placed in front of the pilasters. The ceiling was painted by Domenico Torti and Ludwig Seitz during the years 1883-87, under Leo XIII.

The gallery is divided into six sections, indicated in the following description by Roman numerals.

SECTION I

Right: *statuette of a boy* tossing a walnut with his right hand, while his cloak slips off his left arm. This type of theme is typical of the Hellenistic period (3rd-1st cent. B.C., cf. Boy strangling a goose, p. 68: IV/17). Inv. 2419.

In front of the statuette: *sarcophagus of a boy*; the reclining figure of the dead child is represented on the lid. The relief on the front shows the same child seated on a throne, as in traditional representations of ancient philosophers, surrounded by chubby boys bearing the attributes of the Muses. Rome, about 270-280 A.D. Inv. 2422.

SECTION II

Under the arch, right and left: two *candelabra from Otricoli* (for burning oil, wax or resin). Roman, 2nd century A.D. Inv. 2403, 2408.

On the left: *Ganymede and the eagle*. Pliny (Nat. Hist. XXXIV, 79) refers to a bronze group, by Leochares, portraying Ganymede being carried off by the eagle sent by Zeus. He remarks that the eagle, tenderly grasping the young man by his clothes so as not to harm him, seems well aware of the identity of both the abducted and the abductor. The grandiose, mid-4th century B.C. work by Leochares here appears as the ornamental motif of what was once a table leg, the work of Roman copyists of the 2nd century A.D. Inv. 2445.

In front of the next niche: *sarcophagus with scenes from the myth of Protesilaos*. Left side: Protesilaos bids farewell to his wife, Laodamia. Front: his death on landing at Troy (he was the first Greek to leap from

67

II

A **B** **C** **D**

the ship); Hermes takes him to Laodamia; funeral lament; accompanied by Hermes, he is ferried by Charon across the Styx to the underworld. Right side: Sisyphus, Ixion and Tantalus, the three famous "penitents" of antiquity. From the Appian Way (2nd mile). Roman, about 170 A.D. Inv. 2465.

7

Opposite: *sarcophagus with reliefs depicting scenes from the myth of Orestes:* the slaying of Aegisthus and Clytemnestra; Orestes at Delphi (the Furies). On the sides, sphinxes curled up. Roman, about 160 A.D. Inv. 2513.

8

Behind the sarcophagus: *statue of the Ephesian Artemis,* a copy of the cult statue symbols of fecundity. 2nd century A.D., from Hadrian's Villa. (Cf. p. 131: V/25). Inv. 2505.

III

SECTION III

9-12

Under the four arches, left and right: *two pairs of candelabra,* found in the 17th century near Sant'Agnese on the Via Nomentana. From the time of Trajan (early 2nd cent. A.D.). Inv. 2482, 2487; 2566, 2564.

In the walls, ten fragments of Roman frescoes, from Tor Marancia. 2nd-century A.D. wall decorations.

13

On the right: *statue of Apollo* and, behind, base of Semus Sancus. Contrary to the information given in old catalogues, the statue and base do not belong together. Apollo (Inv. 2585) stands erect, bearing the attributes in his outstretched hands; an archaized work after classical models, 2nd century A.D.

IV

SECTION IV

On the right:

14

Statuette of *Nike* (Victory); the head is that of Athene, and is from another statue. Nike leans on a trophy, her right leg resting on the bow of a ship. A monument to a naval victory. A Roman work of the Imperial Age after a Greek model of the 2nd century B.C. Inv. 2721.

15

Sarcophagus with scene from the myth of Bacchus. Bacchus and his followers find Ariadne. Roman, late 2nd century A.D. Inv. 2698.

On the left:

16

Sarcophagus with reliefs portraying the massacre of the Niobids by Apollo and Artemis, who are shown shooting their deadly arrows (right and left of the scene). Roman, about 160 A.D. Inv. 2635.

17

Boy strangling a goose. The little boy, who is about three years old, is squeezing the goose's neck with both hands, using his full force to overcome the animal's resistance. Marble copy of a bronze original of about 300 B.C. attributed to Boethos of Chalcedon on the ground of an annotation by Pliny: "infans anseren strangulat" (Nat. Hist. XXXIV, 84). Inv. 2655.

18

Opposite: statuette of the *Tyche (Fortune) of Antioch* on the river Orontes, seated on a rock, with a mural crown on her head, ears of wheat in her right hand, and a bust of the river god Orontes at her feet. Roman copy of a Greek original, in bronze, by Eutychides, who made this representation of the city's patron goddess shortly after the foundation of Antioch, in about 300 B.C. Inv. 2672.

V

SECTION V

19

Right: statue of a female runner, known as *Atalanta.* The palm branch on the support is the symbol of victory. A work in the classical style, of the circle of Pasiteles, 1st century B.C. Inv. 2784.

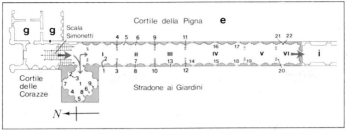

SECTION VI

VI

Right: statue of *Artemis* (Diana); identified by the belt that once carried her quiver. Roman version of a work by Kephisodotos of the early 4th century B.C. The head does not belong to the statue. Inv. 2834.

20

Left: statuette of a *Persian soldier*, identified by the tiara he is wearing. Copy of a statuette from the group of the so-called small shrine of Attalus, which the Pergamenes set up as a votive offering on the Acropolis of Athens in the 2nd century B.C. (the themes are the traditional ones of the Battle of Giants, the Battle of Amazons, and of combats between Greeks and Persians). Inv. 2794.

21

Below the statuette: *sarcophagus with reliefs depicting the abduction of the daughters of King Leucippus by the Dioscuri*, recognizable by their pointed headgear. Castor and Pollux have seized the two girls, and are carrying them away. On the right, a fleeing woman and a warrior (the parents?). On the left, a young warrior prevents a bearded figure from stopping the abductors. On the side, the wedding of the abductors and their victims. As Jupiter had placed the Dioscuri among the stars, they were considered the lords of the astral spheres, and for this reason they frequently appear in funerary representations. About 160 A.D. Inv. 2796.

22

i - Gallery of Tapestries

Tapestry with Christ appearing to the disciples of Emmaus (New School of Raphael, Brussels, 16th cent.), detail

The chiaroscuro decoration of the ceiling of the gallery was carried out in 1789, during the papacy of Pius VI, by Domenico del Frate and Antonio Marini, working on designs by Bernardino Nocchi. It is an allegorical celebration of the glory of the reigning pope. At the time of Pius VI the gallery housed paintings, but after 1838 part of the tapestry collection was transferred here. The works shown here are known as the "New School" tapestries to distinguish them from those of the "Old School" (exhibited in the Pinacoteca), woven in the Brussels workshop of Pieter van Aelst, in the time of Leo X, from cartoons by Raphael. The New School tapestries were made in the same workshop, but from designs by Raphael's students. They were first exhibited in 1531, in the Sistine Chapel.

Also exhibited here is a tapestry from the 16th-century Vigevano workshop (set up in 1503), Lombardy, and others from the Barberini workshop in Rome, set up in 1627 by Cardinal Francesco Barberini, nephew of Urban VIII, and closed down in 1683, after the death of the prelate (1679). The tapestries from the latter workshop depict events from the life of Urban VIII.

Wall opposite the windows, left to right:

Brussels workshop of Pieter van Aelst and school, 16th century, from designs by the school of Raphael: *Adoration of the shepherds*, Inv. 3858; *Adoration of the Magi*, Inv. 3860; *Presentation in the Temple*, Inv. 3857; *Slaughter of the Innocents*, Inv. 3863-3865; *Resurrection*, Inv. 3862; *Jesus Appears to Mary Magdalen*, Inv. 3855; *Supper at Emmaus*, Inv. 3856.

Vigevano workshop, 16th century (Master Benedetto): *Conversion of the centurian Cornelius*, Inv. 3786.

Flemish workshop, 16th century: *Death of Julius Caesar*, Inv. 3788.

Wall between the windows, right to left:

Barberini workshop, 17th cent., Rome: *Maffeo Barberini graduates from the University of Pisa*, Inv. 3918; *Maffeo Barberini controls the level of Lake Trasimene*, Inv. 3919; *Maffeo Barberini is made a cardinal by Paul V*, Inv. 3920: *Maffeo Barberini is elected Pope under the name of Urban VIII*, Inv. 3921; *The Countess Matilda donates her possessions to the Holy See*, Inv. 3922; *Urban VIII annexes the state of Urbino to the Holy See*, Inv. 3924; *Urban VIII begins the building of Fort Urban*, Inv. 3926; *Urban VIII saves the city of Rome from plague and famine*, Inv. 3927.

k - Gallery of Maps

View of the gallery

This gallery was named after the 40 topographical maps (32 frescoes about 320 x 430 cm on the two long walls, and 8 smaller ones at the ends of the gallery) of the regions of Italy, and of the Church's posses- sions that Gregory XIII had painted here between 1580 and 1583, from cartoons by Ignazio Danti, one of the greatest cosmographers of his day. These maps constitute an extremely important record of 16th- century geography and cartography.

The gallery is 120 m long, and 6 m wide, and is covered with a barrel vault. It was built between 1578 and 1580 by Ottaviano Mascherino, who also built the Tower of the Winds, situated above the north end of the gallery, and visible from the gardens. The sundial in the tower was also used to prove the impreciseness of the calendar and the need to reform some aspects of it, which led to the adoption of our present calendar, called Gregorian from the name of that pope.

Ignazio Danti used the Apennines as a dividing line for the arrange- ment of the maps. The regions washed by the Ligurian and Tyrrhenian seas appear on the wall towards the Court of the Belvedere, and the regions surrounded by the Alps and the Adriatic on the wall on the garden side. At the end opposite the present entrance, on both side of the long walls, are maps of ancient and contemporary Italy, which introduce the series of regional maps, each of which has a plan, often in perspective, of its main city.

On the short walls are represented the Siege of Malta, the Battle of Lepanto, the island of Elba, and the Tremiti islands (north, entrance wall), and, opposite, the four great ports of the period: Civitavecchia, Genoa, Venice and Ancona.

Girolamo Muziano and Cesare Nebbia co-ordinated the work, in which they also participated, of the large group of artistis who also decorated the vault with stucco work and a series of 80 episodes from the history of the Church and from the lives of saints; each episode is linked geographically to the region represented below it. In 1631, Urban VIII had the maps "completed" and embellished with further ornamental elements by Lukas Holste.

I - Apartment of St Pius V

Tapestry with episodes of the Passion (Tournai, mid 16th cent.), detail with the Last Supper

This small apartment is composed of the gallery (formerly divided into three rooms), the two rooms to its left and the chapel at its far end; the Sobieski Room was also included. The chapel (the uppermost of three chapels situated one above the other in the edifice built by Pius V), is dedicated to St Michael, and was intended for the pope's familiars. All that remains of the original decorations by Giorgio Vasari and Federico Zuccari is the vault fresco depicting the *Fall of Lucifer and the Rebel Angels*. The frescoes below it were painted in the 19th century.

Today the gallery houses a series of tapestries of various periods and places of origin. The most valuable are those from Tournai (Belgium), the most important centre for quality and quantity of production in the 15th century.

As we enter, above the door:

Barberini workshop (Rome), 17th century: *two friezes of the baldachin of Urban VIII.* Inv. 3730, 3732.

Wall opposite the windows, left to right:

1
2
From Tournai, mid 16th century; *Episodes from the Passion*, with the Last Supper in the center, Inv. 3742; *Tapestry of the Credo*, with the Baptism of Christ in the center, Inv. 3743.

Wall between the windows, right to left:

3
Brussels, 16th century, from cartoons by the school of Raphael: *Coronation of the Virgin*, Inv. 3852.

4
Brussels (Pieter van Aelst): *Religion, Justice, Charity*, Inv. 3866. This once formed the bottom of the throne of Clement VII, and dates back to 1525.

The two rooms on the left are used for temporary exhibits.

72

m - Sobieski Room,
Room of the Immaculate Conception

SOBIESKI ROOM

This room is named after the enormous painting occupying the entire north wall, the work of the Polish artist Jan Matejko. It depicts the victory of John III Sobieski, king of Poland, over the Turks in 1683, outside the walls of Vienna. All the paintings exhibited here were made in the 19th century. Above, fragments of a freize from the time of Gregory XIII.

As we enter, from right to left:

Francesco Grandi, *Martyrdom of Blessed Johann Sarkander*, Inv. 2607.

Cesare Fracassini, *St Peter Canisio and Ferdinand of Austria*, 1864, Inv. 2604.

Cesare Mariani, *St Jean-Baptiste de La Salle*, Inv. 2608.

Cesare Fracassini, *The martyrs of Gorkum*, Inv. 2612.

Jan Matejko, *Sobieski liberates Vienna* (oil on canvas, 458 x 894 cm). This is considered the masterpiece of the Polish artist, who renounced the payment of 80,000 florins on the condition that the painting be presented to Leo XIII on occasion of the bicentenary of the victory of Vienna, 12 September 1883 (the presentation is depicted in a fresco on the vault of the second bay of the Gallery of the Candelabra). Inv. 2613.

The floor is Roman, from Ostia.

ROOM OF THE IMMACULATE CONCEPTION

The room is in the Borgia Tower. Frescoes by Francesco Podesti depict scenes pertaining to the settlement and proclamation of the dogma of the Immaculate Conception by Pius IX in 1854. On the wall opposite the windows, the settlement of the dogma; above, Paradise. On the side walls, the pope incenses the image of the Virgin, and a discussion among theologians. Between the windows, Sibyls. On the vault, medallions with biblical scenes and allegorical figures. The floor is Roman, from Ostia.

At the centre of the room is an elaborate *show-case* (made by Christ-ofle, Paris) displaying ornately bound and decorated volumes, mostly manuscript, given to Pius IX in honour of the proclamation of the dogma of the Immaculate Conception. The volumes contain the text of the papal bull (8 December 1854) translated into an enormous number of languages and dialects. They were donated in 1878 by kings, heads of state, bishops, provinces, dioceses, cities, etc. in response to a proposal by the French priest Marie Dominique Sire.

1

n - Raphael Stanze
Chapel of Urban VIII

Raphael, St Peter delivered from prison, detail (Room of Heliodorus)

The series of rooms known as the "Raphael Stanze" constitutes the official section of the apartment of Julius II della Rovere and his successors, up till Gregory XIII. It is on the second floor of the Apostolic Palace, above the Borgia Apartment. The suite also included the Room of the Swiss Guards, the Room of the Chiaroscuri, the first antechamber, the Chapel of Nicholas V, which was the private chapel of the pope, and the Loggia. Julius II's bedroom ("cubiculum"), now closed to the public, communicated with the chapel and the Room of the Chiaroscuri. It had a small antechamber, the room linking the Chiaroscuri with the Room of Heliodorus. Julius II lived in this apartment from 1507, preferring it to the Borgia Apartment as "non volebat videre omni hora figuram Alexandri praedecessoris sui", according to the master of ceremonies Paris de Grassis.

The decoration of the Stanze was carried out by Raphael and his assistants between 1508 and 1524. The work marked the beginning of the brilliant Roman career of Raphael, who took over from artists then much better known than himself, including his teacher, Perugino, and Baldassarre Peruzzi, Sodoma, and Lorenzo Lotto. Parts of their works were destroyed to make room for those of the young master; the pre-existent paintings of Piero della Francesca, Bartolomeo della Gatta and Luca Signorelli were eliminated completely.

There are four Stanze, built on a rectangular plan, and covered with a cross vault. Except for the Hall of Constantine, which forms part of the 13th-century wing of the Apostolic Palace, they are situated in the wing built under Nicholas V. To the north they look out on the Court of the Belvedere, and to the south on the Court of the Pappagallo.

During most of the year, to avoid overcrowding, a one-way route brings the visitor from this point to an outside balcony. Therefore, the visit to the Raphael Rooms will start from the hall of Constantine. During the other months, the guide book for this section must be read backwards from p. 78.

I, HALL OF CONSTANTINE (1517-24)

This hall, intended for receptions and official ceremonies ("caenaculum amplior"), was decorated by the school of Raphael. Some of the works

74

may be based on Raphael's designs, but most of them were painted after his death in 1520. The iconographical scheme is a continuation of that of the preceding rooms, and its scope is the apotheosis of the Church. The theme here is the Church's victory over paganism, and its establishment in Rome. The main scenes are painted on false arrases, and allegorical figures, popes and virtues appear at the corners.

C D

I

The original beam ceiling was replaced under Pius IV by the present false vault, decorated by Tommaso Laureti and assistants in 1585.

The *Baptism of Constantine*. The setting is the Lateran Baptistry. Pope Silvester has the features of Clement VII. Attributed to Francesco Penni.

1

The *Battle of the Milvian Bridge*. The work depicts Constantine's victory over Maxentius. Some of the details are taken from the reliefs on Trajan's Column. The work is by Giulio Romano.

2

The *Apparition of the Cross*. The group composed of the emperor and surrounding figures is from Trajan's Column and the Arch of Constantine. The fresco is by Giulio Romano.

3

Constantine's (legendary) *Donation of Rome* to Pope Silvester (portrait of Clement VII). Attributed to Giulio Romano and Francesco Penni.

4

If you wish to visit the Room of the Chiaroscuri and the Chapel of Nicholas V, temporarily leave the Stanze at this point.

II, ROOM OF HELIODORUS (1512-14)

II

Raphael decorated this room, the "secret" (private) antechamber of the apartment, as soon as he had finished the Segnatura. The scope of the frescoes here is to illustrate the miraculous protection granted by God to a Church threatened in its faith (Miracle of Bolsena), in the person of its pope (St Peter delivered from prison), in its seat (Attila turned away from Rome), and its patrimony (Heliodorus driven out of the Temple).

The caryatids on the dado are by Francesco Penni, while the small panels were probably re-painted by Carlo Maratta. On the vault: the Sacrifice of Isaac, the Burning Bush, Jacob's Ladder, and God Appears to Noah, all by Raphael.

Attila turned back from Rome. The encounter is thought to have taken place near Mantua, though Raphael has given it a Roman setting. In fact, in the background we can see the Colosseum, an aqueduct, a basilica, and an obelisk. St. Peter and St Paul, armed with swords, appear in the sky, terrifying Attila and his barbarians. On the left, Leo I, with the feature of Leo X, advances on a white mule. Leo X appears twice in the work, as a cardinal and as a pope, because it was begun when he was a cardinal under Julius II, and completed during his papacy. Not completely autograph.

1

The *Miracle of Bolsena*. The work depicts a miracle that took place in 1263. A Bohemian priest who harboured doubts about the presence of Christ in the Eucharist, saw blood pour forth from the sacred host while he was celebrating mass in Bolsena. The prodigy gave rise to Corpus Christi Day, and to the construction of the Cathedral of Orvieto. Julius II is shown kneeling before the altar. The two cardinals of his retinue are Leonardo Grosso della Rovere (the elder of the two) and Raffaele Riario (with clasped hands). Considered one of Raphael's masterpieces.

2

The Expulsion of Heliodorus from the Temple. The work depicts the Biblical story of Heliodorus, who was ordered by the King of Syria to

3

C
D

steal the treasure of the Temple of Jerusalem. On his way out, he was seized by a horseman and two youths, and thrown out of the temple. By means of this episode, Julius II wished to allude to his policy of expelling usurpers from the Church's lands, and to make the message even clearer he had himself portrayed in the scene, on the left. The chair-carrier in German dress is Marcantonio Raimondi, engraver and friend of Raphael, who has portrayed himself as the other chair-carrier. An inscription on the dado below the work records the death of the Constable of Bourbon during the Sack of Rome.

4

St Peter delivered from prison. The angel wakes St Peter (centre), and conducts him out of the prison, past the sleeping guards (right). A soldier with a torch wakes the bewildered guards (left). The face of the apostle is that of Julius II. This fresco, reminiscent of Rembrandt for its use of various light sources, is one of Raphael's most famous works.

III

III, ROOM OF THE SEGNATURA (1508-11)

This was the library and study of Julius II. It was the first of the rooms to be decorated by Raphael, and the works here are almost wholly his own. The iconographical scheme, undoubtedly established by a theologian "ad praescriptum Iulii pontificis", has as its theme the three highest categories of the human spirit according to the neo-Platonic vision: the True, the Good and the Beautiful. Supernatural Truth is represented by the Dispute, rational Truth by the School of Athens, the Good by the Virtues and the Law, and the Beautiful by the Parnassus.

The large vault medallions depicting Theology, Philosophy, Justice and Poetry are closely linked to the wall-paintings, as are the representations of Adam and Eve, the Primum Mobile, the Judgement of Solomon, and Apollo and Marsyas. The decorative scheme of the vault precedes Raphael, and is attributed to Sodoma. The central octagon is by Bramantino. The chiaroscuro works on the dado are by Perin del Vaga, and were made under Paul III. They replaced the wooden panelling by Giovanni Barile and Fra Giovanni da Verona, destroyed during the Sack of Rome in 1527. The caryatids were re-painted by Maratta. The inlaid, polychrome marble floor is ornamented with the crossed keys of Nicholas V, the name of Julius II, and emblems of Leo X.

1

The *Dispute over the Holy Sacrament.* The title ought to be "The Triumph of Religion": above, in the centre, Christ is seated between the Virgin and St John, in Paradise. God is above him, the Holy Ghost below him. The Triumphant Church extends to the sides, above the clouds: saints and Old Testament figures regard the True (the Trinity). On earth, a monstrance, the focal point of the composition, rests on an altar. At the sides of the altar, doctors and theologians of the Militant Church participate in the incarnation of the True through the Eucharist. On the right, in papal dress, are Gregory the Great, in the likeness of Julius II, and Sixtus IV. Behind the latter is Dante. Further right, his head partly concealed by his hood, is Savonarola. The ecstatic-looking old man in Domenican costume on the far left is Fra Angelico. The fresco is wholly the work of Raphael, and though it reveals a certain stylistic hesitance, and a variety of influences (Venice, Leonardo, Umbria), it looks forward to the artist's mature style. During the Sack of Rome soldiers left two graffiti on the fresco, one in praise of Luther, the other of Charles V and of the Constable of Bourbon.

2

The *Cardinal and Theological Virtues.* The cardinal virtues are represented by women: Fortitude holds an oak branch, Prudence observes herself in a mirror, and Temperance holds reins. The theological virtues are represented by cupids: Faith points to the sky, Hope holds a burning torch, and Charity shakes the acorns from an oak-tree. By Raphael.

3

Gregory IX approving the Decretals received from St Raymond de

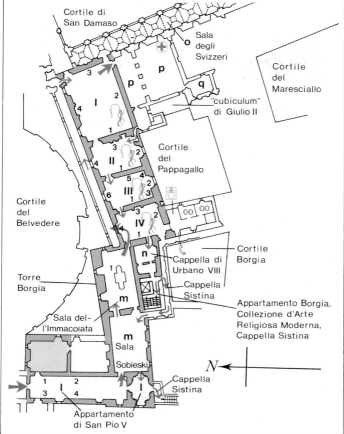

Peñafort (the canonical laws). Next to the pope, who has been given the features of Julius II, are the cardinals Giovanni de' Medici, Alessandro Farnese and Antonio del Monte. Attributed to Raphael's workshop.

Justinian publishing the Pandects (civil laws) *received from Trebonianus.* Attributed to Raphael's workshop.

The *School of Athens.* Ancient philosophers and scientists, some of whom have been given the features of cotemporaries, converse as they stroll within an imposing basilica, designed by Donato Bramante. In the centre, Plato (Leonardo) and Aristotle; one points upward to the world of ideas, the other extends his open hand between the heavens and earth. On the left, Socrates with his characteristic Silenus-like profile. In front of him, Alcibiades and Alexander the Great, the latter in armour. On the right, Diogenes reclining. At the foot of the stair, left, Epicurus wearing a wreath of vine-leaves. Behind him, Averroes watches Pythagoras, who is writing on a black-board. A short distance beyond, the isolated figure of Heraclitus (Michelangelo); Raphael changed his original composition to include this figure, almost a tribute to his rival. Right, Euclid (Bramante) bent over as he draws with a compass; on the neck of his garment, Raphael's signature, "R.V.S.M.". Far right, dressed in white, Sodoma; behind him, Raphael's self-portrait. In the niches, Apollo, god of the Arts and Athene, goddess of Wisdom. In this work Raphael draws toward the full maturity of his style, and creates a series of "types" of which he was to make liberal use later.

III

4

5

The *Parnassus*. Apollo, surrounded by the Muses, is seated in the centre, playing a lyre. On his right, the blind Homer (the features are those of the Laocoön), flanked by Dante and Virgil. Seated below, Sapho. On the right, famous Italian poets and writers: Ludovico Ariosto, Giovanni Boccaccio, Antonio Tebaldeo (in profile, bearded) and Jacopo Sannazzaro (dressed in yellow). With this work, which was painted after the Dispute and the School of Athens, Raphael comes into full possession of his powers of expression.

IV, ROOM OF THE INCENDIO (1514-17)

This was the everyday dining-room ("triclinium penitior"). The kitchens were located in the adjoining room, which is still used as a service-area. It is the last of the rooms decorated by Raphael, who, however, left the execution to his workshop. The chief aim of the frescoes in this room is the illustration of the political ambitions of Leo X, through the depiction of events from the lives of two other popes bearing the same name, Leo III and Leo IV. The vault decorations are by Perugino, and depict allegories of the Trinity. The paintings in the corners of the room, above the dado, represent the Egyptian telamones (supports in the form of statues) found in Tivoli before 1504, and now in the Pio-Clementine Museum. The doors are ornamented with splendid intaglio and inlay work by Giovanni Barile and Fra Giovanni da Verona.

The *Coronation of Charlemagne* in St Peter's. Charlemagne has been given the features of Francis I, and Leo III those of Leo X, an allusion to the concordat reached between France and the Church in Bologna in 1515. Designed by Raphael but carried out by his workshop.

The *Fire in the Borgo* ("Incendio di Borgo"). According to the "Liber Pontificatis", in 847 Leo IV extinguished with the sign of the cross a fire blazing in Borgo Santo Spirito, between St Peter's and the Tiber. In the background, the pope appears on the Loggia of Benedictions of the Constantinian Basilica, extant in Raphael's day. In the foreground are the terrorized crowd and, on the left, the famous pair of figures reminiscent of the episode related by Virgil of Aeneas' flight from Troy with his father on his shoulders. The composition, which anticipates Raphael's late style, is largely attributed to the master.

The *Battle of Ostia*. The work celebrates the victory of Leo IV, in the likeness of Leo X, over the Saracens, and alludes to Leo X's crusade against the Turks. Among the personages in the retinue are the cardinals Bernardo Bibbiena (right) and Giulio de' Medici. Though Raphael made numerous compositional designs, the fresco is the work of his workshop.

The *Self-defence of Leo III*. The work depicts the oath sworn in St Peter's by Leo III to defend himself against the slander of the nephews of Adrian I, while a voice from above admonished, "Dei non hominum est episcopos iudicare". It alludes to the sanctioning by the 1516 Lateran Council of the principle that the pope must answer for his actions only to God. Leo III has been given the features of Leo X. Painted and probably designed by Raphael's assistants.

CHAPEL OF URBAN VIII

This small chapel richly decorated with gilded stucco-work, and frescoes, the work of Pietro da Cortona, was once the private chapel of Urban VIII. The fresco above the altar depicts the Deposition of Christ. The altar frontal is from the small Church, today deconsecrated, of San Filippino on the Via Giulia, which is the only Roman church dedicated to St Filippo Neri.

o - Loggia of Raphael

School of Raphael, The building of the ark

The Loggia may be visited by scholars on request.

The so-called Loggia of Raphael is the second of three arcades built one upon the other, a structure envisaged by Julius II. In 1508 the building of the three arcades was entrusted to Donato Bramante, who was the working on two other Vatican projects, the Court of the Belvedere and the "new" St Peter's. When he died, in 1514, Bramante had completed only the first range of arches. Leo X passed the job on to Raphael, who completed it in 1519, having also decorated the loggia that was to bear his name (the decoration was begun in 1517). Giovanni da Udine decorated the ground-floor loggia and, later (1560-64), the now extensively repainted top loggia, both of which are closed to the public. Gregory XIII and Sixtus V each added an east wing to the structure, thus creating the present Court of St Damasus, which can be seen from the window.

The visitor approaches the Loggia of Raphael from the Hall of Constantine (I) of the Raphael Stanze. The windows along the wall illuminate the Room of the Chiaroscuri (see p. 82), the antechamber of the apartment where Leo X held the "secret consistory", and the Room of the Swiss Guards. A door at the end of the loggia, in the same wall, gives access to a ramp originally designed to be climbed on horse-back, designed by Bramante and largely built by Raphael to link the three floors of the edifice to the Court of St Damasus. The arcades were originally open on the courtside, but in the 19th century they were closed with large windows to protect the frescoes and stucco-work, both of which are now in very poor condition, especially in the lower parts. They must have begun to deteriorate soon after they were made, for they were fist restored in about 1560, by Giovanni da Udine.

Michiel informs us that the gallery was kept closed "et al piacer solum" of Leo X, who arranged in certain of its niches "many statues, kept in private amongst his possessions".

Leo X's antiquarian tastes, typical of his age, are reflected in the loggia decoration. In fact, the themes of the grotesques and stucco ornaments are clearly derived from antiquity, and in particular from the Domus Aurea, with which Raphael and his school were well-acquainted, Raphael having been appointed Superintendent of Antiquities in 1514. Another Renaissance trait present here is the intermingling of

plan →

C
D

biblical and mythological motifs. In order to carry out this complex decorative scheme, Raphael availed himself of the collaboration of Giulio Romano, Francesco Penni, and above all of Giovanni da Udine and Perin del Vaga. However, the work should not be considered the product of "Raphael and assistants", but of teamwork, in the modern sense of the word. Minor contributions were made by Pellegrino da Modena, Vincenzo da San Giminiano, Raffaellino del Colle, Tommaso Vincidor, and the young Polidoro da Caravaggio.

The original majolica floor, by Luca della Robbia the Younger, was removed towards the middle of the 19th century.

There is a great deal of controversy as to the identify of the artists of the single works. It is certain that the stucco ornaments "alla Romana", made with a mixture of lime, plaster and marble sawdust, are by Giovanni da Udine: there is more than one portrayal of himself and Raphael's studio at work, on the pilasters of the first two bays. There is much less certainty as to who painted the biblical scenes on the vaults. They form the so-called Bible of Raphael, and, with the exception of the scenes in the last bay, are based on Old Testament stories. The yoke, ring and feather appearing in the centre of the vaults are motifs from the "device" (insignia and motto) of Leo X.

I
1-4

BAY I
God divides the light from the dark. God divides the land from the waters. God creates the sun and moon. God creates the animals.

II
1-4

BAY II
Creation of Eve. The Original Sin. Expulsion from Eden. Adam and Eve with their sons.

III
1-4

BAY III
The building of the ark. The Flood. Leaving the ark. Noah's sacrifice.

IV
1-4

BAY IV
The victorius Abraham encounters Melchisedec. God's promise to Abraham. The angels visit Abraham. The burning of Sodom.

V
1-4

BAY V
God forbids Isaac to go to Egypt. Abimelech learns that Rebecca is the wife of Isaac. Isaac bleses Jacob instead of Esau. Isaac blesses Esau.

VI
1-4

BAY VI
Jacob's vision. Jacob meets Rachel at the well. Jacob reproaches Laban. Return to Canaan.

VII
1-4

BAY VII
Joseph relates his dreams to his brothers. Joseph is sold by his brothers. Joseph and the wife of Potiphar. Joseph interprets the Pharaoh's dreams.

VIII
1-4

BAY VIII
Moses found in the Nile. The burning bush. The crossing of the Red Sea. Moses makes water spring from a rock.

IX
1-4

BAY IX
Moses receives the tablets of the Law. Worship of the golden calf. God speaks to Moses from a cloud. Moses gives the tablets of the Law to the people.

X
1-4

BAY X
The Ark of the Covenant is carried across the Jordan. The capture of Jericho. Joshua stops the sun. Division of the land of Canaan.

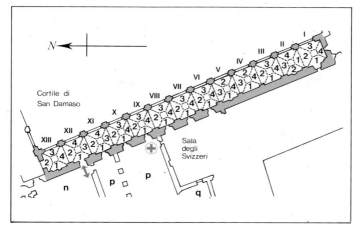

BAY XI
David is anointed King. David kills Goliath. Triumph of David. David's sin.

XI
1-4

BAY XII
The consecration of Solomon. The judgement of Solomon. The Queen of Sheba. The building of the temple.

XII
1-4

BAY XIII
The birth of Christ. Adoration of the Magi. Baptism of Christ. The last supper.

XIII
1-4

p - Room of the Chiaroscuri

View of the room

The Room of the Chiaroscuri, also known as the Room of the Palafrenieri ("footmen"), the first antechamber of the apostolic apartment, is where Leo X used to hold the "secret consistory", i.e. the council of cardinals resident in Rome, and various ceremonies, both public and private, religious and secular. It was also known as the Room of the Pappagallo ("parrot") because as far back as the Middle Ages a cage containing a parrot had been kept in the room. As a reminder of the old name, two parrots, perhaps the work of Giovanni da Udine, are represented on the wall above the door leading to the Room of the Swiss Guards (closed to the public).

This room is in the 13th-century wing of the Apostolic Palace, and is divided in half by a row of columns that mark the beginning of the 14th-century addition, of which the Hall of Constantine (I) of the Stanze forms part.

The present decoration dates back to the 16th century. The ceiling was painted, from a design by Raphael, during the papacy of Leo X. The chiaroscuro figures (from which the room takes its name) of apostles and saints were also made by the school of Raphael. They were partly destroyed in 1558, and were restored by Taddeo and Federico Zuccari in 1560. Further decorations were added by Giovanni Alberti and Ignazio Danti in 1582, during the papacy of Gregory XIII, who also commissioned the present decoration of the Room of the Swiss Guards.

The door bearing the name and coat-of-arms of Julius II leads to the Chapel of Nicholas V. The door next to it leads to the pope's "cubiculum", now closed to the public.

plan
→

Fra Angelico, St Lawrence receiving the treasure of the Church, detail

This chapel is in the Tower of Innocent III, which forms part of the oldest section of the Apostolic Palace. At the end of the 13th century, under Nicholas III, the tower was enveloped by the additions made to the palace round the Court of the Pappagallo. In the 15th century Nicholas V Parentucelli chose the room on the fourth floor as the site of his private chapel.

This relatively small (6.6 x 4 m) room is built on a rectangular plan, and covered with a cross vault. It is approached from the Room of the Chiaroscuri through a door made in the wall during the time of Julius II. The original entrance (now walled up and concealed by a door) is next to the present one. It led to a room used by Julius II as a bedroom ("cubiculum"), a room that was probably once the small study of Nicholas V. In the wall on the left, a low, rectangular window, made toward the end of the 16th century, opens on the Room of the Swiss Guards; it enabled the occupants of the room to follow the mass celebrated in the chapel. In the wall opposite are two long, narrow ogival windows.

The decoration of the chapel was carried out by Giovanni da Fiesole known as Fra Angelico, between 1447 and 1451. The walls are decorated with frescoes depicting events from the lives of St Stephen (above) and St Lawrence (below). The four evangelists and their symbols are portrayed on the starry blue vault, and the doctors of the Church on the pilasters.

The frescoes are masterpieces of the Florentine artist's maturity. As soon as he had finished the chapel he made the decorations, now lost, for the aforementioned study of Nicholas V, and for the Chapel of the Holy Sacrament, now destroyed.

Along the skirting-board are frescoes representing drapery and in the centre, the coat-of-arms of Nicholas V. The embroidered frontal on the altar is a late 16th-century work from the Church of San Filippino, in the Via Giulia. A Flemish tapestry (1520-1530; inv. 3831) replaces the lost altar-piece with the Deposition of Christ that Fra Angelico had painted for the chapel. The floor is the original one, and is by Agnolo Verrone, Florentine marble-worker and contemporary of Angelico. The subjects of the frescoes on the walls and pilasters are as follows (top to bottom):

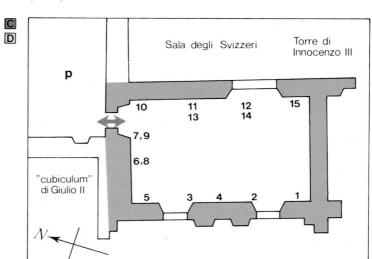

1

Pilaster next to the altar, on the right as we enter: *St Gregory the Great; St Anastasius.*

Right wall:

2, 3

The *Ordination of St Stephen; St Stephen distributing alms.*

4

The *Ordination of St Lawrence.* The figures are probably portraits of the artist's contemporaries; St Sixtus has been given the features of Nicholas V.

5

Pilaster: *St Ambrose; St Thomas Aquinas.*

Entrance wall:

6, 7

St Stephen preaching; St Stephen addressing the Council.

8, 9

St Lawrence receiving the treasure of the Church; St Lawrence distributing alms. St Sixtus is a portrait of Nicholas V.

10

Pilaster: *St Augustine; St Jerome.*

Left wall:

11, 12

The *Expulsion of St Stephen;* the *Stoning of St Stephen.*

13, 14

St Lawrence before Decius; the *Martyrdom of St Lawrence.* In the first scene, the boy who looks away, clasping his hands, is St Roman; further right, the saint, in prison, converts St Hippolytus. As for the second scene, the Martyrdom, all but the upper part was repainted in the 16th century, when the window below it was made.

15

Pilaster: *St Leo the Great; St John Chrysostomos.*

From the Chapel of Nicholas V we proceed left, through the antechamber of the Cubiculum (bedroom) of Julius II, to the Room of Heliodorus.

r - Borgia Apartment

View of the Room of the Mysteries

The Borgia Apartment, which now houses part of the Collection of Modern Religious Art (described in the next section), takes its name from the Spaniard Rodrigo de Borja y Doms, Pope Alexander VI from 1492 to 1503. Today the name is used to indicate only the "secret", i.e. private, rooms which the Borgia Pope had decorated by Bernardino Betti, better known as Pinturicchio.

The Borgia Apartment proper occupied the whole first floor of the Apostolic Palace, built between the 13th century and the end of the 15th century. The Room of the Vestments (X). Room of the Pappagallo (IX, also known as the Dressing-room and Room of the Secret Consistory), Audience-room (VIII) and Room of the Pontifs (VII) belonged to the more official area of the apartment. The Room of the Falda (XII) and another room (XI), the "cubiculum" (bedroom) of Nicholas V, both of which look on to the Court of the Pappagallo, are in the same area. From the Room of the Pontifs one entered the semiofficial area of the apartment, the Borgia Rooms. The Room of the Mysteries (VI), Room of the Saints (V), and Room of the Liberal Arts (IV) are in the 15th-century wing built by Nicholas V. The Room of the Creed (III) and Room of the Sibyls (I) are in the Borgia Tower, built by Alexander VI during the years 1492-94 to complete the fortications of the palace. His bedroom (XIII) is next to the Room of the Liberal Arts, and has two windows looking on to the Borgia Court. The two adjoining rooms probably served as bathroom and as treasury (XXVIII).

Pinturicchio decorated the "secret rooms" in 1492-94, assisted by the members of his workshop, among whom were Benedetto Bonfigli, Pietro d'Andrea da Volterra, and Antonio da Viterbo, known as Pastura.

After the death of Alexander VI, the apartment was abandoned by the popes, who preferred to live elsewhere, and was used as the residence of the "nephew cardinals", including Carlo Borromeo, Pius IV's secretary of state, and nephew.

Pinturicchio's frescoes were repainted and restored in 1816, under Pius VII, when the Vatican Pinacoteca was housed here, and again in 1897, when Leo XIII opened it to the public (the rooms were also restored, and most of the floors reconstructed in copies of the original

85

plan
→

C
D

ceramic tiles, very few of which had survived). A further restoration was carried out in recent times, when the apartment was chosen to house part of the Collection of Modern Religious Art.

I

I, ROOM OF THE SIBYLS

The visit to the Borgia Apartment now begins from this room, situated in the Borgia Tower, and approached from the Raphael Stanze. Tradition has it that Cesare Borgia, known as Valentino, nephew of Alexander VI, had his brother-in-law Alfonso d'Aragona murdered in this room in 1550, and that he was imprisoned here in 1503 by Julius II. The twelve lunettes are decorated with pairs of prophets and Sibyls, from whom the room takes its name. From the wall opposite the window, left to right: Baruch, Samia; Zechariah, Persica; Obadiah, Libica; Isaiah, Ellespontica; Micah, Tiburtina; Ezekiel, Cimmeria; Jeremiah, Frigia; Hosea, Delphica; Daniel, Eritrea; Haggai, Cumana; Amos, Europea, Jeremiah, Agrippina.

The astrological symbols of the seven major planets, and the human activity they were thought to influence are represented in the octagonal panels of the intermediate pendentives: Saturn, with coach drawn by dragons, and works of charity; Jupiter, with coach drawn by eagles, and hunters; Venus, with cart drawn by bulls, and lovers; Mercury, with cart drawn by deer, and merchants; the Moon, with cart drawn by dragons, and fishermen. In the last octagon, astronomers confer beneath an armilllary sphere (an instrument that showed the movements of the planets). The decoration of this room is perhaps the work of Pastura.

III

III, ROOM OF THE CREED

This room, also in the Borgia Tower, is named after the pairs of prophets and apostles, with cartouches bearing verses of the Creed, that appear in the lunettes. Starting from the wall on the side of the Borgia Court, left to right: Peter, Jeremiah; John, David; Andrew, Isaiah; James the Elder, Zechariah; Mathew, Hosea; James the Younger, Amos; Philip, Malachi; Bartholomew, Joel; Thomas, Daniel; Simon, Malachi; Thaddeus, Zechariah; Matthew, Obadiah. Attributed to Pinturicchio's workshop, perhaps Pastura or Tibera d'Assisi.

IV

IV, ROOM OF THE LIBERAL ARTS

This is the first of the rooms located in the wing built by Nicholas V. It was Alexander VI's study, and he also used to dine here; his body was laid out in this room when he died. The name of the room has its origins in the medieval concept of the Arts of the Trivium and of the Quadrivium, which made up the Liberal Arts. The Arts are represented in the lunettes as enthroned women, each identified by an inscription. From the lunette above the window, proceeding right:

1 *Astronomy*; next to her, the geographer Ptolemy wearing a crown.

2 *Grammar.*

3 *Dialectics.*

4 *Rhetoric.*

5 *Geometry.*

6 *Arithmetic.*

7 *Music.*

Some of the figures surrounding the Arts are portraits of contemporaries. The figure of Euclid, kneeling before Geometry, and intent upon

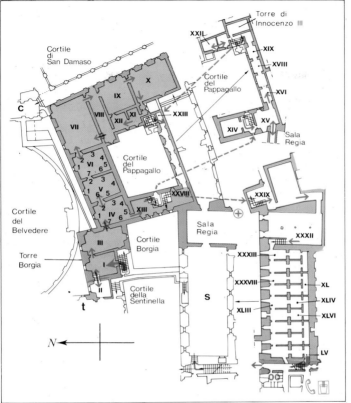

measuring with compasses, may be a portrait of Bramante. Only part of the work is by Pinturicchio, whose name appears on the base of Rhetoric's throne. The rest can be attributed to Tiberio d'Assisi or to Pastura.

The five octagons of the large central arch are 16th-century additions, or perhpas restorations. Depicted here: Jacob takes leave of Laban; the Angels save Lot from the destruction of Sodom and Gomorrah; Justice, Trajan's justice; Justice distributes gifts.

The gilded stucco reliefs on the vault represent the pope's coat-of-arms and devices.

The 16th-century fireplace, carved in "pietra serena" (a Tuscan name for a type of hard sandstone) from a design by Sansovino, is the work of Simone Mosca. Tradition has it that it once stood in Castel Sant'Angelo.

V, ROOM OF THE SAINTS

The hand of Pinturicchio is most evident in this room, for which he planned and exectured most of the frescoes. Starting from the lunette above the window, and proceeding right:

Martyrdom of St Sebastian; in the background, the Colosseum and, further right, Palatine Hill and the churches of St John and St Paul.

Susannah and the elders.

87

3 [C] [D] *Events from the life of St Barbara*; in the foreground, she escapes from the tower, and is sought after by her furious father; in the background, she meets St Juliana and the sherperd who is to hand her over to her father, who is determined to kill her because she became a Christian.

4 *St Catherine disputing* in the presence of the emperor Maximinus; in the background, Constantine's Arch. There are many portraits of contemporaries in this fresco. The man with the drooping moustaches, on the left of the throne, is Andrea Paleologo of the imperial family of Byzantium. Behind him is Antonio da Sangallo the Elder, holding a square, and, on his left, Pinturicchio himself. Prince Djem, guest/hostage of the pope, and friend of Valentino, appears either as the Oriental figure on horseback, or as the figure next to the emperor.

5 The *Meeting of St Anthony Abbot and St Paul the Hermit*.

6 The *Visitation*.

Scenes from the myth of Isis and Osiris are depicted in the spandrels of the vault, according to a "plan" by Antonio da Viterbo; their presence, together with that of the bull Apis, is an allusion to the pope, as a bulla appears in his device. In the cross-vault near the window: Osiris teaches the Egyptians to till the earth, and to plant vines and apple-trees; wedding of Osiris and Isis. In the other cross vault: Seth (Typhon) kills Osiris; Isis finds the limb of Osiris; Osiris leaves the pyramid in the from of the bull Apis; Apis is carried in triumph by the people.

On the large arch, scenes from the myth of Io and Argus: Mercury lulls Argus to sleep with the music of a syrinx; Hera asks Zeus to hand over Io; Io is tempted by Zeus; Isis enthroned between Horus and Mercury; Mercury kills Argus.

Above the door leading to the Room of the Mysteries: Madonna and Child by Pinturicchio, possibly a portrait of Giulia Farnese.

VI

VI, ROOM OF THE MYSTERIES

This is the last of the rooms decorated by Pinturicchio, who left a large part of the actual painting to his assistants. The Mysteries of the Faith are depicted in the lunettes. From the lunette above the window, proceeding right:

1 The *Ascension*.

2 The *Pentecost*.

3 The *Assumption of the Virgin*.

4 The *Annunciation*.

5 The *Nativity*.

6 The *Adoration of the Magi*.

7 The *Resurrection*.

Several portraits of contemporaries appear here. In the Resurrection there is a splendid portrait of Alexander VI, kneeling; the central soldier, with a lance, may be a portrait of Cesare Borgia. The figure on the right in the Ascension may be Francesco Borgia, the pope's "cubiculario" (manservant).

Eight tondi with busts of prophets, each identified by an inscription on the frame, decorate the spandrels of the two vaults: Micah, Joel, Jeremiah, Sophonias, Isaiah, Solomon, Malachi, David.

VII, ROOM OF THE PONTIFFS

With the Room of the Pontiffs we enter the official wing of the apartment. This room is the section built in the 14th century, and was used for formal audiences, banquets, consistories and official functions in general. The present false vault replaces the original beam ceiling, which collapsed in 1500, nearly killing Alexander VI. The ceiling decoration consists of stucco ornaments and grotesques made by Perin del Vaga and Giovanni da Udine, under Leo X. It depicts the twelve signs of the zodiac, the constellations, the seven planets known then, and, in the centre, dancing angels.

A series of inscriptions above the lunettes celebrates popes Stephen II, Adrian I, Leo III, Sergius II, Leo IV, Urban II, Nicholas III, Gregory XI, Boniface IX, and Martin V. The room was probably named after these inscriptions.

ROOMS VIII-XIII

Alexander VI's private Audience Room (VIII) is adjacent to the Room of the Pontiffs. The vault frescoes, painted 1576-77 by Lorenzo Sabbatini and assistants, depicts St Peter and St Paul, and eight stories from the Acts of the Apostles. This room communicates by way of a small stairway (not open to the public) decorated with frescoes by Simone Lagi (c. 1630) with the Raphael Stanze.

VIII

One door in the Audience Room leads to the Room of the Falda (XII), and another to the room now known as Second of the Vestments (IX, once called Room of the Pappagallo and, later, Dressing-Room and Room of the Secret Consistory; the Room of the Chiaroscuri, above, was used for the same purposes during the second half of the 16th century). Here the pope donned his vestments, and also met with cardinals, prelates and ambassadors, dealt with ordinary problems, and conducted special ceremonies like the Benediction of the Golden Rose, and the Christmas Benediction of the Sword; the "secret consistory" was also held here. The richly carved and decorated ceiling was made in 1563, under Pius IV, and restored under Gregory XIII; the central section with the Pentecost is by Girolamo Muziano (1576). The frieze dates back to the time of Pius IV, and is attributed to Giovanni Battista Lombardelli, Paris Nogari and others.

XII
IX

The next room is the Room of the Vestments (X), so called because the cardinals dressed here. The ceiling and frieze are of the same period as those of the preceding room.

X

This room give access to the Ducal Room (Sala Ducale) and the Royal Hall (Sala Regia), both closed to the public.

The "cubiculum" (XI) of Nicholas V communicates with the Room of the Vestments, and is adjacent to the Room of the Falda. The panelled ceiling, with a representation of St Peter in the centre, was made under Nicholas V. The many representations of the coat-of-arms of Sixtus IV suggest that the ceiling was restored during his papacy.

XI

Alexander VI's bedroom (XIII), where he died, is adjacent to the Room of the Liberal Arts. The low, richly carved wooden ceiling is decorated with elements in stucco of the Borgia coat-of-arms. The small frieze is of a later period.

XIII

r - Collection of Modern Religious Art

Ben Shahn, Third Allegory, detail

This is the new collection of paintings, sculpture and graphic art set up by Pope Paul VI as a record of the capacity of contemporary art for religious expression. He inaugurated the collection, comprised exclusively of donations, in 1973. The works occupy the apartment of Alexander VI (on the first floor of the Apostolic Palace), the two floors of the so-called Salette Borgia, a series of rooms on the ground floor, and a series of rooms below the Sistine Chapel. The last used to be the study of the "Magistri Caeremoniarum" (persons who directed proceedings on formal occasions, and performed what would now be called secretarial duties). Also included in the itinerary is a room in the tower built by Innocent III in the 13th century; it lies below the Chapel of Nicholas V, and has fragments of fresco decorations dating back to the papacy of Nicholas III.

The itinerary begins in the Room of the Sibyls (I) of the Borgia Apartment, and in the small room that adjoins it (II), where works by F. Goya, A. Rodin and H. Matisse (decorations and ornaments for the Chapel of Vence) introduce the collection of religious art. This and the following rooms include paintings by Italian artists of the so-called Novecento movement (O. Rosai, A. Soffici, F. Casorati, M. Sironi and V. Guidi), and by artists associated with the "Corrente" movement (B. Cassinari, R. Guttuso, A. Sassu) and the "Roman School" (C. Cagli, D. Purificato, F. Gentilini, F. Pirandello). A more decisive aim to revive religious art is expressed in the paintings of M. Denis, G. Desvallières and Père Couturier, founders of the "Atéliers d'Art Sacré", in France, and in the works of G. Previati, A. Carpi, B. Saetti, S. Consadori, L. Filocamo, F. Ferrazzi, R. Brindisi and M. Avenali. Sculpture is represented by a series of sketches by A. Biagini, F. Nagni and A. Monteleone for the doors of St Peter's; by L. Minguzzi and L. Fontana for the doors of the Cathedral of Milan; by E. Greco for those of the Cathedral of Orvieto; and by bronzes by E. Barlach, F. Messina, A. Berti, P. Fazzini and E. Manfrini.

G. Manzù, "Chapel of Peace", a homogeneous collection of vestments and vessels for church ceremonies from Sotto il Monte (Bergamo), birth-place of John XXIII, has been reconstructed on the upper floor of the Salette Borgia (Room XIV). The artist himself planned the layout of the exhibits.

Room XV* is devoted to the works of G. Roualt. Rooms XVI-XVIII contain works by late 19th-century artists who reacted against Impressionism: P. Gauguin, E. Bernard, O. Redon, the "Nabis" painters M. Denis and F.E. Vallotton, and the "École de Paris" painters M. Chagall, O. Zadkine, S. Dalì, T. Foujita and M. Utrillo. The graphic arts section (XIX-XXII) contains drawings and engravings by G. Morandi, F. Casorati, A. Bucci, M. Marini, A. Modigliani, H. Moore, G. Sutherland, B. Nicholson, P. Klee, W. Kandinsky, Le Corbusier, G. Braque and E. Munch.

plan p. 87

On the upper floor of the Salette Borgia (XXIII-XXVIII) are exhibited works by G. Balla, M. Sironi, C. Carrà, O. Rosai, A. Martini, P. Semenghini, A. Tosi, V. Guidi, F. De Pisis, L. Spazzapan, C. Levi, E. Morlotti, G. Omiccioli, T. Longaretti, F. Tomea and high-fired ceramics by A. Biancini.

Rooms XXIX-XXXII, on the ground floor, house various large works: mosaics by D. Cantatore and F. Ferrazzi; stained glass windows by F. Léger, R. Bissière, J. Villon, J. Thorn-Prikker and H. Campendonk; bronzes by A. Selva, J. Meštrović, L. Scorzelli, Mirko, F. Bodini, V. Ciminaghi, L. Baskin and E. Hillebrand; marble and stone sculpture by L. Fontana, U. Mastroianni, M. Marini, and G. Mazzullo; paintings by B. Buffet and G. Hajnal.

Most of the works exhibited in Rooms XXXIII-LV, below the Sistine Chapel, are arranged by nationality and artistic movement. First comes the United States donations, comprising works by Ben Shahn, Ph. Evergood and J. Levine, painters/witnesses of post-Depression America, and works by L. Feininger, M. Weber, J. Lipchitz, A. Rattner and F. Watkins, artists connected with early 20th-century European vanguards. Room XXXVIII contains a large group of works by G. Severini; they date back to the fifties and sixties, and record the artist's activity as decorator for the Cathedral of Cortona, the Church of St Pierre in Fribourg, and the university of the same city. Rooms XL-XLIII contain an outstanding series of Expressionist paintings, most of which are by German artists; the collection ranges from works by Paula Modersohn-Becker and the Belgian painter J. Ensor, precursors of Expressionism, to works by the "Brücke" group (E.L. Kirchner, E. Heckel, K. Schmidt-Rottluff, E. Nolde, C. Rohlfs), to O. Dix, M. Beckmann and O. Kokoschka. They are followed by ceramics by Picasso, paintings by F. Bacon and G. Sutherland, opposite extremes of the new tendencies in British painting, and paintings by D. Rivera, J.C. Orozco, D.A. Siqueiros and R. Tamayo, better-known for their large mural paintings in Mexico (Rooms XLIV-XLVI). Spain is represented by works of E. Chillida, P. Serrano Aguilar, and B. Palencia; Yugoslavia by works of J. Meštrović, I. Dulčić, and naïfs of the so-called School of Hlebine; France by works of J. Bazaine, A. Manessier, J. Villon and J. Fautrier. The collection finishes with works of U. Mastroianni, C. Capogrossi, F. Botero, Djanira, R.A. Crooke, L. Zack, K. Azuma, S. Hantai and E.G. Hansing.

*

Room XV leads on to a balustrade overlooking the Royal Hall, formerly used for receiving ruling monarchs and ambassadors and for other ceremonies; it was renovated by Antonio da Sangallo the Younger under Paul III, and the frescoes, by Late-Renaissance artists, illustrate episodes from the history of the papacy.

s - Sistine Chapel

View of the chapel

The Sistine Chapel is in an edifice standing at the southwest corner of the old medieval section of the Apostolic Palace, and takes its name from Pope Sixtus IV della Rovere, who had it built between 1477 and 1480. At present, entrance to the chapel is through a small door in the wall behind the altar, reached by coming down from the Raphael Stanze, or up from the Collection of Modern Religious Art. The official entrance is in the Royal Hall (Sala Regia), the hall where the pope publicly received royal and imperial ambassadors.

Built by Giovannino de' Dolci on a plan by the Florentine architect Baccio Pontelli, the Sistine edifice was designed for the dual purpose of housing the new palatine chapel, and defending the Apostolic Palace. The defensive nature of the building is evident from the stern massive appearance of its exterior, and from the battlements at the top. The structure includes an area below ground level, a mezzanine, and the chapel, above which is a spacious attic and, on the outside, a gallery for the guards. The mezzanine, which now houses part of the Collection of Modern Religious Art, was once occupied by the offices of the "Magistri Caeremoniarum", among whom were Giovanni Burcardo, a contemporary of the Borgia Pope; Paris de Grassis, a contemporary of Julius II and Leo X; and Biagio da Cesena, a contemporary of Paul III. The chapel is still used for some papal functions and for the conclave, which originally assembled in the nearby Chapel of the Holy Sacrament.

The latter, frescoed by Fra Angelico, was pulled down during the papacy of Paul III to enlarge the Stairway of the Maresciallo. The Sistine Chapel is built on a simple rectangular plan. It has no apse, and is 40.23 m long, 13.41 m wide, and 20.7 m high. It is covered with a barrel vault, with weight-bearing vaulting cells that descend between the twelve arched windows. The floor is in inlaid marble of different colours. A marble transenna, a free interpretation of the Byzantine iconostasis, separates the area of the presbytery reserved for the officiating clergy from that of the congregation. It was originally joined to the choir, but was moved back during the papacy of Gregory XIII to enlarge the presbytery. Both the transenna and the choir are ornamented with extremely fine reliefs, the work of Mino da Fiesole, who may have been assisted by Andrea Bregno and Giovanni Dalmata.

The decoration of the walls with events from the lives of Moses and Christ, and with portraits of popes, was carried out by a team of painters originally composed of Perugino, Sandro Botticelli, Domenico Ghirlandaio and Cosimo Rosselli, assisted by members of their workshops, among whom were Pinturicchio, Piero di Cosimo and Bartolomeo della Gatta. They were later joined by Luca Signorelli, who painted the last two frescoes of the Mosaic series. Pier Matteo d'Amelia painted a simple, starry sky on the vault. The work was begun in 1481, and completed in 1483. On 15 August of the same year, Sixtus IV consecrated the new chapel, dedicating it to the Virgin Mary. The work of the various artists was probably co-ordinated by Perugino, who was the first to be engaged, and who had painted the lost altar-piece with the Virgin Mary, and the first two panels of both the Mosaic and Christian cycles, works that were destroyed by Michelangelo to make room for the Last Judgement. The only signature which has been found is that of Perugino.

The three popes who succeeded Sixtus IV left the chapel as they had found it. It was only in 1506 that Julius II della Rovere, nephew of Sixtus IV, decided to change the vault decoration. In 1508 he entrusted the task to Michelangelo Buonarroti, who tried in vain to resist the will of the masterfull pope. Tradition has it that it was Donato Bramante, envious of his rival's success, who suggested that Michelangelo be commissioned to do the job. On 10 May 1508 Michelangelo began work on the ceiling, with the help of assistants such as Jacopo d'Indaco and Francesco Granacci. He dismissed his assistants as soon as he had learnt the fresco technique, which was entirely new to him at that time. By September 1510 he had finished half the vault (from the entrance to the Fall). On 14 August 1511, Julius, impatient to see the work, had the scaffolding taken down, and it is said that when Raphael saw the paintings on the vault he changed his style. The ceiling was completed in October 1512, and on All Saints' Day (1 November) Julius II inaugurated it with a solemn high mass. Towards the end of 1533 Clement VII de' Medici commissioned Michelangelo to paint the Last Judgement on the altar wall, and the Fall of the Rebel Angels, which was never executed, on the opposite wall. The placing of the Last Judgement over the altar is unusual in that the subject, for liturgical reasons, was traditionally depicted on the entrance wall; the pope may have had it placed on the altar wall to serve as a reminder of the Sack of Rome, in 1527, which many had interpreted as divine punishment for the corruption of the times. Once again Michelangelo reluctantly accepted the commission, though he did not begin work on the painting until 1535, and then only under pressure from Paul III, Clement VII's successor. The 15th-century paintings on the wall were destroyed, and the wall covered with a slightly sloping layer of bricks. Unaided by assistants, Michelangelo began to paint on this surface in the summer of 1536, completing the immense painting (which occupies 200 square metres, and represents 391 figures) in the autumn of 1541. On 31 October of the same year, Paul III, who had followed the artist's progress with great impatience, celebrated vespers in front of that extraordinary painting which, according to Giorgio Vasari, aroused "the wonder and astonishment of the whole of Rome".

scheme →

93

scheme
→

A
B
C
D

SIDE WALLS AND ENTRANCE WALL

The wall frescoes representing the lives of Moses and Christ are closely related, and the Latin inscription above each fresco emphasizes this relationship. The inscriptions sometimes refer to a principal episode in the frescoes, and sometimes to a secondary episode, whose counterpart appears on the opposite wall, illustrated by a similar inscription. Therefore a full understanding of the cycle requires that the two Lives be viewed together. The complicated iconographic scheme was undoubtedly established by Sixtus IV or one of his court theologians, and has a precise political aim; in effect, the choice of the episodes tends to stress the role of Christ and his "precursor", Moses, as leaders of the people, legislators and priests. In the Handing over of the keys (see below: 10), Christ, with a symbolic gesture, transmits these roles to Peter, founder of the papacy. The Payment of the Tribute, in the background of the same painting, alludes to the independence of spiritual from temporal power, and independence also recognized by the emperor Constantine (whose triumphal arch appears twice) with his legendary donation to Pope Silvester. The fresco with the Punishment of Korah (see below: 9) alludes to the divine punishment awaiting those, including persons within the Church, who question the authority of the papacy. Similar messages are contained in the gallery of portraits of the first thirty popes (only 26 remain as the first four on the altar wall were destroyed), which serve as a record of the historical origins of papal power. The interpretation of the cycle now begins with the two panels at the sides of the altar wall.

1

South wall: the *Journey of Moses*. In the background, Moses takes leave of his father-in-law before returning to Egypt. In the foreground, on the left, the prophet meets the angel sent to punish him for not having circumsized his son; on the right, the Circumcision, the episode to which the inscription of the panel refers. The fresco is by Perugino.

1a
1b

— The two popes next to the window are *Clement I* (right), by Ghirlandaio, and *Evaristus* (left), by Botticelli.

2

North wall: the *Baptism of Christ*. The scene appears in the centre, and the inscription refers to this episode. In the background, left, a sermon by the Redeemer; right, a sermon by John the Baptist. The fresco is by Perugino, whose signature appears on the marble frame above the tondo of God. — The popes are *Anaclete* (left), by Ghirlandaio, and

2a
2b

Alexander I (right), by Fra Diamante.

3

South wall: *Events from the life of Moses*. Right to left: Moses kills the Egyptian who maltreated an Israelite; he escapes from Egypt; he defends Jethro's daughters from the shepherds, and helps the girls to water the flock; he takes off his shoes and prostrates himself before the burning bush (the inscription refers to this epidosde); he leads the

3a
3b

jews out of Egypt. Fresco by Botticelli. The popes are *Sixtus I*, artist unknown, and *Hyginos*, by Ghirlandaio.

4

North wall: the *Temptations of Christ*. The temptations, to which the inscription refers, appear in the background. In the foreground, the Purification of the leper. There are several portraits among the onlookers; the figure on the far right, with a baton, is Girolamo Riario, the pope's condottiere. By Botticelli. The popes are *Telesphorus*, by Fra

4a
4b

Diamante, and *Pius I*, by Botticelli.

5

South wall: the *Crossing of the Red Sea*. Left, the jubilant people gather round Moses (the inscription refers to this episode); right, the Egyptians are swept away by the sea. In the background, Moses and Aaron before Pharaoh. There are many portraits: the old man holding a case, on Moses' right, is Cardinal Bessarione; the youth in black, on the left, is Piero di Cosimo; the warrior with his back almost turned to the viewer is Roberto Malatesta. By Cosimo Rosselli. The popes are

5a,5b

Anicetus and Eleutherius, both by Fra Diamante.

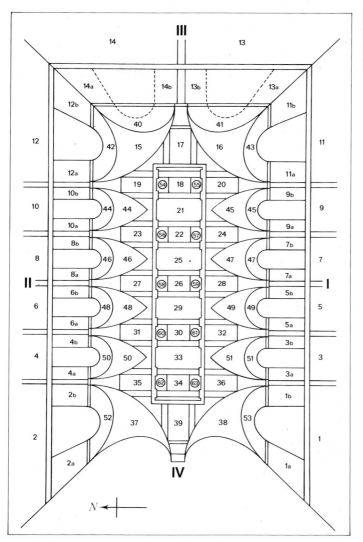

SCHEME OF THE WALLS AND CEILING

I   South wall: life of Moses
II   North wall: life of Christ
III East entrance wall
IV   West wall with the Last
     Judgement (see scheme on p. 99)

Ceiling frescoes not mentioned in text

The Ancestors of Christ
40 Lunette with Eleazar, Matthan
41 Lunette with Jacob, Joseph
42 Lunette with Azor, Zadoch
43 Lunette with Achim, Eliud
44 Lunette and vaulting cell with Josiah,
    Jeconiah, Shealtiel
45 Lunette and vaulting cell with
    Zerubbabel, Abiud, Eliakim
46 Lunette and vaulting cell with Hezekiah,
    Manesseh, Amon
47 Lunette and vaulting cell with Azariah,
    Jotham, Ahaz
48 Lunette and vaulting cell with Asa,
    Jehoshaphat, Joram

49 Lunette and vaulting cell with Rehoboam,
    Abjijah
50 Lunette and vaulting cell with Jesse,
    David, Solomon
51 Lunette and vaulting cell with Salmon,
    Boaz, Obed
52 Lunette with Nahshon
53 Lunette with Amminadab

Monochrome medallions with stories
from Genesis, II Samuel, and II Kings
54 Joab, nephew of David, kills Abner
55 Bidgar throws King Joram from the cart
56 Death of Uriah, husband of Bathsheba
57 Jehu destroys the image of the god Baal
58 David before the prophet Nathan
59 Destruction of the tribe of Achab
60 Death of Absalom
61 Medallion with no story
62 Sacrifice of Isaac
63 Elija ascends to Heaven on a chariot of
    fire

95

scheme
←

6

6a, 6b

North wall: the *Calling of the first apostles*. In the foreground, Peter and Andrew kneel before Christ (the inscription refers to this episode); in the background, their vocation, and that of John and James. Among the portraits: the old man in the foreground is the humanist Argiropolos, and on his right are Giovanni Tornabuoni, the pope's treasurer, with his son Lorenzo. By Ghirlandaio. The popes are *Soter* and *Victor*, both by Ghirlandaio.

7

7a, 7b

South wall: *Moses receives the tablets of the Law*. Centre, he receives the tablets; below, the people worship the golden calf; foreground, Moses breaks the tablets. Right, in the background, the Punishment of the idolaters; left, Moses returns with the tablets of the Law (the inscription refers to this episode). By Cosimo Rosselli. The popes are *Zephyrinus* and *Urban I*, both by fra Diamante.

8

8a, 8b

North wall: the *Sermon on the Mount*. In the centre, the sermon, to which the inscription refers; right, the Healing of the leper. Among the portraits: the two figures standing in the foreground, left, are Jaime (in Oriental dress) and Fernando de Almeida; further left, standing, the queen of Cyprus; behind her, in black, Cosimo Rosselli, the painter of the fresco. The popes are *Calixtus I*, by Rosselli, and *Pontianus*, by an unknown artist.

9

9a
9b

South wall: the *Punishment of Korah, Datan and Abiron*. On the right, the Attempted stoning of Moses, to which the inscription refers. In the background, centre, Constantine's Arch; on the right, the Septizonium. Among the portraits: left, behind the bearded figure of Moses, Alessandro Farnese and Pomponio Leto; far right, behind Moses, dressd in black, Botticelli, the painter of the fresco. The popes are *Anteros*, by Fra Diamante, and *Cornelius*, by Botticelli.

10

10a
10b

North wall: the *Handing over of the keys*, in the foreground; further back, left, the Payment of the tribute; right, the Attempted stoning of Christ, to which the inscription refers. In the background, Constantine's Arch (shown twice). Among the portraits: the second figure from the right is Giovannino de' Dolci, the third Baccio Pontelli, the fourth Pinturicchio, the fifth (in black) Perugino, the painter of the fresco; far left, Alfonso di Calabria. The popes are *Fabian*, by an unknown painter, and *Lucius I*, by Botticelli.

11

11a
11b

South wall: the *Testament of Moses*, shown in the foreground, right (the inscription refers to this episode); left, Moses gives his staff to Joshua. In the background, right to left: the angel shows Moses the promised land; Moses descends from Mt Horeb; the Death of Moses. Among the portraits is that of the artist of the fresco, Luca Signorelli (third figure from the left in the background). The popes are *Stephen I*, by Botticelli, and *Dionysus*, by Rosselli.

12

12a
12b

North wall: the *Last Supper*, in the foreground, to which the inscription refers; in the windows, the Prayer in the garden, Christ taken prisoner, the Crucifixion. By Rosselli. The popes are *Sixtus II*, by Botticelli, and *Felix I*, by Ghirlandaio.

13

13a,13b

Entrance wall, south side: *Disputation over the body of Moses*, by Matteo da Lecce (1571-72). It replaces the lost masterpiece by Signorelli. The popes are *Eutychianus*, by Ghirlandaio, and *Marcellus I*, by an unknown artist.

14

14a,14b

Entrance wall, north side: the *Resurrection*, by Arrigo Paludano (van den Broeck, 1571-72). It replaces the masterpiece by Ghirlandaio. The popes are *Marcellinus*, by Botticelli, and *Caius*, by Ghirlandaio.

THE CEILING

scheme
←

Michelangelo's original idea was to portray the twelve apostles in the vaulting cells, and a series of architectural elements on the vault, but then he decided to represent the history of mankind before the coming of Christ, thus linking the ceiling decoration with that of the walls. Without seeking illusionistic effects, he divided up the vault by painted monumental architecture into panels, each enclosing a separate scene.

The nine panels depict events from Genesis. Five Sibyls and seven prophets, pagan and Hebrew harbingers of the future Grace, are represented in the spaces between the vaulting cells. The corner-spandrels contain the miraculous Salvations of Israel, prefigurations of the redemption, which form a thematic link with the 15th-century cycle on the walls. In the vaulting cells and the lunettes below them (the inscriptions on the plaques probably identify the figures portrayed within) are the Ancestors of Christ (see 40-53, scheme p. 95). The nude youths to the sides of the panels containing the stories from Genesis have both an ornamental and a symbolic function. They have been variously interpreted as geniii of the golden age of Julius II, personifications of various kinds, expressions of Michelangelo's Neoplatonist ideas, etc. In any case, they have a function similar to that of the putto plaque-bearers (between the lunettes) and to the "bronze" nudes (above the vaulting cells). Each pair of the nude youths holds a monochrome medallion with stories from Genesis, II Samuel, and II Kings (see 54-63, scheme p. 95).

Contrary to custom, Michelangelo began painting the ceiling from the entrance end, working towards the altar, probably because the crowded scenes in this area presented fewer technical and compositional problems to an artist as yet unfamiliar with the fresco technique.

With our backs turned to the wall opposite the Last Judgement, we see in the right corner-spandrel *Judith and Holofernes*; Judith covers the head of the dead man, a presumed self-portrait of Michelangelo; on the right, the headless body. In the left corner-spandrel: *David and Goliath*; David is about to cut off the head of the giant Philistine. — In the centre, in the triangle between the two spandrels, the prophet *Zechariah* thoughtfully leafs through a book.

15
16
17

Central Panel: the *Drunkenness of Noah*; Cam, in the foreground, his head turned away from the viewer, mocks his sleeping father, while Japheth covers his father, and Shem reproaches Cam; on the left, Noah plants the vine. — On the right, the *Delphic Sibyl*, asborbed in a sudden prophecy as she reads. The prophet, on the left, is *Joel*, a presumed portrait of Donato Bramante, who studies a parchment.

18
19
20

Central panel: the *Flood*. Painted between December 1508 and January 1509, it was the first of the Histories to be depicted. An explosion in Castel Sant'Angelo in 1797 caused a triangular portion of the right-hand side of the fresco to fall off. In the background, centre, the ark represented as a house; in front of the ark, a boat sinks for excessive weight; on the right, on a small island, underneath a cloth, the multitude of the selfish prevents others from reaching dry land, while on the left, in contrast, an old man "has clasped someone who is half dead, and is striving his utmost to save him"; on the left, in the foreground, the multitude of the generous, among which is a series of famous groups: the embracing lovers awaiting death together, the mother with her terrified children, and the fierce-eyed nude carrying his wife on his shoulders.

21

Central panel: *Noah's sacrifice* after the flood. The episode follows the Flood in order of time, but was placed here because it requires less space. — The prophet is *Isaiah*, distracted by the call from heaven. The female figure is the *Erythraen Sibyl*, whose lamp is being lit by a putto.

22
23
24

scheme
←

25   A B C D   Central panel: the *Fall*. On the left, Adam and Eve, the loveliest of the nudes painted by Michelangelo, are tempted by the demon in the guise of an anthropomorphic serpent; right, the Expulsion from Eden. This panel marks the beginning of the stylistic maturity of Michelangelo, who, especially in the Temptation, draws towards forms of increasing grandeur.

26   Central panel: the *Creation of Eve*. Next to Adam, who is "enslaved by sleep", is the stump of a tree, a symbolic allusion to the Cross. — The

27
28   wrinkled female figure is the *Cumaean Sibyl*, who searches for a passage in a book. The prophet is *Ezekiel*, wearing a Syriac turban and holding a scroll of prophecies, who is seized by inspiration.

29   Central panel: the *Creation of Adam:* iconographically new because represented in the moment the Creator instills life into Adam with a gesture of his hand.

30   Central panel: the *Division of the land from the waters*. The nude youth at the base of the panel, on the left, was inspired by the Belvedere

31   Torso (see p. 46: III/1). — The prophet is *Daniel*, his hair and clothing ruffled by the breeze of the spirit, who is intent upon making notes

32   from a text. The elderly female figure, bent with age, is the *Persian Sibyl*.

33   Central panel: the *Creation of the Heavens*. On the right, God creates the sun and moon, while on the left, his back toward the viewer, he creates the plant life on the earth.

34
35
36   Central panel: the *Division of day from night*. — The female figure is the *Libyan Sibyl*, who has just stopped reading and is about to rise from her chair. The prophet is *Jeremiah*, tragic symbol of the melancholy of knowledge, in whom Michelangelo has expressed his immost self, and possibly his own face.

37   In the right corner-spandrel (looking towards the altar): the *Bronze Serpent*, with which Moses saved the Israelites from divine punish-

38   ment. In the left corner-spandrel: the *Punishment of Haman;* on the right, the recumbent Ahasuerus calls Mordecai; on the left, the council called by the king to decide the condemnation of Haman; in the centre, the crucified figure of Haman, which Michelangelo drew from the Laocoön (see p. 41: VIII/5). — In the centre, in the triangle between the

39   two spandrels, the monumental figure of the prophet *Jonah*, prefiguration of Christ, and symbol of the Faith.

scheme
→

THE LAST JUDGEMENT

Conceived as a monumental structure of human figures, the Last Judgement is the masterpiece of Michelangelo's maturity. He was in his sixties when he began the painting, which took about 450 "days" to complete. The work has various sources: the Bible, and Ezekiel in particular, the Dies Irae, Dante (but only as regards the presence of Charon and Minos), and the motives of pre-Tridentine religious polemic. The plan is the traditional one, figures arranged on different levels, but the whole composition is absorbed into the dynamic vortex created by the blast of the trumpets, and Christ's gesture of condemnation.

1, 2   In the two lunettes are the symbols of the Passion borne by angels, among whom is *Gabriel*. Further down, in the centre, *Christ the Judge*, an anti-classical and anti-traditional image, with the features of the

3
4, 5
6   Apollo Belvedere (see p. 41: VIII/3), and Herculean limbs; next to him is the *Virgin,* who turns away her head in pity; at their feet, the patron saints of Rome: *St Lawrence* with the gridiron, and *St Bartholomew* with the human skin (the head of which is a *sorrowful self-portrait of the artist*).

On the right: *Peter* with the keys; *Adam* and *Eve* (or Job and his wife); the reconciling embrace of *Esau* and *Jacob* (or a husband and wife after their earthly separation); *Simon of Cyrene* (or Dismas) with the cross on his shoulders; *St Sebastian* holding an arrow; *St Catherine of Alexandria* with the cog-wheel; *St Blaise* with the iron combs; *Dismas* (or St Philip) with the cross; *Simon Zelotes* with the saw. On the left: *St Andrew* with the cross; *John the Baptist* with animal-skin cloak; the *group with the personification of the mother*, the *nude Eve*, and *Virgil*. On the "level" below: centre, the *trumpeting angels*; right, the damned are hurled down by demons; left, the elect ascend: of particular interest are the *two redeemed suspended by a rosary*, a clear anti-Lutheran allusion. On the earth below: left, the resurrected, whose bodies are being re-formed; right, hell with two Dantesque figures: *Charon,* who, unlike his counterpart in the Divine Comedy, pushes the damned out of the boat; and *Minos,* to whom Michelangelo gave the feature of Biagio da Cesena, the master of ceremonies of Paul III who had expressed strong criticism of the work.

The frescoes are being restored with astounding results as regards our knowledge of Michelangelo's pictorial technique and his use of colour. The project, begun in 1981, will last until 1993.

7-9
10, 11
12
13, 14
15, 16
17, 18
19
20, 21
22, 23

24

25
26

t - Vatican Library

Cross-reliquary of Paschal I, in pale gold leaf and enamel (9th cent.), detail; Roman fresco known as the Aldobrandini Wedding (1st cent. B.C.), detail; Armillary sphere (17th cent.); Great Hall of Sixtus V or Salone Sistine

As a result of the new "one-way" system, the visit now begins in the Room of the Addresses to Pius IX (XIII), and ends in the Profane Museum (I).

XIII

ROOM OF THE ADDRESSES TO PIUS IX (XIII), originally set up to preserve addresses, messages of homage sent to the Pope by the faithful throughout the world. In the centre of the room: show-case containing objects from excavations at Pompeii unearthed in the presence of Pius XI on 22 October 1849. Remarkable among these is the *bas-relief with galloping horseman*, a Greek original of the mid-4th century B.C.

XII

CHAPEL OF ST PIUS V (XII), built between 1566 and 1572; decorated by Jacopo Zucchi, from designs by Giorgio Vasari, with *stories from the life of St Peter the Martyr.* In the show-case are objects from the treasury of the Sancta Sanctorum. The following are worth noting: *ivory with the Healing of the Blind Man*, once the lid of a case belonging to a physician, perhaps an oculist; 6th century. *St Peter* and *St Paul*, two figures forming a diptych; Roman school, about 7th century. *Silver shrine* with representation of Christ enthroned between St Peter and St Paul; on the sides, scenes from Christ's childhood, The shrine, which was made in Rome in the 9th century for Paschal I, contained the *enamelled cross with stories of Christ,* of the same period. *Reliquary of the head of St Praxedes*; on the sides, saints; on the enamelled lid, the Deesis surrounded by tondi of the apostles; 11th century, from Byzantium. The ring with the seal of Nicholas III was found inside the reliquary.

100

On the floors immediately above and below (see p. 72) are two other chapels of St Pius V, built by the same pope.

plan
pp. 24-25

ROOM OF THE ADDRESSES (XI), used under Gregory XVI for the display of Byzantine icons and "primitive" paintings (now in the Pinacoteca), and so called because the addresses sent to Leo XIII and Pius X were kept here. It contains Roman and early Christian glassware, and church ornaments, vestments and cult objects in enamel, ivory and precious metals, dating from the Middle Ages on. The following are worth noting: *Rambona diptych*, with enthroned Madonna and Crucifixion; made by a northern Italian workshop (c. 900) for Abbot Olderico of the monastery of Rambona (show-case 12). *Cover of the Codex Aureus of Lorsch*; in the centre, Christ tramples a dragon and a lion; at the sides, two angels. Carolingian copy of the diptych of Anastasius (517); made in the Convent of St Gall, Switzerland (show-case 12). *Christ and 5 apostles,* a series of enamels from the antependium of the "Confession" in the Constantinian basilica of St Peter's; Limoges, 13th century (show-case 8). *Encrusted drinking-glass with sea-animal designs*, made in Cologne c. 300 A.D.; from the Catacombs of St Calixtus.

XI

ROOM OF THE ALDOBRANDINI WEDDING (X), built in 1611, under Paul V, and decorated by Guido Reni, with stories of Samson. Back wall: large Augustan Age fresco representing wedding preparations; known as the *Aldobrandini Wedding* because its first modern owner was Cardinal Pietro Aldobrandini. Side walls: *fresco cycle with landscapes and scenes from the Odyssey* (Odysseus among the Laestrygones, and in Circe's palace, and his voyage to the underworld); 1st century B.C.

X

ROOM OF THE PAPYRI (IX), so called because it was set up to house papyri from Ravenna (6th-9th cent.); decorated under Pius VI by Anton Raphaël Mengs. In the show-case are gilded, early Christian glass objects with pagan and sacred scenes, among which are the full-length *portrait of the ship-builder Dedalo* with six scenes of carpenters at work (c. 300, from the Catacomb of St Saturninus on the Via Salaria), and the *Resurrection of Lazarus* and *Wedding at Cana* (4th cent.). On the ceiling is a fresco commemorating the inauguration of the Clementine Museum (1773).

IX

CHRISTIAN MUSEUM (VIII), set up in 1756, under Benedict XIV, to house early Christian antiquities, displayed in the show-cases. Of special interest is the mosaic *travelling-icon with St Theodore*, which is similar to those preserved in the monasteries of Mt Athos; probably Oriental, 12th/13th century.

VIII

GALLERY OF URBAN VIII (VII), created to house manuscripts of the Palatine Library. In the lunettes, *views of buildings constructed or renovated during the papacy of Benedict XIV.*

VII

SISTINE ROOMS (VI), two rooms laid out by Sixtus V to house documents and registers of the papal archives. On the walls *episodes from the papacy of Sixtus V*. In the first room, in the larger lunettes which face each other, are two frescoes from 1590 by Cesare Nebbia and Giovanni Guerra: *View of St. Peter's according to the project by Michelangelo* and the *Transportation of the obelisk to St. Peter's Square in May-September 1586.*

VI

SALONE SISTINO (V). This Great Hall was set up by Sixtus V as the Library reading-room. In the lunettes above the entrance and the exit of the small Gallery are two frescoes facing one another with views of *the popes' Lateran Palace* before and after its reconstruction by Sixtus V in 1598. In the Vestibule are representations of the papal chapels of the basilicas of *St Lawrence's Outside the Walls, St Paul's Outside the Walls, Santa Maria Maggiore, Santa Maria del Popolo* and also of

scheme
→
V

scheme
→
V

plan
pp. 24-25

IV

III

II

I

the *Third Lateran Council*, and those of *Florence* and *Trent*. In the lunettes, *episodes from the papacy of Sixtus V*; in the other frescoes, the *history of the book* and the *Councils of the Church*; on the pilasters, the *inventors of the alphabet*. The decoration is the work of several painters under the direction of Cesare Nebbia, who also made the designs.

The Salone periodically hosts exhibitions of books and manuscripts from the Library collections.

PAULINE ROOMS (IV), set up under Paul V. The *episodes from the papacy of Paul V* were painted by Giovanni Battista Ricci in 1610-11.

ALEXANDRINE ROOM (III), set up in 1690, by Alexander VIII; decorated under Pius VII with *episodes from the papacy of Pius VI*, about 1818. In one of the show-cases, *embroidered linen altar-cloth from the Sancta Sanctorum*, 11th century, probably from the north.

CLEMENTINE GALLERY (II), set up by Clement XII; divided into five rooms by Pius VI. On the walls, *episodes from the papacy of Pius VII*, painted in about 1818. In the show-cases, Gian Lorenzo Bernini's *models* of Charity, the prophet Habakkuk, and Daniel in the lions' den, and *studies* for the Chigi Chapel in Santa Maria del Popolo (1655-56), and for the monument to Urban VIII in St Peter's (1628-47). In the room that precedes the Profane Museum, two porphyry columns with *reliefs of the Tetrarchs* (provincial governors of the Roman Empire in the 3rd and 4th centuries A.D.).

PROFANE MUSEUM (I). Founded by Clement XIII in 1767, the museum contains material of various periods—Etruscan, Roman, medieval—and places of origin, arranged in a typically late 18th-century fashion. This is what remains of the great collection taken to Paris in 1797. The rich furniture is by Luigi Valadier.

When we leave the Profane Museum of the Vatican Library, we find ourselves once again in the Vestibule of the Four Gates. On the left is the Atrium of the Four Gates and, beyond, the small portico and the Court of the Pinacoteca, which form part of the Museums entrance already described on p. 28. The Court of the Pinacoteca, which was planned by the architect Luca Beltrami (1932), faces the Vatican Gardens, beyond which we can see Michelangelo's dome on the Basilica of St Peter. The avenue on the left runs along between the gardens and the wing of the Apostolic Palace that houses the exhibition galleries of the Vatican Library and, on the floor above, some galleries of the Museums. The small tower above the building is the Tower of the Winds, built for the observations that led to the adoption of the Gregorian calendar in 1582.

From here we approach the self-service restaurant, the Pinacoteca (p. 104), and the Gregorian Profane, Pio Christian, Missionary-Ethnological, and Carriage Museums (pp. 113-154).

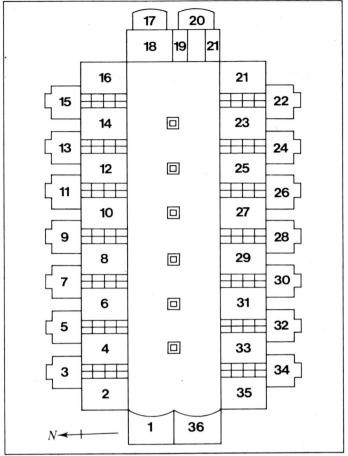

SCHEME OF THE LUNETTES AND WALLS OF THE SALONE SISTINO

In the left aisle:

1 Allegory of the emendation of public
  customs in Rome under Sixtus V
2 Fourth Council of Constantinople (870)
3 Chapel of the Crib in Santa Maria
  Maggiore (1586)
4 Second Council of Nicaea against the
  Iconoclasts ((790)
5 Erection of the obelisk in Piazza del
  Popolo (1588)
6 Third Council of Constantinople (680)
7 Ponte Sisto and the Hospice of
  St John Calabita
8 Second Council of Constantinople (553)
9 Erection of the statue of St. Paul above
  the Aurelian Column (1588)
10 Council of Chalcedon (451)
11 Removal of the body of St Pius V to
   Santa Maria Maggiore (1588)
12 First Council of Ephesus (431)
13 Obelisk and Square of Santa Maria
   Maggiore (1587)
14 First Council of Constantinople (381)
15 The Galleys of Sixtus V (1588)
16 Burning of the Arian books by
   Constantine (? 325)
17 Incoronation of Sixtus V on the steps
   of St Peter's (1 May 1585)
18 First Council of Nicaea (325)

In the right aisle:

19 Sixtus V accepts the plan of the new
   library from Domenico Fontana (1587)
20 Sixtus V takes possession of the Lateran
   in a papal cavalcade (May 1585)
21 The Jewish library founded by Moses
22 Allegory of the fight against the brigands
23 The library of Babylonia
24 St Peter's Square in 1586
25 The library at Athens
26 Allegory of the abundance produced
   by the good government of Sixtus V
27 The library of Alexandria, Egypt
28 The erection of the statue of St Peter
   above Trajan's Column
29 The Roman library founded by
   Tarquinius Superbus
30 Papal procession to S. Maria Maggiore
   for the opening of the 1585 Jubilee
31 The episcopal library of Jerusalem
   (ca. 250)
32 The new Lateran Palace and the
   obelisk erected in 1588
33 The episcopal library of Caesarea in
   Palestine (ca. 230)
34 The "Aqua Felix" at Piazza
   San Bernardo (1585-87)
35 The apostolic library with portraits of
   St Peter, Nicholas V, Sixtus IV, etc.
36 Plan of the city of Rome according to
   projects by Sixtus V

103

Raphael, Transfiguration, detail

The Pinacoteca houses paintings and tapestries dating from the 11th to the 19th century. Each room is devoted to one or more schools of painting, to a period, or to individual artists. In the vestibule, on the left as we enter, is Enrico Quattrini's bust of Pius XI, who established the Pinacoteca in its present site (see pp. 3, 14-15 for the history of the Pinacoteca).

ROOM I
(Primitives)

1 Vittore Cavalli, known as Vitale da Bologna, *Madonna and Child* (tempera on wood, 96 x 68 cm). Signed VITALIS DE BONONIA F.; at the bottom, left, a group of kneeling monks, perhaps the donors. Formerly in the Vatican Library collection. Inv. 17.

2 School of Giunta Pisano, *St Francis and stories of his life* (tempera on wood, 66 x 86,5 cm). Very similar to two panels in the churches of San Francesco in Assisi and Pisa. In the centre, the figure of the saint; at the sides, four of his miracles; the Healing of the benumbed child, the Healing of the cripple, the Possessed woman freed of the demon, an Old man praying before the altar of the saint. Formerly in the Vatican Library collection. Inv. 23.

3 Giovanni and Niccolò, *Last Judgement* (tempera on wood, 288 x 243 cm), Roman school, datable to the second half of the 12th century. The panel is from the oratory of San Gregorio Nazianzeno (St Gregory Nazianzen), near Santa Maria, Campus Martius. It was commissioned by two Benedictine nuns, represented at the bottom, left, and identified by the Latin inscription "Domna Benedicta ancilla Dei et Constantia abbatissa". The shape of the panel—round, with a rectangular piece attached to the base—is unusual. The various scenes are arranged on different levels. At the top, Christ with seraphim and angels. Below, Christ, with symbols of the Passion, stands behind an altar, surrounded by apostles. Further down, from left to right: the resurrected, led by St Paul and Dismas, the good thief; the Virgin; the saintly Innocents; St Stephen; the Works of Mercy depicted in three episodes. Next level: the Resurrection of the dead; on the left, those devoured by wild animals and fishes; on the right, Those who were buried; in the centre, two allegories of classical derivation, of the Sea and the Earth. On the lowest level: Paradise, left, and the torments of Hell, right. Inv. 526.

104

Margaritone di Arezzo, *St Francis* (tempera on wood, 127.2 x 53.9 cm). **B**   4
One of the earliest representations of the saint. Signed MARGARITO **D**
DE ARITIO ME FECIT. Formerly in the Vatican Library collection. Inv. 2.

Giovanni Baronzio, *The guardian angel with the child John the Bap-*   5
tist (tempera on wood, 40 x 46.5 cm). Probably part of a predella;
the other parts are in the former Sterbini Collection and in the Berlin
Museum. Inv. 185.

Allegretto Nuzi, *Madonna and Child, St Michael and St Ursula* (tem-   6
pera on wood; central panel 116.2 x 57.8; side panels 83.8 x 33 cm).
The triptych is signed ALEGRITTUS NUTII ME PINXIT A.M. CCCLXV
(1365). In the central panel; the group of donors kneeling at the
Virgin's feet. Formerly in the Vatican Library collection. Inv. 204.

Giovanni del Biondo, *Madonna of the Apocalypse with saints and*   7
angels (tempera on wood, 75.4 x 43.4 cm). Left: St Stephen, St
Anthony, St Lawrence, St Francis. Right: St Mary Magdalen, St Catherine of Alexandria, St Clare, St Catherine of Siena. Below, a skeleton
devoured by worms. Formerly in the Vatican Library collection. Inv. 14.

Giovanni Bonsi, *Madonna and Child with saints* (tempera on wood, 166   8
x 232 cm). Centre, the Virgin and Child; left, St Honophrius and St
Nicholas; right, St Bartholomew and St John the Evangelist. The only
work certain to be by the hand of Bonsi. Signed (1371): AD. M.
CCCLXXI. IOHES BONSI DE FLORENTIA. ME PINSIT. Inv. 9.

ROOM II   II
(School of Giotto, and Late Gothic painters)

Giotto, *Stefaneschi triptych* (tempera on wood; central panel 178 x 88   1
cm; side panels 168 x 82 cm; predella: central panel 44 x 85 cm; side
panels 44 x 82 cm). Painted by Giotto and assistants for Cardinal
Jacopo Caetani Stefaneschi. It may have been painted in about 1315,
since Celestine V, among the donors, is haloed (he was canonized in
1313). It is from the Sacristy of the Basilica of St Peter's, and was
originally made for the high altar of Constantine's Basilica. Painted on
both sides. Front: central panel, Christ enthroned, with angels and the
donor (Cardinal Stefaneschi); side panels, Beheading of St Paul, and
Crucifixion of St Peter. Back: central panel, St Peter enthroned, surrounded by angels and donors (Cardinal Stefaneschi offers the polyptych, and Celestine V offers a manuscript); side panels, St Mark and St
John the Evangelist, right, and St James and St Paul, left. Predella
front: centre, the Madonna enthroned, surrounded by angels. St Peter
and St Paul; on the right and left, apostles. Predella back: three saints,
including St Stephen; the side panels have been lost. Inv. 120.

Jacopo del Casentino, *Madonna and Child* (tempera on wood, 56 x 39   2
cm). One of the few works attributable to this Florentine painter, who
was born in 1297 and died in 1358. Inv. 179.

Pietro Lorenzetti, *Christ before Pilate* (tempera on wood, 38 x 27.5   3
cm). Formerly in the Vatican Library collection. Inv. 168.

Simone Martini, *Redeemer giving his blessing* (tempera on wood 39 x   4
29 cm), about 1320. It may have been the crown of an altar-piece.
Formerly in the Vatican Library collection. Inv. 165.

Bernardo Daddi, *Madonna of the Magnificat* (tempera on wood, 86.7 x   5
52.6 cm). The upper part has been restored. Formerly in the Vatican
Library collection. Inv. 174.

Florentine school, 14th century (in the manner of Jacopo di Cione),
Coronation of the Virgin (tempera on wood, 116 x 64 cm). Formerly in   6
the Vatican Library collection. Inv. 8.

<table>
<tbody>
<tr><td>

II

7
8

</td><td>

[B]
[D] Giovanni di Paolo, the *Prayer in the garden* (tempera on wood, 33 x 32.5 cm), and the *Deposition* (tempera on wood, 33 x 32.5). Panels of the predella of a polyptych; the other panels are in Philadelphia and Altenburg. Made between 1436 and 1440. Formerly in the Vatican Library collection. Inv. 129, 124.

</td></tr>
</tbody>
</table>

9   Stefano di Giovanni, known as Sassetta. *St Thomas Aquinas before the Crucifix* (tempera on wood, 25 x 28.5 cm). Once part of the predella of the polyptych made for the Arte della Lana (now dispersed among Siena, Budapest, London and the Vatican), painted 1423-26. Inv. 234.

10   Lorenzo Monaco, *Stories from the life of St Benedict* (tempera on wood, 30 x 65 cm). The saint frees a monk from the temptations of the devil, and saves a boy. Formerly in the Vatican Library collection. Inv. 193.

11-14
11, 12
13
14   Gentile da Fabriano, *Stories of St Nicholas* (tempera on wood): the *Birth of the saint* (36 x 36 cm); *St Nicholas gives three golden balls to three poor girls* (36.5 x 36.5 cm); *St Nicholas revives three children found cut up in pieces in a barrel* (36.5 x 36.5 cm); *St Nicholas saves a ship* (39 x 62 cm). The panels belong to the predella of the polyptych painted by Gentile for the Quaratesi Chapel in the Church of San Niccolò, Florence. The other parts of the polyptych are in the Uffizi, Florence, and in the National Gallery, London. Inv. 247-250.

15   Stefano di Giovanni, known as Sassetta, *Madonna and Child* (tempera on wood, 54.5 x 73 cm). Inv. 2139.

ROOM III
(Fra Angelico, Filippo Lippi, Benozzo Gozzoli)

III

1   Tommaso di Cristoforo Fini, known as Masolino da Panicale, *Crucifixion* (tempera on wood, 53.1 x 31.6 cm) and *Burial of the Virgin* (tempera on wood, 19.7 x 48.4 cm). Originally they were probably the crowning and one of the predella panels of the Colonna altarpiece, formerly in Santa Maria Maggiore (1428). Inv. 260, 245.

2   Fra Giovanni da Fiesole, known as Fra Angelico, *Madonna and Child with St Dominic, St Catherine and angels* (tempera on wood, 24.4 x 18.7 cm), about 1435. Formerly in the Bisenzio Collection, then Lord Dudley's collection; it came to the Vatican in 1867. Inv. 253.

3, 4   Fra Angelico, *Stories of St Nicholas of Bari* (tempera on wood, 33 x 63 cm each). Two panels of the predella of the large altarpiece made in 1437 for che Chapel of St Nicholas in the Church of San Domenico, Perugia; probably commissioned by Bishop Guidalotti. The third panel and the other parts of the altarpiece are now in the National Gallery of Umbria, Perugia. The *Birth of St Nicholas, his vocation, and the alms to the three poor girls* are represented on one panel; on the other, the *Meeting with the emperor's messenger, and the miraculous rescue of a sailing-boat.* Inv. 251, 252.

5   Filippo Lippi, *Coronation of the Virgin* (tempera on wood; central panel 170 x 95 cm, side panels 164 x 83 cm). The triptych was painted in about 1460 for the Chapel of St Bernard in the Monastery of Monteoliveto, Arezzo. It was commissioned by Carlo Marsuppini, secretary of the Republic of Florence, who appears, kneeling, in the left panel. When the order was suppressed, the triptych went first to the Lippi familiy of Arezzo, and then, in 1841, to Ugo Baldi. It was bought by Gregory XVI for the Lateran Pinacoteca, and later transferred to the Vatican. Inv. 243.

6   Benozzo Gozzoli, *Madonna of the Girdle* (tempera on wood, 113 x 164 cm). On the predella are the Birth of the Virgin, the Wedding, the Annunciation, the Nativity, the Circumcision, and the Death of the Virgin. The opening at the Virgin's feet appears to have been used for communicating nuns in seclusion. Painted in 1450 for the Church of San Fortunato, Montefalco. Formerly in the Lateran Pinacoteca. Inv. 262.

plan
→

ROOM IV
(Melozzo da Forlì, Marco Palmezzano)

B
D

IV

Melozzo da Forlì, *Sixtus IV and Platina* (fresco transferred to canvas, 370 x 315 cm). The fresco originally decorated one of the rooms of the library of Sixtus IV. It was painted in 1477, and represents the nomination of Bartolomeo Platina as prefect of the Vatican Library (1475). The figure dressed as a cardinal is Giuliano della Rovere, nephew of Sixtus IV, and the future Julius II; the others are Raffaele Riario, Girolamo Riario and Giovanni della Rovere. Inv. 270. In this room are also displayed fragments with *Musical Angels* from the fresco painted by Melozzo in the apse of the Basilica dei Santi Apostoli which represented the Ascension of Christ. Inv. 269 A-O.

1

Marco Palmezzano. *Madonna and Child with saints* (tempera on wood. 340 x 226.5 cm). At the foot of the throne are the saints Francis, Lawrence, John the Baptist. Anthony, Dominic and Peter. Made for the Church of the Carmine, Cesena. Formerly in the Lateran Pinacoteca. Signed MARCHUS PALMEZANUS PICTOR FOROLIVIENSIS FACIEBAT, MCCCCCXXXVII (1537). Inv. 619.

2

ROOM V
(Various 15th-century painters)

V

Ercole de Roberti, *Miracles of St Vincent Ferreri* (tempera on wood, 30 x 215 cm). The predella of the altar-piece painted by Francesco del Cossa for the Griffoni Chapel in San Petronio, Bologna. The central panel of the altar-piece is in the National Gallery, London: the side panels are in the Brera Gallery, Milan. The following miracles are depicted: the Revival of a child killed by his mad, pregnant mother: the Extinguishing of a fire; the Rescue of a youth in danger; the Resurrection of the Jewess; the Healing of the crippled woman. Inv. 286.

1

Lucas Cranach the Elder, *Pietà* (tempera on wood, 54 x 74 cm). Cranach's monogram, a small winged snake, appears at the base of the tomb. Inv. 275.

2

Benedetto di Buglione, *Coat-of-arms of Innocent VIII Cybo* (enamelled terracotta). From the door of Palazzetto del Belvedere. Inv. 4087.

3

ROOM VI
(Polyptychs)

VI

Carlo Crivelli, *Madonna and Child* (tempera on wood, 148 x 67 cm). Made for the Church of San Francesco at Force, in the Marches. Formerly in the Lateran Pinacoteca. Signed OPUS CAROLI CRIVELLI VENETI, dated 1482. Inv. 297.

1

Carlo Crivelli, *Pietà* (tempera on wood. 105 x 205 cm). From the Marches. Transferred to the Vatican by Gregory XVI. Signed OPUS CAROLI CRIVELLI VENETI. Inv. 300.

2

Niccolò di Liberatore, known as Alunno, *Camerino triptych* (tempera on wood: central panel 110 x 48 cm, side panels 93 x 25 cm). From the Collegiate Church of Camerino, where it was purchased by Pius IX for the Vatican Pinacoteca. Central panel, Christ crucified, the two Marys, and St John. Left panel, St Peter and St Venantius. Right panel, St Porphyry and St John the Evangelist. In the pinnacles: centre, the Resurrection: right, David: left, Isaiah: the missing pinnacles are in the Louvre. Inv. 287.

3

Antonio Vivarini, *St Anthony Abbot and other saints* (tempera on wood; lower panels 105 x 30 cm; upper central panel 80 x 50 cm; upper side panels 53 x 30 cm). A complex polyptych comprising a wooden statue of St Anthony, and a series of panels painted with the figures of Christ in the tomb, and saints Peter, Paul, Jerome, Benedict, Christopher, Venantius, Sebastian and Vitus, identified by their attributes. Made for the Church of Sant'Antonio, Pesaro. Formerly in the Lateran Pinacoteca. Signed ANTONIUS DE MURANO PINXIT, dated 1469. Inv. 303.

4

plan
→
VII

⊡ B
⊡ D

ROOM VII
(15th-century Umbrian School)

1

Bernardino di Betto, known as Pinturicchio, and Giambattista Caporali, *Coronation of the Virgin* (tempera on canvas, transferred: 330 x 200 cm). At the Virgin's feet are the apostles, and saints Francis, Bernardino, Anthony of Padua, Louis of Toulouse, and Bonaventura. Painted in about 1502 for the Monastery of the minor order of Umbertide near Perugia. Inv. 312.

2

Pietro Vannucci, known as Perugino, *Madonna and Child with saints* (tempera on wood, 193 x 165 cm). Commissioned in 1483, but completed only shortly after 1495, for the chapel of the Palazzo dei Priori of Perugia. Taken to Paris in 1797. The crown, with a representation of Christ in the tomb, is in Perugia, as is the original frame. At the Virgin's feet are the patron saints of the city: Lawrence, Louis, Herculanus and Constant. Signed HOC PETRUS DE CHASTRO PLEBIS PINXIT. Inv. 317.

3

Giovanni Santi, *St Jerome enthroned* (tempera on canvas, 189 x 168 cm). A mediocre work by Raphael's father. It was once a processional standard, and is from the Church of St Bartholomew, Pesaro. The signature, IOHANNES SANTIS DE URBINO P., appears on the step of the throne. Inv. 326.

VIII

ROOM VIII
(Raphael)

1

Raphael, *Coronation of the Virgin* (central panel, oil on canvas - transferred - 267 x 163 cm, predella, oil on wood, 38.8 x 189.3 cm). The apostles, and saints Thomas, Peter, Paul and John witness the event. On the predella: the Annunciation, the Adoration of the Magi, and the Presentation in the temple. Painted in 1502-03 for the Oddi family, it once adorned the Church of San Francesco, Perugia. Taken to Paris in 1797, and transferred to canvas. Inv. 334, 335.

2

Raphael, *Madonna of Foligno* (oil on canvas - transferred - 301 x 198 cm). Commissioned in about 1512 by Sigismondo de' Conti, who is shown kneeling before St Jerome, as an "ex voto" for the protection of his house from lightning. Originally positioned in the church fo Ara Coeli, in 1565 his nephew placed it in the church of the monastery called of the Contesse di Foligno. Taken to Paris in 1797, and transferred to canvas. Inv. 329.

3

Raphel, *Transfiguration* (oil on wood, 410 x 279 cm). Above, Christ between Moses and Elijah, with saints Peter, John, James and, at the side, Julian and Lawrence, Below, the apostles and the episode of the possessed child, whose relatives beg for God's mercy. Commissioned in 1517 by Cardinal Giulio de' Medici, who intended to donate it to the Cathedral of Narbonne; it was completed shortly before the artist's death in 1520. It is entirely from the hand of Raphael, and any contributions by his workshop are of minor importance. This masterly work can be considered the "manifesto" of the artist's style in his last years. In 1523 the cardinal donated it to the Church of San Pietro in Montorio, Rome. In 1797 it was taken to Paris. Inv. 333.

4

5
6
7,8
9, 10
11
12, 13
14

In the show-cases: tapestry of the *Last Supper* (A, inv. 3789), presented by Francis I to Clement VII in 1532 and woven from the painting by Leonardo, and the *tapestries of Raphael* showing ten stories from the lives of St Peter and St Paul, eight of which are exibited: *St Paul in prison* (B, inv. 3875), *St Paul's sermon in Athens* (C, inv. 3876), the *Sacrifice of Lystra* (D, inv. 3874), the *Conversion of St Paul* (E, inv. 3872), the *Stoning of St Stephen* (F, inv. 3871), the frieze of the *Hours* (F, inv. 3878), the *Miraculous draught of fishes* (G, inv. 3867), the frieze of the *Seasons* (G, inv. 3867a), the *Healing of the cripple* (H, inv. 3869), the *Handing over of the Keys* (I, inv. 3868). Those not exhibited are: the *Death of Ananias* (inv. 3870) and the *Blinding of Elima* (inv.

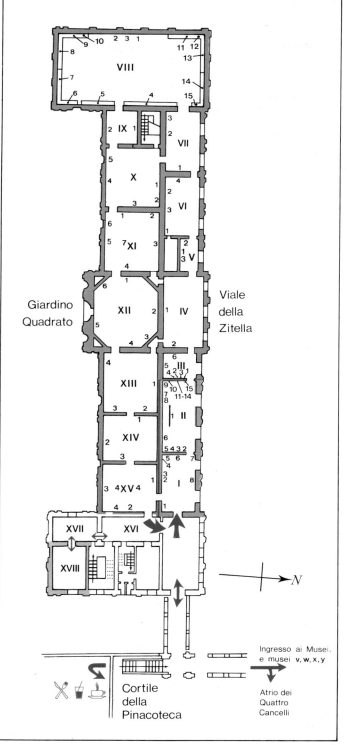

Giardino
Quadrato

Viale
della
Zitella

N

Ingresso ai Musei.
e musei v, w, x, y

Cortile
della
Pinacoteca

Atrio dei
Quattro
Cancelli

B
D

15

3873). Commissioned by Leo X in 1515 to decorate the side walls of the presbytery of the Sistine Chapel. Raphael, assisted by his students, among whom was Perin del Vaga, made the cartoons (now in the Victoria and Albert Museum, London), and entrusted the execution to Pieter van Aelst of Brussels. The tapestries were first displayed in the chapel on St Stephen's Day 1519. Also on show are two *friezes* dating from the time of Clement VII.

IX

ROOM IX
(Leonardo and other 16th-century artists)

1

Leonardo da Vinci, *St Jerome* (tempera on wood, 103 x 75 cm), about 1480. Once owned by Angelika Kauffmannn, then lost. Cardinal Joseph Fesch found it in two pieces; the part with the saint's torso was being used as a coffer lid in the shop of an antique dealer, and the part with the head was being used as the seat of a stool in a shoemaker's shop. Bought by Pius IX. Inv. 337.

2

Giovanni Bellini, *Pietà* (tempera on wood, 107 x 84 cm). The dead Christ, Mary Magdalen, Nicodemus, and Joseph of Arimathea àre depicted. This is the top of the altar-piece painted by Bellini in about 1470-71 for the Church of San Francesco, Pesaro. The altar-piece and predella are in the Civic Museum of Pesaro. The Pietà was removed by the French to Paris, whence it came to the Vatican Pinacoteca. Inv. 290.

X

ROOM X
(Titian and 16th-century Venetians)

1

Titian, *Madonna of San Nicoletto dei Frari* (oil on canvas, transferred; 388 x 270 cm). At the Virgin's feet are saints Sebastian, Francis, Anthony of Padua, Peter, Nicholas, and Catherine of Alexandria. The altar-piece was painted in 1528 for the Church of San Niccolò dei Frari at Venice Lido; the upper part has been lost. Signed TITIANUS FACIEBAT. Inv. 351.

2

Paolo Caliari, known as Veronese, *St Helen* (oil on canvas, 166 x 134 cm). Formerly belonging to the Pio di Carpi family, it was bought by Benedict XIV for the Capitoline Pinacoteca and later transferred to the Vatican. Inv. 352.

3

Paris Bordone, *St George and the dragon* (oil on wood, 290 x 189 cm). From the parish church of Noale, Treviso; formerly in the Quirinal. Inv. 354.

4

Giulio Pippi, known as Giulio Romano, and Francesco Penni, *Coronation of the Virgin* (oil on canvas, 354 x 232 cm). Painted in about 1525 for the nuns of the Convent of Monteluce in Perugia. The upper part is probably the work of Giulio Romano, and the lower part that of Penni. The commission was originally given to Raphael, but the altar-piece was painted by his two students, according to his designs, after his death. In 1797 it was taken to Paris. Inv. 359.

5

Titian, *The doge Niccolò Marcello* (oil on canvas, 103 x 90 cm). A posthumous portrait. Niccolò Marcello is thought to have introduced the custom of dogal garments interwoven with gold. Painted in about 1542. Bought by Leo XII from the Aldrovandi Collection of Bologna. Inv. 445.

XI

ROOM XI
(Late 16th century)

1

Giorgio Vasari, the *Stoning of St Stephen* (oil on wood, 300 x 163 cm). From one of the chapels of St Pius V in the Vatican. Inv. 363.

Giuseppe Cesari, known as Cavaliere d'Arpino, *Annunciation* (oil on canvas, 290 x 184 cm). Signed IOSEPH ARPINAS F.; dated 1606. Inv. 365.

🅱 🅳

2

Girolamo Muziano, the *Resurrection of Lazarus* (oil on canvas, 295 x 440 cm). Michelangelo's praise of this work made the artist famous. Formerly in Santa Maria Maggiore, then in the Quirinal; in the Vatican since 1870. Signed HIERS. MUTIANUS FECIT AC DEDIT. Inv. 368.

3

Niccolò Filotesio, known as Cola dell'Amatrice, *Assumption* (tempera on wood; central panel 200 x 183 cm, side panels 115 x 160 cm). Left panel, St Lawrence and St Benedict; right panel, Mary Magdalene and St Catherine. Formerly in the Lateran Pinacoteca. Signed COLA AMATRICIUS FACIEBAT MDXV (1515). Inv. 372.

4

Federico Barocci, *Rest on the Flight into Egypt (Madonna of the Cherries)* (oil on canvas, 133 x 110 cm). Commissioned in 1573 by Simonetto Anastagi of Perugia, who donated it to the Church of the Jesuits in the same city. After the Society was suppressed, the painting was brought to Rome, to the Quirinal, and thence, after 1802, to the Vatican. Inv. 377.

5

Federico Barocci, the *Blessed Michelina* (oil on canvas, 252 x 171 cm). Commissioned in 1606 by Alessandro Borignani for the Borignani Chapel in the Church of San Francesco, Pesaro. Taken to Paris, in 1797. Inv. 378.

6

Pierino da Vinci, *Cosimo I dei Medici as patron of Pisa* (Carrara marble, 74 x 108 cm). After 1549. Originally the property of the Salviati family, later in the Cavaceppi collection. Bought by Visconti for the Pio Clementine Museum. Inv. 742.

7

ROOM XII
(Baroque)

XII

Jean de Boulogne, known as Valentin, *Martyrdom of St Processus and St Martinian* (oil on canvas, 302 x 192 cm). Painted for an altar in St Peter's, where it was replaced by a mosaic copy. Formerly in the Quirinal; taken to Paris in 1797. Inv. 381.

1

Domenico Zampieri, known as Domenichino, *Communion of St Jerome* (oil on canvas, 419 x 256 cm). Painted in 1614 for the Church of San Gerolamo della Carità, it was removed to Paris in 1797. Signed DOM. ZAMPERIUS. BONON. F.A. M.D.XIV; dated 1614. Inv. 384.

2

Michelangelo Amerighi, known as Caravaggio, *Deposition* (oil on canvas, 300 x 203 cm). Commissioned by Francesco Vittrice, it was painted in 1604 for the Church of Santa Maria in Vallicella (Chiesa Nuova), Rome. Taken to Paris in 1797. There are versions by Rubens and Cézanne of this painting. Inv. 386.

3

Guido Reni, *Crucifixion of St Peter* (oil on canvas, 305 x 171 cm). Commissioned by Cardinal Scipione Borghese for the Abbey of San Paolo delle Tre Fontane, Rome. Taken to Paris n. 1797. Inv. 387.

4

Giovan Francesco Barbieri, known as Guercino, *St Mary Magdalen* (oil on canvas, 222 x 200). Painted in about 1623 for the now-destroyed Church of Santa Maria Maddalena delle Convertite, Rome. Formerly in the Quirinal. Inv. 391.

5

Nicholas Poussin, *Martyrdom of St Erasmus* (oil on canvas 320 x 286 cm). Commissioned by Cardinal Francesco Barberini; painted in about 1630 for the left tribune of St Peter's where it was replaced by a mosaic copy. Perhaps the largest painting made by the artist. Signed NICOLAUS PUSIN FECIT. Inv. 394.

6

plan
←

XIII	B D

ROOM XIII
(17th and 18th century)

1 Anton van Dyck, *St Francis Xavier* (oil on canvas, 210 x 145 cm). Painted during the artist's stay in Rome, 1622-23, for the Church Il Gesù. Inv. 756.

2 Pietro Berrettini da Cortona, *The Virgin appears to St Francis* (oil on canvas, 227 x 151 cm). Inv. 405. A mature work; there is a copy in Leningrad. Inv. 405.

3 José de Ribera, known as Spagnoletto, *Martyrdom of St Lawrence* (oil on canvas, 200 x 152 cm). A work of the artist's youth; by some attributed to his student Hendrick van Somer. Inv. 408.

4 Nicolas Poussin, *The battle of Gideon* (oil on canvas, 98 x 13.7 cm). An early work, made soon after he came to Rome, about 1624. Inv. 815.

XIV

ROOM XIV
(Various subjects)

1 Erasmus II Quellinus and Daniel Seghers, *Garland of flowers with Madonna and Child* (oil on canvas, 118 x 85 cm). Inv. 416.

2 Pietro Navarra, *Flowers and fruit* (oil on canvas, 135 x 98 cm). Inv. 427.

3 Donato Creti, *Astronomical observations (the sun, moon, Mercury, Venus, Mars, Jupiter, Saturn and a comet)* (oil on canvas, 51.5 x 35 cm each). Executed for the astronomical observatory of Bologna. Inv. 432-439.

XV

ROOM XV
(Portraits)

1 Thomas Lawrence, *George IV of England* (oil on canvas, 292 x 204 cm). Signed SIR THO. LAWRENCE, on the lower part of the curtain. Donated by George IV to Pius VII. On the table, the opened letter, dated 1816, sent by the pope to the king. On the king's left leg, the badge of the Garter. Inv. 448.

2 Carlo Maratta, *Clement IX* (oil on canvas, 145 x 116 cm). From the Rospigliosi Gallery; donated by Louis Mendelssohn of Detroit. Painted in 1669 and signed CARLO MARATTA. Inv. 460.

3 Giuseppe Maria Crespi, *Benedict XIV* (oil on canvas, 260 x 180 cm). Painted for Prospero Lambertini while he was still a cardinal, and Archbishop of Bologna; when he was elected pope, the cardinal's robes were repainted as papal vestments. Inv. 458.

4 In the show-cases, Antonio Canova and assistants, *original models and projects* for the monument to Pius VI in St Peter's. Only the figure of the pope was ever carried out. Gift of the Pontificio Seminario Romano Maggiore.

XVI Room XVI is used for temporary exhibits.

XVII Room XVII contains the original models for the bronze sculptures by Bernini, built for the Chapel of the Holy Sacrament (kneeling angel) and for the Cathedra (standing angels and heads of the doctors of the Church) in St. Peter's.

XVIII Room XVIII contains the Byzantine Icon collection. The 115 paintings of tempera on wood, dating from the 15th to the 19th century, are Slavic and Greek in origin. They represent biblical subjects and evangelical calendars with saints.

View of the museum

This museum contains the collection of antiquities formerly housed in the Lateran Museum. The collection was set up in the Lateran Palace by Gregory XVI, and inaugurated on 14 May 1844. John XXIII had it transferred to this new building, and it was opened to the public in 1970.

Most of the material is from sites in the Vatican State. The main sections of the museum are as follows: Roman Imperial Age (1st-3rd cent. A.D.), copies and versions of Greek originals of the classical age (5th-4th cent. B.C.), and various Roman sculptures arranged in chronological order: historical portraits and reliefs, urns, funeral monuments, sarcophagi, cult sculpture, and decorative reliefs.

In the vestibule, to the right of the entrance: coloured mosaic representing a basket of flowers; original of the 2nd century A.D., from the Appian Way (cf. p. 49: I/8).

On the wall left of the entrance: *inscription* commemorating the foundation of the three ex-Lateran museums (Gregorian Profane, Pio Christian, Missionary-Ethnological). Just inside the entrance, on the right: marble bust of *Gregory XVI*, founder of the Gregorian Profane Museum; cast-iron bust of *Pius IX*, founder of the Pio Christian Museum, with commemorative plaques of the same period.

1

2
3

SECTION I
(Greek originals)

I

In the late fifties, the fragments of 5th-4th century B.C. Greek statues and reliefs that were scattered throughout the Vatican Museums were brought together on the top floor of the Belvedere Palace, at the end of the Gregorian Etruscan Museum and the Antiquarium Romanum. Recently, in 1988, a new arrangement was established at the entrance to the Gregorian Profane Museum.

On the wall facing the entrance: a thin, very tall *funerary stele of a*

4

plan
→
I

B
D
youth, crowned with a palmette, on a base bearing an inscription, once stood on a burial mound. The dead youth is shown raising his arm in greeting; a boy brings palestra articles: a round "aryballos" and a strigil. To render so perfectly the sense of a youthful presence in a significant and illuminating form: this is "classic" Greek art of about 450 B.C. Inv. 559.

To the right of the stele are three marble fragments of the original sculptural decorations of the Parthenon in Athens, built between 448 and 432 B.C., product of the combined efforts of Pericles, the commissioner, of Iktinos, the builder, and of Phidias, the sculptor.

5
Fragment of a horse's head from the western pediment of the Parthenon. A drawing of 1674 by Jacques Carrey shows how the pedimental decoration appeared before it was destroyed in 1687. Athene and Poseidon, both on bigae, are shown competing for dominion over Attica. As the heads of three other horses have been preserved, this must be the fourth, that belonging to the front horse of Athene's cart, a fact also borne out by its appearance, size and stylistic features. Inv. 1016.

6
Fragment of relief with the head of a boy from the north frieze of the Parthenon. This frieze surrounds the cella, is 160 m long, and represents the procession of the Panathenaea, a festival in honour of Athene. More than three hundred men, and two hundred animals are represented in the frieze. This fragment with the head of a boy, who carries a tray of votive cakes (skaphephoros), is from the 5th slab of the north wall. Inv. 1014.

7
Bearded head from the 16th metope of the south side. The identification is based on Carrey's drawing, and his indications of material, size and style are consistent with this fragment. The decorations on the 92 metopes of the Parthenon represent the struggles of the gods and heroes of prehistory to establish world order. On the south wall is the Battle of the Centaurs, and in the centre, on the 16th metope, is a figure presumed to be that of Erechtheus, a son of Earth and king of Athens; it is his head that appears on the fragment exhibited here. Inv. 1013.

8
Head of Athene. An acrolith originally belonging to a statue made of other material (e.g. wood covered with precious metal leaf). The inserted eyeballs are in hard grey stone (chalcedony), the irises and pupils (lost) in vitreous paste, eyebrows of thin bronze foil. Jewels were affixed to the ear lobes. The holes on the forehead and temple were for attaching a helmet, which Athene was the only goddess to wear. Presumably belonged to a cult statue of Magna Graecia, of about 460 B.C. Inv. 905.

9
Fragment of relief with horseman, part of a funeral monument of about 440-430 B.C. It recalls the horseman frieze of the Parthenon. Inv. 1684.

10
Votive relief: three *male figures in "himation"*; the two bearded figures are unidentifiable heroes, the youth the offerer. Late 5th century B.C. Inv. 9984.

11
Heroic relief with representation of a horseman, altar and worshippers. Attic, c. 400 B.C. Inv. 1900.

12
Large votive relief with *Aesculapius on a throne, Hygeia and the children of Aesculapius*, and worshippers (smaller). Attic, 4th century B.C. Inv. 739.

13
Crowning-piece of a funeral monument, the deceased emerges from an acanthus tuft. Attic, 3rd century B.C. Inv. 886.

14
Fragment of relief with representation of a Theoxenia: a banquet in

B
D

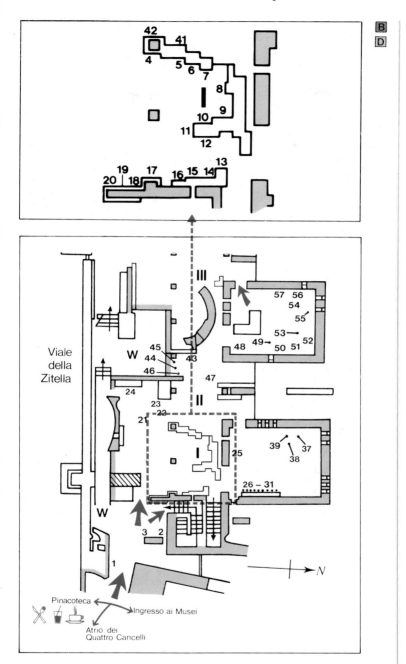

homage to the god Dionysus, who is also present. Votive relief, 2nd century B.C. Inv. 1346.

I

Relief with funeral banquet. Hades (with a crown, a sign of divinity) on a "kline"; at his feet are Kore-Persephone and a group of worshippers. Attic, 2nd half of the 4th century B.C. Inv. 1348.

15

Votive relief: *Aesculapius on a throne with Hygeia* and the dedicator

16

plan
← I

B
D

(the smaller figure). Probably made around the end of the 5th century B.C. as the Aesculapius cult was introduced into Athens only in the second half of the 5th century; in any case, Hygeia's hair-style, and the manner in which the heads are carved would tend to rule out an earlier dating. Inv. 799.

17

Fragmentary relief with the seated Penelope. The portrayal of Ulysses' wife, who remained alone for twenty years, wistful and self-absorbed, is a subject that we know from numerous replicas; it is unquestionably identified by the inscriptions that accompany some of them, as well as by the very fixity of the theme, which is as constant as a quotation. The fragment belongs to a Boeotian funerary relief. C. 450 B.C. Inv. 1558.

18

Figure of seated woman with head covered as a sign of mourning: Electra at the tomb of her father, Agamemnon, waiting for Orestes, the avenger (?). From Taranto, 4th century B.C. Inv. 2050.

19

Aphrodite leaning against a female herma crowned with polos. Attic, early 4th century B.C. Inv. 9561.

20

Votive relief dedicated to the *Nymphs*, three of whom dance in a circle. About 400 B.C. Inv. 1345.

II

SECTION II
(Roman Imperial Age copies and versions of Greek originals, 1st-3rd century A.D.)

Turning our back to the entrance of the museum, to the left we will see ephebic torsos, early Roman Imperial Age copies and versions of classical Greek works (5th-4th cent. B.C.).

21, 22
23

At the back, opposite the entrance: copies of Myron's famous bronze group of Athena and Marsyas and a cast of the Lancellotti Athena. *Statue of Marsyas*, from the Esquiline, Inv 9974. *Torso of Marsyas*, from Castel Gandolfo, Inv. 9975. *Fragment of the head of Athene*, completed in plaster, Inv. 9970. The bronze group by Myron of Eleutherae was placed as a votive offering in the Athenian Acropolis around the mid-5th century B.C. It is described by Pausanias (I, 24, 4) and Pliny (Nat. Hist. XXXIV, 57), and depicted on coins; only parts of it have been preserved through Roman copies in marble. The imperious gesture of the goddess prevents the satyr Marsyas from snatching the double flute which she has just invented and discarded.

24

Among a group of heads on the left: *basalt head,* copy of a Greek honorary statue known as "Idolino"; it represents a young athlete, victor at the Olympian or Delphic games, offering a libation with a sacrificial patera. In the style of Polyclitus, about 440 B.C. Inv. 10134.

Crossing again the section of the Greek originals we enter the Room of the Asaroton Mosaic; on the wall to the left on entering:

25

Hellenistic relief, perhaps of the 1st century B.C., with figures of a woman and a poet holding a theatrical mask; in the centre, table with two other masks. The male figure may be Menander, the most distinguished author of Greek New Comedy (Attic comedy of the 4th cent. B.C.); the female figure may be a Muse or a personification of Comedy. Inv. 9985.

Large floor mosaic reconstructed from fragments found in an ancient building on the Aventine. The central part has been lost and only parts of the two framing strips have survived. The inner one is decorated with figures of Nile fauna set against a dark background. The outer strip shows the floor of a dining-room covered with the scraps of a rich banquet (note the mouse gnawing a nut), on a white background. This still-life theme is known by the Greek name of Asaroton. Along one side of the white stripe are six theatrical masks and other objects; below them, the words in Greek, "made by Heraclitus". However, the mosaic is not by Heraclitus, but is a copy of the famous Hellenistic mosaic by Sosus, in Pergamum. We know from Pliny the Elder (Nat. Hist. XXXVI, 14) that the centre of the mosaic contained a bowl and doves, a scene similar to that of the well-known mosaic, now in the Capitoline Museum, from Hadrian's Villa. 2nd century A.D. Inv. 10132.

B
D

On the right: gallery of hermae. Originally, hermae were pillars terminating in a head or bust of the god Hermes, which stood as the protective guardians of roads and city gates in Ancient Greece, but the word is now used to indicate any statue in the form of a pillar. *Bearded god* (Dionysus?), Inv. 10120, 10119, 10068, 10069. *Apollo*, Inv. 10070. *Hercules* (identified by the hero's headband), Inv. 9800, 10118. *Dionysus*, Inv. 10121. *Hercules*, Inv. 10067.

26-29
30
31, 32
33, 34

Colossus of *Poseidon* (Neptune). The god of the sea rests his right foot on the bow of a ship, next to which is a large dolphin that supports the statue. The downcast eyes suggest that the statue once stood in an elevated position. The crown of flowing hair and the expression of controlled passion underline the grandeur of the figure. The model of this work was probably a bronze of the 4th century A.D., one obviously famous in its day as it was depicted on silver coins of the Hellenistic period (the dolphin was added by the copyist). Inv. 10315.

35

Triangular base with reliefs depicting Dionysian festivals. The form of the base corresponds to that of the Athenian bases used to support the votive tripods offered by the winning chorus of the drama competitions held during the Dionysian Festival. A finely carved 1st-century Neo-Attic work in Pentelic marble, inspired by a Greek original of the 4th century B.C. Inv. 9987.

36

Dionysiac figures. Copies of the "resting satyr" attributed to Praxiteles. One of the most famous, and most frequently copied works of the great Attic sculptor of the 4th century B.C. Here the animal nature of the satyr is only hinted at, in the pointed ears, and perhaps in the woolly hair and cunning expression. (Cf. copies p. 44: V/7, and p. 37: 15). Inv. 9980, 5330, 10292.

37-39

Just outside the room: relief with *Medea and the daughters of Pelias*. The witch Medea convinced the daughters of Pelias that they could rejuvenate their father by cutting him into pieces and boiling him with magic herbs, a scheme designed to restore her husband Jason (winner of the Golden Fleece) to the throne usurped by his uncle Pelias. The relief shows Medea throwing the magic herbs into a cauldron attended by one of the daughters, while the other daughter thoughtfully holds the sword. The artist has invested the scene with a strong sense of dramatic tension. Three-figure reliefs of this type, the most famous of which is the relief of Orpheus and Eurydice, are linked to the dramatic trilogies performed in Athens during the Festival of Dionysus. They are thought to have been votive offerings for success in the drama competitions. Neo-Attic copy of the 1st century B.C. of a late 5th-century Greek original. Inv. 9983.

40

Leaving the room, on the trellis to the left:

Portrait head of Demosthenes (died in 322 B.C.), Athenian orator and politician. The head, found in the Lateran, is a Roman copy of a bronze original made by Polyeuktos around 280 B.C. for the agora in Athens (Cf. Braccio Nuovo, p. 36: 9). Inv. 20725.

41

Head of Achilles, part of a group showing the hero struggling with Penthesilea, a Hellenistic work of the 2nd century B.C. Inv. 4632.

42

On the opposite side is a *statue of the Athenian tragic dramatist Sophocles* (496-406 B.C.); found at Terracina in 1839, and donated to Gregory XVI by the Antonelli family. Inv. 9973.

43

B
D

On the metal trellis to the left: *portrait head of Sophocles*, Inv. 4528.

The identification of the statue from Terracina is confirmed by the small bust with inscriptions in the Room of the Muses (see p. 47: III/12). Both are Roman Imperial Age copies of Greek originals in bronze. Literary sources mention two portraits of Sophocles, one commissioned after his death by his son Iophon (Vita Sophoclis, 11), and the other, in bronze, commissioned, together with portraits of Aeschylus and Euripides, by the orator Lycurgus for the 110 Olympiad (340-336 B.C.; Pseudo-Plutarch, Vita X oratorum, Lycur, p. 841). They are probably the portraits that Pausanias saw in the Theatre of Dionysus in Athens (I, 21, 1). On stylistic grounds, the Terracina marble is thought to be a copy of the portrait in the Theatre of Dionysus. The portrait head mentioned above, Inv. 4528 (known as the Farnese type because of a copy once belonging to the Farnese Collection), is linked to the portrait commissioned by Iophon. The dramatist is shown in his prime, composed and self-confident, his cloak thrown casually round his shoulders, his gaze fixed on something in the distance. The head band indicates his status as priest of the cult of Aesculapius; when the cult first appeared in Athens, Sophocles introduced it into his own household. After his death he was heroized by the Athenians. His contemporaries called him "favourite of the gods" (theophilés) and "blessed" (eudaimon), yet the 7 of his 123 plays that have suvived reveal that he was capable of penetrating to the depths of human passion.

On the same trellis:

45   Portrait herma of *Homer*, now broken (for this type, cf. p. 47: III/17). Inv. 7112.

46   Left: portrait of the Greek lyric poet *Anacreon* (c. 572-487 B.C.). Marble copy of a portrait statue which Pericles probably commissioned from Phidias in 440 B.C. for the Athenian Acropolis. Inv. 4563.

47   In the room with the glass wall, to the right of the statue of Sophocles: *robed male torsos*. Roman copies or versions of Greek statues of heroes or gods. The copyists may have added portrait heads of Roman personages to indicate their divine or heroic status.

Facing the reconstruction of a circular tomb near Vicovaro (see below), we have on our right the entrance to the Room of the Chiaramonti Niobid, which contains copies of female statues of the classical age.

48   On the right: upper part of a statue of *Artemis* in the severe style; the remaining fragments of a goat are visible on the left arm, Inv. 9833.

49   *Headless statuette* with peplos. The outstretched right hand probably held a sacrificial patera. The original was probably of the Diana of Ariccia type of 430-420 B.C. Inv. 9569.

50   Torso of a statue of *Athene of the Rospigliosi type*. The original is associated with the work of Timotheos (c. 360 B.C.). Inv. 5377.

51   *Female head* in the severe style. Inv. 10313.

52, 53   Two *draped female statues of Aurae* (personifications of light breezes). Copies, probably from Palestrina. Until 1956 they adorned the roof of the Round Room (Pio-Clementine Museum). Originally, they served as ornaments (acroteria) at the corners of the tympanum of a temple. Neo-Attic-Hellenistic works of the 1st century B.C. after classical models of about 400 B.C. Inv. 15046, 15047.

54   *Chiaramonti Niobid*. One of the daughters of Niobe, wife of Amphion, king of Thebes, by whom she had seven sons and seven daughters. Niobe boasted of her many children to Leto, who had only two, Apollo and Artemis. Leto's divine pair, angered by the insult to their mother, killed Niobe's children, the Niobids, with arrows. The statue here repre-

plan
←
II

sents one of Niobe's daughters. The identification is based on the existence of a counterpart, in the Uffizi in Florence, which was in turn identified by the circumstances of its discovery. Pliny the Elder (Nat. Hist. XXXVI, 28) speaks of a group of dying Niobids ("Niobae liberos morientes"), the work of Skopas or Praxiteles, kept in the Temple of Apollo Sostianus in Rome. The Chiaramonti Niobid is probably an isolated copy of one of the original group. (Cf. the representation of this myth on the sarcophagi p. 127: IV/9, and p. 68: IV/16). Inv. 1035.

Head of a Muse with ivy garland, in the style of Praxiteles; made for a statue. Found near the Lateran. Roman copy of a 4th-century B.C. original. Inv. 9969.

55

Portrait of Cleopatra VII, the famous Egyptian queen who reigned between 51 and 30 B.C. The head was detached from a statue to which it did not belong, displayed in the Room of the Greek Cross (Pio Clementine Museum), and exhibited here in 1987. Inv. 38511.

56

Torso of a statue of *Diana* (Artemis) the huntress. The swift forward movement of the figure is accentuated by the flowing drapery. Roman copy of a Greek original of the 4th century B.C. Inv. 9567.

57

This room leads to a new section devoted to Roman sculpture, arranged in chronological order.

plan
→
III

SECTION III
(Roman sculpture of the 1st and early 2nd century)

The first part of this section consists of Roman portraits from the late Republic and early Empire.

Two *portraits of the same person*. It has been suggested that the subject is Virgil, though unfortunately there is no way of proving this. Inv. 10162, 10163.

1, 2

Three *funeral reliefs* with portraits of the families of Roman freedmen, of the 1st century B.C.: the *gens Numenia* (Inv. 10490), the *gens Servilia* (Inv. 10491), and, further along the trellis, the *gens Furia* (Inv. 10464).

3-5
3
4, 5

Round altar dedicated to Mercy; decorated with garlands of fruit, and ten-stringed citherns. Under each garland, four attributes of Hephaestus (Vulcan): hammer, tongs, anvil and pileus (cap worn by artisans, and associated with Hephaestus). a Copy of the altar dedicated by Scribonius Libo, in the Forum Romanum, known from coins of the Emilia and Scribonia "gentes" (families). The finely carved, gracefully arranged ornaments on this altar are reminiscent of the magnificent festoons of the Ara Pacis of Augustus. Found at Veii; 1st century A.D. Inv. 10455.

6

Idealized statue with mantle round the hips, and portrait of Germanicus (15 B.C.-19 A.D.), brother of emperor Claudius. From Veii, 1811. Inv. 10434.

7

Twenty-one marble fragments of a *round tomb near Vicovaro* have been assembled so as to give a general idea of the appearance of the original structure. The surviving pieces include four fragments, with palmette frieze, of the upper edge of the drum; eight fragments of the cornice at the top of the drum; and nine roof blocks, arranged in alternating horizontal and vertical courses. The outer surface is decorated with reliefs of ox skulls and festoons. The diameter of the roof, and hence of the drum and cornice, has been estimated at about 10 metres. The ornaments and shape of the tomb suggest that it was built during the time of Tiberius or Claudius (c. 20-40 A.D.).

8

plan
→
III

B
D   Sculptures of the 1st century A.D., found in the area of the Roman municipality of Cerveteri (ancient *Caere*) in 1840-46, are arranged within and in front of the hemicycle formed by the Vicovaro Tomb. Inv. 9949, 9962.

9   Pair of *sleeping sileni*; their heads rest on a wineskin that probably served as a fountain (from the theatre of Caere). Roman copies of Hellenistic originals. Inv. 9949, 9962.

10   *Toga-clad statue* with portrait of an important personage connected with the Julian-Claudian imperial family, as yet unidentified. Inv. 9951.

11   *Draped female figure*. Copy of a Greek original of the 4th century B.C. The head is modern. Inv. 9954.

12   *Reliefs with personifications of the three Etruscan cities* (names inscribed) *of Vetulonia, Vulci and Tarquinia:* a man standing under a pine-tree, with an oar on his left shoulder; a veiled woman sitting on a throne, holding a flower (?) in her right hand; a man, standing, wearing a toga, his head covered (possibly Tarchon, the mythical founder of Tarquinia). These figures were evidently copied from statues, and their only link here is the garland held above them by a putto. On the back, small altar with a boar in front of a laurel. The relief was found together with other statues of members of the Julian-Claudian imperial family and was probably part of the facing of an altar for the imperial cult. The altar, whose preserved fragment constituted half of the left side, was decorated with personifications of peoples in the Etruscan League, which was originally formed of twelve cities, but in the period between Augustus and Claudius was by imperial decree refounded and extended to include fifteen. Inv. 9942.

13   Colossal seated statue of the emperor *Claudius* (41-54 A.D.), *of the Capitoline Jove type*. It is unlikely that the head belongs to the statue. Claudius is wearing the civic crown of oak leaves. Inv. 9950.

14   Plaster mould of the *head of Augustus* in the Louvre (MA 1246). The original, together with other imperial portrait statues from Cerveteri, was found in 1840. However, since it was not acquired by the Papal State, it ended up in Paris by way of the Campana collection. The portrait belonged to a seated statue similar to those of Tiberius and Claudius (nos. 13, 16); identified only recently, its mould was put on display in 1988.

15   Colossal head of *Augustus* (31 B.C.-14 A.D.), found at Cerveteri in 1846, probably (unlike the other imperial portraits) in the theatre. Inv. 9953.

16   Colossal seated statue of the emperor *Tiberius* (14-37 A.D.), *of the Capitoline Jove type,* with civic crown of oak leaves. From Cerveteri. (Cf. below: 29). Inv. 9961.

17   *Toga-clad statue with portrait head not belonging to it*, probably representing a member of the Julian-Claudian family. Inv. 9955.

On the metal trellis: inscriptions, from the area of the Theatre of Caere, in honour of Augustus, Germanicus Caesar, Drusilla, Agrippina the Younger and Claudius.

In front of the hemicycle:

18   *Altar dedicated to C. Manlius*, censor of Caere, by one of his clients. Front: the sacrifice of a bull (the inscription is above the garland). Back: a female deity sits on a rock, surrounded by worshippers. The deity may be Fides. On each side: a lar dances between two olive-trees. 1st century B.C. Inv. 9964.

19, 20   Two *laurelled statues*: one headless, and of high accomplishment (Inv.

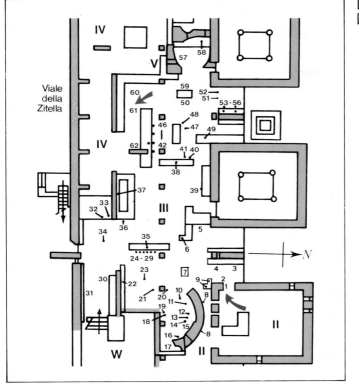

9948), the other with the portrait possibly of *Drusus* (38-9 B.C.) brother of the emperor Tiberius. Inv. 9963.

III

Draped female statue with the portrait possibly of Agrippina the Younger (15-59 A.D.), wife of the emperor Claudius, and mother of Nero. The hair-style is typical of the early Empire, and the face bears a strong resemblance to members of the Julian-Claudian family. The body, copy of a Greek original of the 5th century B.C., idealizes the empress in that it gives her the appearance of a goddess. Inv. 9952.

21

Opposite the Caere group, at the back: relief known conventionally as the *Altar of the Vicomagistri*. Found 1937-39 in the Campus Martius area (on the site of the present Palace of the Apostolic Chancery). The relief, of which only two non-adjacent strips remain, probably decorated the base of a large altar of the Imperial Age. It depicts a sacrifical procession: two consuls accompanied by lictors; pipers; the three victims accompanied by sacrificers; flautists and cithern-players; five veiled youths; figures wearing togas and laurel wreaths which had been interpreted as the Vicomagistri. The youths preceding the Vicomagistri hold statuettes in their left hands. One represents two dancing lares with drinking-horn, the other a toga-clad figure, the Genius Augusti, a sort of tutelary spirit of the emperor. The duties of the Vicomagistri included the care of the cult of the Lares Compitales in each of the "vici", the small districts into which Rome was divided. One of the changes made by Augustus in the period 14/13-7 B.C. was the introduction of his own Genius into the cult. In fact, the high number of "vici", the importance of the sacrifice to which even consuls (the highest-ranking Roman magistrates) are present, and the fact that the so-called Vicomagistri wear patrician footwear in contrast with the humble social extraction from which they were usually drawn, leads one to

22

plan
←
III

B
D
suppose that these are the lares of Rome itself, whose temlple was in the vicinity of the Forum Romanum. The high priests shown here therefore are probably those responsible for this important central cult of the Roman state. Tiberian-Claudian age. C. 30-40 A.D. Inv. 1156, 1157.

23 Turning away from the Altar of the Vicomagistri, we see: *Altar of Augustus Pontifex Maximus* (from 12 A.D.). All four sides are decorated with reliefs. Front: winged Victory with round shield, on which appear the words. "The senate and people of Rome have dedicated this altar to the emperor Augustus, son of the divine Caesar, in his capacity as Pontifex Maximus". Back: apotheosis of Caesar. Sides: a sacrifice to the lares, and the prophecy made to Aeneas regarding the sow of Lavinium. Inv. 1115.

24-29 On the next trellis: *portraits of the Julian-Claudian age* (first half of the 1st cent. A.D.). From left to right:

24 Portrait of *Livia*, second wife of Augustus, born in 57 B.C., and died in 29 A.D., At the age of 86; deified under Claudius, in 41 A.D. Inv. 10204.

25 Colossal head of *Augustus,* from Veii. Born 63 B.C., adopted by his great-uncle Caesar in 44 B.C., became emperor in 31 B.C. (date of the naval victory at Actium), proclaimed "Augustus" by the Senate in 27 B.C., died at Nola 19 August 14 A.D., at the age of 76. This portrait was made after his death (cf. above: 15, and. p. 35: 2). Inv. 10222.

26-28 *Princes of the Julian-Claudian family.* Inv. 10194, 10198, 10221.

29 *Tiberius,* stepson and successor of the emperor Augustus (14-37 A.D.). (Cf. above: 16). Inv. 4060.

Behind the wall of the Vicomagistri: funeral urns and altars of the 1st century A.D. The remains of the cremated were placed in urns of various shapes—round, square, rectangular, with lids in the form of a sloping roof, or in ossuaries in the form of an altar. Most of the funeral altars exhibited here were found in 1825, in the Volusii Columbarium on the Appian Way, near the Vigna Ammendola.

30 To this group belongs the *cinerary urn in the form of a richly decorated altar* (in the area below the stairs, left). Two candelabra (or censers) are represented at the corners. On the face are the inscription, the head of Medusa, and a large festoon. The charming scene below shows the end of a cockfight organized by two cupids. The winning cock, holding a wreath with its claws, is embraced by its master. Other wreaths and palms appear on the table. The other cock is carried away by its weeping master. On the other sides: festoons, and nests of newly hatched birds being fed by their parents. An example of rare workmanship. 1st century A.D. Inv. 9820.

31 At the outer wall: *cinerary urn with vintage*; on the front, between hermae, two men press grapes in a vat. Inv. 10531.

Turning away from the area below the stairs:

32 *Funeral altar of Claudius Dionysius,* shown standing, holding his wife's hand. Mid-1st century A.D. Inv. 9836.

33 *Funeral relief showing the same Claudius Dionysius* lying in bed, his wife sitting next to him. The woman's hair-style is typical of the Claudian age. Mid-1st century A.D. Inv. 9830.

34 *Altar of Gaius Julius Postumus.* The decorations suggest that the deceased was a child. On the front: a boy feeds grapes to a hare held in his tunic; next to him, a taller boy wearing a toga. On the right side:

a boy plays with a dog. Left side: a child in a carriage drawn by a boy. [B]
Until 1925 this funeral altar was used as a stoup in the Church Santa [D]
Maria in Domnica, on the Caelian Hill. 1st century A.D. Inv. 9934.

Leaving the section devoted to urns and funerary altars, we see on the
trellis on the right: *ornamental reliefs with Bacchic scenes* represented
among leaves and saplings; finely carved reliefs, evidently used as wall
decorations. 1st century A.D. Inv. 10111-10117.

35

On the left: *base of a column* from the Julian Basilica in the Forum
Romanum; an example of the high skill achieved in the carving of
marble architectural ornaments in the early Flavian Age. Inv. 9788.

36

The two large reliefs that follow are known as the *Chancery Reliefs*
because they were found under the Palace of the Apostolic Chancery,
in the Campus Martius, 1937-39.

37, 38

Left: *Frieze B, with the "adventus" (arrival) of the emperor Vespasian*
(69-70 A.D.) in Rome. The emperor is recognizable in the noble-
looking, toga-clad figure on the right-hand side of the frieze. Domitian,
Vespasian's son, also wearing a toga, welcomes his father in his
capacity as "praetor urbanus". The scene is set on the outskirts of
Rome. Among the emperor's retinue are a winged Victory, holding a
wreath of oak leaves over his head, and lictors. Domitian is flanked by
the Genius of the senate, and the Genius of the people; the latter rests
one foot on the boundary stone. Vespasian's greeting includes the city
of Rome, enthroned on the left, surrounded by Vestal Virgins. Vespasian returned to Rome as emperor in 70 A.D.; this representation of
the historic event was commissioned by Domitian, who later became
emperor (81-96 A.D.). Inv. 13392-13395.

37

Right: *Frieze A, with the "profectio" (departure) of the emperor Domitian (Nerva).* The emperor is dressed in a tunic and "paludamentum"
(travelling-cloak), and is surrounded by deities, genii, lictors and soldiers. He is preceded by Minerva, Mars, lictors, and Victory, whose left
wing is visible (about a metre of the left slab is missing). Virtue leads
the emperor by the arm. The Genius of the Senate and the Genius of
the people, both behind the emperor, bid him farewell. They are followed by a condottiere and soldiers. The emperor holds a scroll in one
hand, and raises the other hand in a gesture of command. Domitian's
head is recognizable from the hair-style; his face was later eliminated,
and replaced with that of Nerva, his successor (96-98 A.D.). In fact,
after Domitian's death, his face and his name were removed from all
public monuments by decree of the Senate ("damnatio memoriae").
Inv. 13389-13391.

38

On the wall, on the right: fragment of a portrait of the emperor *Titus*
(79-81 A.D.). Most of the skull-cap, the nape of the neck, and part of
the forehead and right eye are missing. What remains of the face
reveals a splendidly modelled portrait, untouched by the hands of
restorers. Inv. 4066.

39

Beyond Frieze A of the Chancery Reliefs are 39 fragments from the
Haterii Tomb, excavated in 1848. The tomb was discovered outside
Porta Maggiore, near Centocelle. Further excavations carried out in
early 1970 resulted in the discovery of new epigraphical and sculptural
material (now the property of the Italian State). A description of *some
of the Haterii Tomb fragments* follows.

40-48

On the other side of the trellis where Frieze A of the Chancery Reliefs
is exhibited: *shrines with the busts of a man and woman* of the Haterii
family, in almost perfect condition. The man has an expressive face,
short, curly hair, combed forward, and prominent, bristly eyebrows. His
only garment is a cloak thrown over his left shoulder. The bust is

40, 41

B
D supported by a writhing serpent, an allusion, perhaps, to the heroic status of the subject. Inv. 10025, 10026.

On the trellis on the right:

42   *Fragmentary relief* with lemons and quinces, and, above, frieze with masks. Inv. 10024.

43   *Relief representing five buildings of ancient Rome.* They have been identified as follows, from left to right: 1) Arch with three barrel-vaults and the inscription "Arcus ad Isis". This was the monumental entrance to the Temple of Isis and Serapis in the Campus Martius. In the 11th century it was known as the Arch of Camigliano or Arch of Camillo. It stood at the Piazza del Collegio Romano end of the Via Pie' di Marmo, and was probably erected to commemorate the victory over Judaea. 2) The Flavian amphitheatre, known as the Colosseum (begun by Vespasian 70-76 A.D., and dedicated by Titus in 80 A.D.), with a reproduction of the main entrance, an arch surmounted by a quadriga. 3) Triumphal arch, generally identified as the one erected 80-81 A.D., in honour of Titus, at the east entrance to the Circus Maximus; through the passage we can distinguish the "Magna Mater in Circo Maximo", enthroned between lions. 4) Triumphal arch with the inscription "Arcus in Sacra Via Summa". This is the arch erected, in honour of Titus, on the Via Sacra, at the highest point of the Velia. 5) Temple of the Thunderer at the approach to the Capitoline Hill. Behind the altar is a cult statue of Jove, with thunderbolts and sceptre; similar representations appear on contemporary coins. The temple was destroyed by fire in 80 A.D., and reconstructed during the time of Domitian. This relief from the Haterii Tomb is now interpreted as follows: the tomb was built, for himself and his family, by a building contractor (this theory is supported by the presence of a crane in the relief Inv. 9998, see below: 46) who had been involved in the erecting or reconstruction of the edifices depicted here, all of which are of the Flavian age. Inv. 9997.

44   *Relief* (in two pieces) *with scene of corpse and mourners.* Lamps and torches are arranged round the large funeral bed, which is in the atrium of a house. Behind the bed, the wailing-women; below, mourning servants and a flautist. Inv. 9999.

45   *Fragment of a portal with busts of the four gods of the underworld*: Mercury, Proserpine, Pluto and Ceres. The underside, which would have been visible from below, is also decorated. Inv. 10018.

46   *Relief representing a funeral edifice and crane.* The temple-like building stands on a high podium; it is lined with columns and pilasters, and is richly decorated, with the busts of three children and, on the pediment, the bust of a woman, probably the deceased. The scene above the building shows the inside of the tomb, with the dead woman lying on a funeral bed. Below, an old woman performs a sacrifice at a burning altar, in front of which three children are playing. On the right, is a small shrine with a statue of Venus; three portrait masks crown the small chapel. Below the stairs on the podium are a canopied altar and what is probably an "ustrinum", or place of cremation. The crane, on the left, extends to the top of the relief; the machine was operated by the force of the weight of the workmen inside the wheel. Inv. 9998.

On the floor, in front of the trellises:

47   *Quadrangular cinerary urn*; the decorations represent water spouting from a shell, and fish, dolphins and ducks; at the corners, ram-heads. Inv. 10000.

48   *Pillar of the roses.* Two sides are ornamented with the same motif, a candelabrum with roses and, below, olive branches; above, two long-tailed birds (parrots?). One of the finest examples of Roman decorative art. Inv. 10029.—This concludes our description of the major finds from the Haterii Tomb. **B** **D**

In the first window compartment, on the right: *bust of L. Iulius Ursus,* friend of the emperors Domitian and Trajan; it was he who prevented the execution of the empress Domitia Longina (Cassius Dio, LXVIII, 3, 1; 4, 2); made consul for the third time in 100 A.D. Identified from another portrait bust with inscription, property of the Duke of Wellington. Inv. 10210.

49

Further on, on a trellis apart: *relief with procession of Roman magistrates before a temple.* The magistrates are accompanied by lictors. The upper part, with the columns and pediment of a temple, is a cast of the original fragment in the Museo Nazionale Romano. The myth of Rhea Silvia, the twins and the wolf is depicted on the temple pediment. The head of Trajan, the second figure, is a restoration by the Danish sculptor Bertel Thorvaldsen. Inv. 9506.

50

Second window compartment:

At the front: two *ancient columns,* decorated. Inv. 10096, 10097.

51, 52

Behind the columns, on the wall:

On the right, above: *fragment of a tomb relief.* The central slab, with inscription, is missing. Left, toga-clad figure offering a libation. Below, a man asleep in a grotto, holding a poppy pod, possibly a representation of the deceased. Above, a cockfight and cupids carrying garlands. C. 100 A.D. Inv. 9822.

53

Below: *tomb relief with circus races.* A quadriga races along the "spina" (wall separating the two tracks). Against the spina are several "metae" (signposts), an obelisk, two columns with statues, and, between the statues, a shrine with four dolphins on the roof. A victor holding a palm leaf leans against the group of metae on the left. The large figure on the left is the deceased, dressed in a toga, and holding a scroll in his left hand. His right hand is extended towards his wife ("dextrarum iunctio"). The races are in honour of the dead man. C. 100 A.D. Inv. 9556.

54

On the left, above: *fragment of a pediment* of a funeral monument on the Appian Way. Cupids support the bust of Claudia Semne (identified by the circumstances of its discovery). The bust represents the "anima" of the dead woman. Inv. 10528.

55

Below: *tomb relief of Ulpia Epigone.* The subject is shown lying on a couch, a sewing box at her feet, a lap-dog under her arm. The hairstyle is typical of the Flavian-Trajan period. Inv. 9856.

56

As we leave the compartment, we see a small hemicycle on the right:

Colossus of a barbarian prisoner. His costume and physiognomy identify him as a Dacian (a Balkan people conquered by Trajan). Although the most celebrated, Trajan's Column was not the only monument to the Dacian campaign. This unfinished statue, together with similar statues that were re-used in The Arch of Constantine, is from another monument celebrating the same event. 2nd century A.D. Inv. 10534.

57

Fragment of relief with military insignia identified as that of the twelfth "Fulminata" by the thunderbolt on the shield. 2nd-3rd century A.D. Inv. 9508.

58

On the trellis in front of the hemicycle: *fragment of relief with standard-bearer.* The insignia is that of the Praetorian Guards, and it appears

59

125

plan
III ←

B
D frequently on columns erected by Trajan and Marcus Aurelius. Standard-bearers are always shown with their heads covered with a skin. This fragment was evidently part of a military scene, perhaps from a triumphal arch. 2nd century A.D. Inv. 9507.

Most of the architectural fragments are from Trajan's Forum.

60, 61

Proceeding right, we see on the trellis: *two fragments of the same architectural frieze*, probably from Trajan's Forum. The two pieces form a scene that wâs probably repeated along the frieze. The relief decorations on the amphora depict a satyr and two maenads. At the sides of the amphora two cupids are watering griffins. The cupids' legs are transformed into acanthus leaves and spirals that harmonize with the luxuriant floral decoration. 2nd century A.D. Inv. 9700, 9648.

62

Above the passage to Section IV; *fragment of architectural frieze* with motifs. In spite of the abundant foliage, the basic design is clearly visible. 2nd century A.D. Inv. 9715.

plan
IV →

SECTION IV
(Sarcophagi)

The reliefs in the Gallery of the Sarcophagi are arranged by subject. The description begins with those having mythological themes.

On the left:

1

Below: *fragment of sarcophagus with the labours of Hercules*: the capture of the Cretan bull, the capture of the mares of King Diomedes, the victory over Geryon. Inv. 9803.

2

Above: *sarcophagus front with scene of Meleager killing the Caledonian boar.* Inv. 10404.

On the right, in front of the trellis:

3

Sarcophagus with scenes of the myth of Adonis. Left, the young hunter Adonis takes leave of Aphrodite, who sits on a throne surrounded by cupids. Right, the boar is about to attack; Adonis falls, mortally wounded. Centre, Adonis enthroned next to Aphrodite. The goddess was inconsolable after the loss of her beloved youth, and begged the god of the underworld to let Adonis spend six months of the year on earth—a reference to the theme of life after death. The faces of Adonis and Aphrodite are portraits. C. 220 A.D. Inv. 10409.

4

Lid on the Adonis sarcophagus with scenes from the saga of Oedipus (lid does not belong to the sarcophagus). Left to right: Laius' sacrifice before the Delphic Apollo; Laius and the exposure of Oedipus; Oedipus flees from Corinth. The two series are separated by a pilaster. Second series, right to left: Oedipus kills Laius (in the chariot); the riddle of the Sphinx, and its interpretations by a Theban shepherd. Inv. 10408.

On the other side of the pillar:

5

Left: *sarcophagus slab with the myth of Adonis.* Adonis takes leave of Aphrodite, and the struggle with the boar. (Cf. above: 3; the style and treatment are different). C. 300 A.D. Inv. 9559.

6

Right: *sarcophagus* (with fragments of the original lid) *with scenes from the myth of Phaedra and Hippolytus.* Left to right: Phaedra, wife of Theseus, and stepmother of Hippolytus, reveals her love for the youth through his nurse. Hippolytus, departing for the hunt, rejects the offers of his stepmother. On the right, Hippolytus hunting a boar; he is

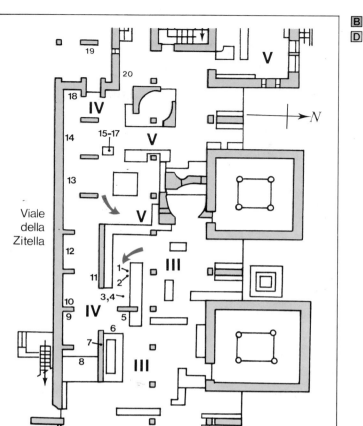

accompanied by a female figure wearing a helmet, a personification of courage. On the fragments of the lid, hunting scenes. Left side, sacrifice to Artemis; right side, hunters on horseback. C. 220 A.D. Inv. 10400.

IV

The next three *sarcophagi*, at the back of the gallery, left, were found together in a tomb near the Porta Viminalis, in 1839. The tiles of the tomb bear seals from the years 132 and 134 A.D.

7-9

On the left: *sarcophagus with scenes from the myth of Orestes*. From left to right: Orestes and Pylades at the tomb of Agamemnon, who appears as a shadowy figure below the vault; death of Aegisthus, from whom Orestes takes the royal cloak; murder of Clytemnestra, and two Furies with serpent and torch; Orestes' purification at Delphi, to which the tripod, laurel and omphalòs allude. Right side: a seated Fury. Left side: the shadowy figures of Aegisthus and Clytemnestra on Charon's boat. Lid: Orestes and Iphigenia in Tauris. Inv. 10450.

7

On the right: *Sarcophagus with two Gorgonian masks and festoons of fruit* supported by a small satyr, in the middle, and two cupids. On the ends, candelabra with pairs of griffins. On the lid, cupids race on various animals. Inv. 10443.

8

Sarcophagus representing the slaughter of the Niobids. Lid: the very small figures at the sides are Apollo and Artemis, who, to avenge their

9

plan
←
IV

B
D

mother, shoot arrows at Niobe's helpless children. The parents, power-less, are forced to watch: Amphion, left, his shield raised, and Niobe, right, her cloak blowing in the wind. Left end: shepherd with oxen, in a rocky landscape, and nymph. Right end: Niobe and Amphion at their children's tomb. (Cf. p. 118: II/54). Inv. 10437.

10   On the outer wall of the next compartment: *sarcophagus slab with myths of Mars and Rhea Silvia* (left), *and Selene and Endymion* (right). The two myths symbolize the participation of mortals in the lives of the gods. In the first case, a girl is found worthy of the love of a god; in the second, a youth is found worthy of the love of a goddess. The heads of Mars and Rhea Silvia are probably portraits; those of Selene and Endymion, unfortunately, are restorations. C. 250 A.D. Inv. 9558.

11   Opposite: *sarcophagus with Bacchic scene*. Two satyrs, in the centre, support a shield designed to contain the inscription. Left, Dionysus (Bacchus) in a chariot drawn by two centaurs; right, Ariadne in a similar chariot. Both are accompanied by followers. The sarcophagus is in excellent condition, as is the lid, decorated with Bacchic scenes and two satyr-heads. A fine example of a Roman sarcophagus in its origin-al state. 2nd century A.D. Inv. 10425.

12   In the next compartment, in front of the outer wall: *sarcophagus with Bacchic scene*. The triumphant Dionysus (Bacchus) returns from his conquest of India (this legend was introduced into the myth after Alexander the Great's eastern campaigns). Nike (Victory) crowns the god, who stands on a chariot drawn by two elephants. The lion, panther and giraffe (visible in the centre, above Silenus) add an exotic touch to the otherwise traditional retinue. The various elements are successfully combined into a lively composition. Both the workmanship and state of preservation are excellent. 3rd century A.D. Inv. 10428.

This is followed by sarcophagi with cupids, masks and festoons (left wall), vintagers (in front of the pillar), and medallions (next compart-ment). Of special interest among these:

13   *Sarcophagus with the Seasons*. Centre, two cupids hold a medallion bearing the rough portrait of a woman. Below, a cupid disguises him-self with a large mask of Silenus to frighten his small companion. On the right and left, four more cupids, two on each side, appear as traditional representations of the Seasons. However, the Seasons are no longer true to type, their distinguishing features having become confused when their original significance was forgotten. The execution is also marked by a certain decadence. 3rd century A.D. Inv. 10411.

14   In the next compartment, on the outer wall: *large sarcophagus front with philosophers*. The sage is enthroned in the centre. He reads from a scroll to a man and two veiled women. The attitude of the woman on the left recalls the traditional representation of Polyhymnia, one of the nine Muses. The other woman holds a closed scroll. Bearded figures, facing outward, appear at both sides of the central scene. On the right, traces of a sundial. The imposing central figure is thought to be the philosopher Plotinus, who came to Rome from Alexandria in 244 A.D., lived here, and died at Minturnum in 270; however, there is no proof that this is his portrait. C. 270 A.D. Inv. 9504.

Opposite:

15   *Fragment of an oval sarcophagus*. On the right side, bearded philo-sopher, and the hands of a cloaked figure holding a scroll. Inv. 9524.

16   Left: *fragment with lion-hunt* (traces).

17   The *fragment of a lid* with representation of a cock-fight may belong to the fragments mentioned above. Inv. 9523.

At the end of the Gallery of the Sarcophagi, to the left of the glass door: *sarcophagus of a child, with representations of athletes* engaged in boxing, wrestling and the pancratium (contest consisting of boxing and wrestling), and paying tribute to the winner. The bearded figures holding palms are the judges. On the left a victor is being crowned. A herald blows his trumpet to announce the victory. C. 210 A.D. Inv. 9495.

plan
←
IV
18

Outside the french window: *plaster cast of the Laocoön group*, dating from before the 1957-60 restoration (see p. 41, 42)

19

Our description concludes with: *sarcophagus with representations of the growing and processing of wheat* (left, in front of the stairs). The rough-hewn relief is divided, into two levels. In the upper part: a peasant works a plough drawn by two oxen, and another digs the ground; on the right, the harvest. In the lower part, right to left: a cart takes the wheat to the mill; two workmen turn the millstone; the baking of the bread. In the centre, portrait of the deceased, dressed in a toga, and holding a scroll. On the lid: the name of the deceased, and an ironic Latin verse (from a Greek epigram) in which he dismisses Hope and Fortune, for whom he has no further use, leaving them to make fools of others. 3rd century A.D. Inv. 10536.

20

SECTION V
(Roman sculpture of the 2nd and 3rd century)

plan
→
V

We now return to the area where the capitals are exhibited.

The Ionic and Composite capitals in the centre are probably from Trajan's Forum.

On the wall (behind which the statue of the Dacian is exhibited): three *fragments of a large historical frieze* from the time of Hadrian (Inv. 9916, 9922, 9921). The *figure in toga* and patrician boots (Inv. 9922) is probably the emperor Hadrian (117-138 A.D.). His *portrait* is displayed a short distance beyond (Inv. 4068). A *portrait of a member of his retinue* appears on the left (Inv. 9921); it may be one of the Caesernii brothers, known to have accompanied Hadrian. They have been tentatively identified in the tondi, from the time of Hadrian, on the Arch of Constantine.

1-3
2
4
3

Proceeding left:

Statue of Antinous. Though the original head has been lost (the present one is a restoration), the statue is probably a representation of Hadrian's young favourite, in the guise of Vertumnus, a god of changing seasons. (Cf. p. 48: II/3 and II/7). Inv. 9805.

5

Portrait of bearded man with Greek helmet. The facial type, and treatment of the eyes would indicate a late work of the time of Hadrian. Probably from a statue alluding to Mars. Inv. 10150.

6

Fragments of relief with two wrestlers. The skilfully carved figures are almost detached from the background. The relief probably decorated a large monument. It was known to Raphael, who made a drawing (now lost) of it, filling in the missing parts. 2nd century A.D. Inv. 9504, 9502.

7, 8

On the opposite side of the trellis: *funeral relief*. This heavily restored relief depicts a young warrior on horseback greeting a woman sitting on a throne; in the background, a slave holds his master's spear. The laurel and serpent are an allusion to the heroization of the deceased. Inv. 9977.

9

plan
→
V

10-13 [B] [D] Left: *fragments of toga-clad statues in porphyry.* This stone was reserved for representations of Roman emperors. Inv. 10478, 10480, 10481, 10483.

14 Right: *torso wearing a lorica.* A masterly work in porphyry, probably a representation of Trajan or Hadrian. Inv. 10482.

15 In the first window compartment, on the left: *relief from the Fountain of Amalthea.* A nymph offers water to a young satyr from a large, horn-shaped vase. Young Pan plays his syrinx in a grotto nearby. Water spouted from the hole in the drinking horn. A Roman-Hellenistic work of the 2nd century A.D. Inv. 9510.

16 In front of the partition that separates the two windows: eight Roman portraits of the first half of the 3rd century A.D., among which is that of the *young Caracalla* (211-217 A.D.), son and successor of Septimius Severus. Inv. 19627.

In the second window compartment:

17, 18 Right: two *fragments of ornate pillar facings.* A vine grows from a vase, filling the background with its foliage and fruit. The scene is interspersed with cupids and animals. Inv. 10087, 10089.

19 Opposite: *statue of Omphale* with portrait head. The statuary type recalls Aphrodite, though the club and lion-skin identify the subject as Omphale, the Lydian queen whom Hercules was ordered to serve (their roles were reversed, and she took his attributes). The portrait dates back to the early 3rd century A.D. Probably a funeral statue. Inv. 4385.

Next come Roman portraits of the 3rd century A.D.

20 Left wall, before the entrance to the next room: toga-clad statue of *Dogmatius* (Gaius Caelius Saturninus); the base is probably the original one. The inscription lists the offices held by the subject, a consul and intimate of the emperor Constantine. Stylistically, the portrait corresponds to the period 323-337 A.D., though the style and treatment of the toga are typical of the time of Hadrian (2nd cent. A.D.). It is therefore likely that the potrait of Dogmatius was added, in about 330 A.D., to a pre-existent toga-clad statue. Inv. 10493.

Turning right, we come to a room of Roman statues associated with chthonic and mystery cults (Room of the Statue of Mithras).

21 *Omphalòs wrapped in bands,* attribute of the Delphic Apollo. Apollo took these sacred navel-stones from the goddess of the earth, the original mistress of Delphi, and they remained a feature of the chthonic earth goddess cult up to the time of the Roman Empire. The impression of a foot on the upper surface indicates that the piece probably formed part of a statue. Inv. 9978.

22 *Triangular base of a candelabrum.* All three sides are decorated: Poseidon with cloak and trident, one foot resting on a mound of earth (see the omphalòs above): Pluto with cornucopia; goddess with peplos and sceptre. A neo-Attic work of classical inspiration made during the Roman Imperial Age. Inv. 9967.

23 *Mithraic group.* Mithras kills the primigenial bull. The god, in Persian dress, is shown plunging his sword into the bull's neck. Followers of the Mithras cult believed that life on earth originated from the death of the primigenial bull. The five ears of corn on the tail are symbols of vegetative energy. The dog seizes the soul by drinking the blood; the serpent and scorpion, forces of Darkness and Evil, try to impede the act of creation by devouring the life-giving blood and seed of the bull. 3rd century A.D. (Cf. p. 43: IV/3). Inv. 9933.

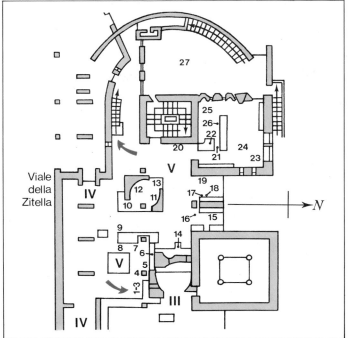

V
24

Altar with the twelve labours of Hercules. The inscription explains that with this altar, Publius Decimus Lucrio has fulfilled a vow to Hercules. The three-line inscription is divided by a relief depicting Hercules and Minerva standing at an altar. Below, the labours of Hercules, from left to right: the Nemean lion, the Hydra of Lerna, the Boar of Mt Erymanthus; the Hind of Ceryneia, the Stymphalian birds, the cleaning of the stables of Augeas, the victory over the Amazons, the horses of Diomedes, the Cretan bull; the struggle against Geryon, the capture of the dog Cerberus from the underworld, the apples of the Hesperides. 1st century A.D. Inv. 9811.

25

Diana of Ephesus. Her attributes symbolize her power to influence growth. She is an Asian deity similar to the Great Mother of the gods.

The Acts of the Apostles (19, v. 27 et seq.) refer to the extent and power of her cult; in response to Paul's attempt to convert them, the Ephesians cried, "Great is Diana of the Ephesians". The town scribe reassured the people with the words, "Men of Ephesus, who knoweth not that the city of the Ephesians is temple-keeper of the great Diana and of the image that fell down from the skies?" (Cf. p. 68: II/8). Inv. 10410.

26

Statue of *Asclepius* (Aesculapius), identified by the staff with a snake coiled round it. He is shown leaning on the staff, his long cloak thrown over his left shoulder, his chest bare. The representation probably goes back to an original by Bryaxis, known through literary sources. From the time of Trajan. 2nd century A.D. Inv. 9910.

27

In a semicircular court outside this room is one of two *floor mosaics* discovered in 1824 in two exedrae of the central room of the Baths of Caracalla. We get a good view of the first mosaic as we go up the stairs. A winding band divides the mosaic into series of squares and

plan
←
V

B
D

rectangles, which contain representations of Roman referees or "coaches" (toga-clad figures), and athletes (nude figures), who hold their characteristic attributes: the boxer's baskets, the disc, sword, and palm of victory. Some squares contain representations of objects that allude to the training exercises that went on at these baths: a strigil, an ointment jar, weights, discs, a crown, and a palm. 3rd century A.D.

JEWISH LAPIDARIUM FORMERLY IN THE LATERAN

The catacomb of Monteverde (probably the oldest Jewish catacomb in Rome) was discovered by Bosio in 1602, but was only fully explored by Muller in 1904-1906. The majority of the tombstones exhibited in this lapidarium come frome it, as do the other items, pagan in origin but re-used in the Jewish catacomb, such as roof tiles and bricks used to close the loculi. The markings on these tiles and bricks enable us to date the period of use of the catacomb, from the 1st to the 3rd century. The epitaphs, many of which begin with the formula *enthàde kèitai* ("here lies...") and end with the words *en eirène he kòimesis autù* ("may your rest be in peace"), give us the name of communities (Augustans, Agrippans, etc.), political or religious functions and relations of the deceased. There are also many traditional symbols, such as the candleholder (*menorah*), horn (*shofar*) or the sacred ark of the law (*torah*). The tombstones also reveal that the Jews of Rome spoke Greek (75%), Latin (22%) and Aramaic (3%).

plan
p. 135

Beyond the last part of the corridor is a semicircular balcony, the "Belvedere". The Pio Christian Museum begins here.

28

From the "Belvedere" we have a view of the *second mosaic from the Baths of Caracalla*, also decorated with the figures of athletes and referees (cf. above: 27).

The Good Shepherd, detail

This museum contains the collection of Christian antiquities housed in the Lateran Palace until 1963.

It was founded by Pius IX in 1854, two years after he set up the Commission for Christian Archeology to supervise the excavation and maintenance of the catacombs; monuments which could not be preserved "in situ" were placed in the museum. The museum was arranged by Father Giuseppe Marchi and G.B. De Rossi. It consists of two sections, the first devoted to sculpture, mosaics and architectural fragments, the second to epigraphical material. The first section, the only one at present open to the public, places special emphasis on the collection of sarcophagi, arranged by subject (as far as possible) and by type. The second section contains historical inscriptions pertaining to public monuments and places of worship, poems of Pope Damasus I, tomb inscriptions bearing consular dates, or pertaining to Christian dogmas or the ecclesiastical hierarchy, and symbolic inscriptions.

For visitors coming up from the Gregorian Profane Museum, the visit begins at the end of the museum, i.e. from the "Belvedere" above the Baths of Caracalla mosaic.

One of the most interesting pieces of the fine collection of Christian epigraphs in the "Belvedere" is the *cippus of Albercio*, Bishop of Hieropolis in Phrygia in the time of the emperor Marcus Aurelius (161-180 A.D.). Two fragments, now reassembled, were discovered in 1883 by W. Ramsay, at Hieropolis, near Synnada, Phrygia. One was presented to Pope Leo XIII by the Sultan, and the other by Ramsay. The inscription on the fragments was immediately identified as part of a metrical epigraph dictated by the bishop before his death, and recorded in the "Life of Bishop Abercius of Hieropolis" in the Acta Sanctorum (to the left of the fragments is a tentative *plaster reconstruction of the cippus*). Albercius, who in the early part of the text proclaims himself "disciple of the pure shepherd who leads his sheep to graze on the hills and plains...", mentions, in these fragments, his voyage to Rome, where he saw a "queen in golden robes and golden shoes. And I also saw a people which possess a golden seal". Having mentioned other travels, he adds: "Faith led me everywhere

1

2

133

plan
→

B
D

and set before me to eat in every place fish from the springs, big and clean, caught by a pure virgin. And this she (Faith) offered always her friends to eat, and together with it a fine wine, and to mix with the wine she offered bread". If the Christian interpretation of the text is correct, then the Cippus of Albercio is one of the most important Christian epigraphs of Eucharistical content in existence, and certainly the earliest datable one.

3

We now come to a narrow passage. Beyond the stairway on the left and the cast of Hippolytus, on the wall opposite the large window: *sarcophagus front* from St Lawrence Outside the Walls. It represents a young, beardless Christ, in short tunic and mantle, among the twelve bearded apostles (the first two are Peter and Paul). The fifteen sheep in the foreground symbolize the Christian Flock. At the corners, two shepherds in dress similar to that of the Good Shepherd. From an iconographical point of view, the figure of the Good Shepherd, which is reminiscent of classical models, is not a Christian invention as this manner of representing the shepherd was known in the Mediterranean area as far back as the 7th century B.C. (e.g. the famous "moskophoros" in the Acropolis Museum, Athens). But here the theme is new: the statuette is not the temple offering of antiquity, but a depiction of the Good Shepherd himself: "And when he has found it (the lost sheep), he lays it on his shoulders, rejoicing" (Luke 15, 4-5), and "I am the good shepherd..." "I came that they may have life, and may have it abundantly" (John, 10, 11; 10, 10). Inv. 31534 (ex 177).

4

As we emerge from the narrow passage, we see on the left, beyond the window: the *statue of the Good Shepherd*. This statue belonged to the Mariotti Collection in the 18th century, before it was transferred to the Vatican Museums, and thence to the Lateran. The figure is that of a young, beardless shepherd with long curly hair, dressed in a tunic, and carrying a bag across his shoulders. There is very little free-standing early Christian sculpture, perhaps because of an ideological prejudice towards statues as a potential source of idolatry. The statue was extensively restored in the 18th century. Inv. 28590 (ex 103).

5

Beside the statue there is a *sarcophagus decorated on all four sides*, found near the Cemetery of Pretestatus, on the left side of the Appian Way. Front side: three shepherds standing on ornate pedestals; the shepherd in the centre is bearded, and holds a ram on his shoulders; the two at the sides are beardless, and each holds a sheep. The short tunics, leggings, ankleboots, staffs and sacks complete the conventional representation of the shepherd. The background is filled with a crowded vintage scene showing winged genii climbing the vine shoots, picking clusters of grapes, and putting them into a vat to be pressed (below, on the right). On the right a small Psyche offers grapes to a resting genie. Below, on the left, another genie milks a goat. The decorations on the ends of the sarcophagus are on two levels, with scenes of country life symbolizing the four seasons. The back is decorated with triangle motifs. 2nd half of the 4th century. Inv. 31554 (ex 191 A).

6

A short distance beyond, on the left: *sarcophagus in the form of a bath*, found in 1881 on the Via Salaria near the mausoleum of Lucilius Poetus, and purchased by Leo XIII in 1891. In the centre, a shepherd with a ram on his shoulders, and two other rams at his feet. Left, a bearded man, in philosopher's dress, seated between two listeners. Right, three women, one of whom is seated. The scene is enclosed at either end by two large rams. The frieze is faithful to the compositional convention of placing all the heads at the same level, regardless of the height or attitude of the various figures; as a result, the two seated figures, probably the occupants of the tomb, are decidedly larger. Probably about the mid-3rd century. Inv. 31540 (ex. 181).

7

In front of a small niche in the outer wall (right): *sarcophagus with lid*, found in 1818 at Tor Sapienza on the Via Prenestina, on an estate of

B
D

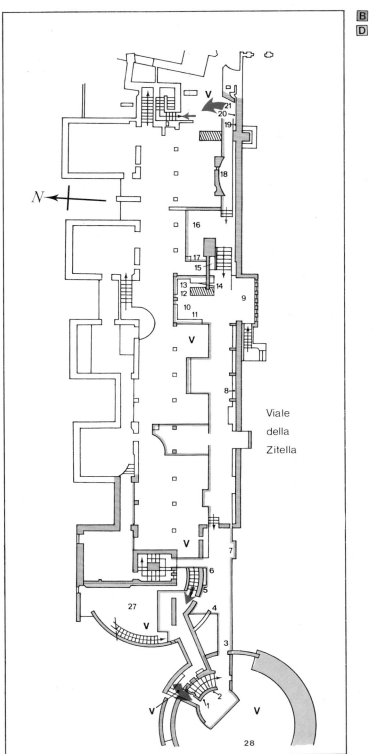

N

V

21
20
19

18

16

17
15

13
12
14

9

10
11

V

8

Viale
della
Zitella

V

7

V

6

5

27

V

4

3

2
1

V

V

28

135

plan
←

B
D

the Massimi family. It is in very good condition, and is the only one in the collection that still retains traces of its original colours (blue, red, gold).

On the lid: centre, the tabula inscriptions, with three Bs; left, hunting scenes; right, bust of a man against a background of drapery (parapétasma) supported by small genii. On the sarcophagus: left, a bearded shepherd carrying a ram on his shoulders (and therefore not the Good Shepherd!); right, a woman in prayer against a background of drapery; centre, lively agricultural and pastoral scenes. Late 3rd/early 4th century. Inv. 31485 (ex 150).

8

We now go down a few steps, and about half-way through the next gallery. On the outer wall (right): *sarcophagus front with lid* (they may not belong together) from the Cemetery of St Calixtus. On the sarcophagus, from the left: Resurrection of Lazarus; Multiplication of the loaves and fishes; Miracle of Cana; Praying woman between Peter and Paul; Healing of the bleeding woman; Peter taken prisoner; Miracle of the spring. On the lid, left of the tabula inscriptions, the manger scene; right, scenes from the Book of Jonah. The long metrical inscription on the upper edge and on the tabula states that Crescens was buried here after only four months of marriage, and that his widow had him placed here against the wishes of her father-in-law, and with the help of her mother-in-law. Early 4th century. Inv. 31484 (ex. 148).

9

At the end of the gallery we come to a large, dimly lit room. On the right is the large *"dogmatic" sarcophagus*, found in the foundations of St Paul's Outside the Walls. Only the front is decorated, with two rows of reliefs. The busts of the dead couple, in the central clipeus, are only rough-hewn. Top row, from the left: God creates man and woman; Christ gives Adam a sheaf of corn, and Eve a sheep, symbols of their condemnation to work for their food and clothing; behind Eve is the tree of the knowledge of Good and Evil. To the right of the clipeus: the Wedding at Cana; Miracle of the loaves; Resurrection of Lazarus. Bottom row, from the left: Adoration of the Magi; Healing of the blind man; Daniel in the lions' den; Prophecy of Peter's denial; Peter taken prisoner; Miracle of the spring. 1st half of the 4th century. Inv. 31427 (ex 104).

10

On the left side of the same room, under the ambo: *cast of the sarcophagus in the Basilica of Sant'Ambrogio, Milan.* All four sides are decorated with reliefs. The various scenes are set against a background representing the city walls of the heavenly Jerusalem. Front: Christ and the apostles. Right: Elijah ascends to Heaven before the eyes of Elisha (Second Book of Kings, 2, 11-12); Noah leaves the ark; below, the smaller figures of Adam and Eve under the tree of knowledge of Good and Evil. Back: Christ and the twelve apostles. Left side: Sacrifice of Isaac, and four apostles. The back corners of the roof-shaped lid are decorated with sculptures of heads; in the centre, two winged genii support a clipeus containing a portrait of the dead couple; right, the Epiphany; left, the three young Judeans, Shadrach, Meshach and Abednego, refuse to worship the statue erected by Nebuchadnezzar (Daniel 3, 1 et seg.), or, according to other interpretations, the Magi before Herod. On the right tympanum of the lid, the manger scene; left tympanum, monogram of Christ within a laural wreath; doves and Alpha and Omega, the two apocalyptic letters. Late 4th century.

Along the metal trellis marking the boundary of the left side of the room, proceeding clockwise:

11

Sarcophagus front with two rows of reliefs depicting Old and New Testament scenes. In the centre, shell with portrait of couple. Early 4th century. Inv. 31532 (ex 175).

12

Sarcophagus front with two rows of reliefs, from the Basilica of San Sebastiano. In the central shell, portrait of couple. Reliefs: scenes from the Old and New Testaments. Early 4th century. Inv. 31535 (ex 178).

Sarcophagus front with two rows of reliefs, from the vicinity of the Basilica of San Sebastiano. In the centre, shell with portrait of couple. Top row, from the left: Christ's entry into Jerusalem; Christ between Adam and Eve—Adam has a sheaf of corn, and Eve a sheep (cfr. above: 9); Moses receives the tablets of the Law. To the right of the central shell: the hand of the Angel of the Lord stops the sacrifice of Isaac; Resurrection of the youth from Naim; Multiplication of the loaves. Bottom row, from the left: Miracle of the spring; Peter taken prisoner; Prophecy of Peter's denial; Daniel in the lions' den; Healing of the man with palsy, of the man born blind, of the bleeding woman; Miracle at Cana. 1st half of the 4th century. Inv. 31551 (ex 189).

B **D** **13**

Sarcophagus front with two rows of reliefs, friezes and medallion, from Palazzo Carpegna. In the central clipeus, busts of couple: the beardless husband, in tunic and toga, holds a scroll; his wife is dressed in a tunic and cloak. Top row, from the left: Miracle of the loaves; Prophecy of Peter's denial; Moses receives the Law on Sinai. To the right of the clipeus: Sacrifice of Isaac; Healing of the man born blind; Resurrection of Lazarus. In the unfinished bottom row: praying woman between apostles; Peter taken prisoner; three genii symbolizing the seasons (rough-hewn, may be part of an initial decorative scheme that was later abandoned); Daniel in the lions' den; Miracle at Cana; Healing of the man with palsy; Miracle of the spring. Early 4th century. Inv. 31546 (ex 184).

14

As we go down the stairs, we see on the left: *sarcophagus with decorated ends*, lid and inscription, from the Vatican Necropolis. The inscription reads: "To my dearest wife Agapene who lived with her husband 55 years, one month and five days, and who was laid to rest 23 December. Crescentianus made this (sarcophagus) when he was alive". After his death, the following was added in less careful lettering: "buried 30 August at the age of 101". The front of the sarcophagus is divided into seven niches by spiral fluted columns supporting alternating tympana and arches. From the left: Sacrifice of Isaac; Moses receives the Law on Sinai; Christ heals the man born blind; Christ prophesies Peter's denial; Healing of the bleeding woman; Multiplication of the loaves; Miracle of the spring. On the left side: the Original Sin. Right side: the three youths in the furnace. This subject is repeated on the lid, to the left of the tabula inscriptions; on the right, scenes from the Book of Jonah. 2nd half of the 4th century. Inv. 31489 (ex 152).

15

Beyond the stairs, in the centre of the wide raised podium: *cast of the sarcophagus of Junius Bassus.* The original was found in 1595, under the "Confession" of St Peter's, and is now kept in the Room of Junius Bassus in the Treasury of St Peter's. The cast is exhibited here because of the iconographical importance of the monument.

16

At the left end of the podium: *sarcophagus with five niches,* from the hypogeum of the "Confession" of St Paul's Outside the Walls. In the centre, a cross: on the vertical limb, the monogram of Christ within a laurel wreath; on the cross-limb, two doves. At the sides, two sentinels; one sleeps, and the other contemplates the symbol of Christ, triumpher over death. In the other niches formed by olive-trees, from left to right: God with Abel and Cain; Peter taken prisoner; Martyrdom of Paul; Job, scolded by his wife for his patience, is comforted by his friends. 2nd half of the 4th century. Inv. 28591 (ex 164).

17

Down a few steps, on the left, in the centre of the niche: *sarcophagus with the Crossing of the Red Sea.* On the left, Pharaoh and the Egyptian army pursue the people of Israel, who pass "into the midst of the sea upon the dry ground, while the waters were a wall unto them on their right hand and on their left" (Exodus 144, 22). On the right, Moses stretches out his hand towards the sea, and the waters close over the Egyptian army. Further on, Miriam, prophetess, and sister of Aaron, sings a hymn of victory and thanksgiving. Late 4th century. Inv. 31434 (ex. 111).

18

plan
←

[B]
[D] A short distance beyond, at the end of the outer (yellow) wall is a series of fragments of sarcophagi depicting the Nativity and the Epiphany. From the 2nd century on, the Epiphany was one of the most common themes in early Christian art. St Augustine (Sermon 203, 3) explains the reason for this: "The Magi were the first pagans to know Christ our Lord, and these early Gentiles deserve to symbolize all peoples". The Magi are depicted in short tunics and Phrygian caps, and are accompanied by their camels. St Matthew (2, 2-12) writes that the Magi came from the East, led by a star, to the Temple of Herod in Jerusalem. Herod directed them to Bethlehem, where they found the Messiah, worshipped him, and offered him gifts of gold, frankincense and myrrh. Irenaeus, Bishop of Lyon in the 2nd century, explains the significance of the threefold gift of the Magi (Adversus Haeres, III, 9): "The myrrh because He came into the world to die and be buried for mortal man; the gold because He is king of the Everlasting (Luke 1, 33); the frankincense because God manifested himself in Judaea (Psalms 75, 2) and He revealed himself to those who had not sought him".

Worth noting among these fragments:

19

Front of a sarcophagus lid. From the left: the enthroned Madonna holds the Child, to whom the Magi offer gifts; in the background, their camels. Next: the manger scene between two palms; the swaddled Child in a wicker cradle, an ass and an ox. Centre: Daniel in the lions' den. Next: the deceased (Crispina) is shown reading a codex bearing the engraved monogram of Christ, the Lex Christi, which was given to her at her baptism, and which guided her through her earthly life. On the right side: the Miracle of the loaves (a youthful Christ in tunic and cloak); Peter taken prisoner; the Miracle of the spring. Mid-4th century. Inv. 31552 (ex 190).

20

Fragment of the front of a sarcophagus lid, with the star at the corner of the stable roof (cf. Matthew 2, 9: "... and Lo, the star, which they saw in the east, went before them, till it came and stood over where the young Child was"). Inv. 31563 (ex 204).

21

Front of a sarcophagus lid, with the theme of the Epiphany occupying the right side: the first king offers the Child a golden crown with his left hand, and points to the star with his right. Late 4th century. Inv. 31463 (ex 126).

Ceremonial mask of the Baluba tribe, Zaire

The Missionary-Ethnological Museum was first established in the Lateran Palace, by Pius XI, who inaugurated it on 21 December 1926. John XXIII had it transferred to the Vatican, and set up in this new building. The museum contains extra-European artefacts from the Missionary Exhibition (1925), from the Borgia Museum, and from donations made by various missionary congregations and private donors.

The museum is divided into two sections, the Main itinerary and the Secondary itinerary. The former is designed for the general public, and comprises objects illustrating the various forms of religion of extra-European countries. The Secondary Itinerary includes ethnographical collections, and is intended for scholars.

In view of the didactic nature of the exhibits, visitors are advised to follow the itinerary indicated by the arrows.

CHINA

At the entrance, two Takuchai (guardian lions) in enamel, from Peking; the male faces the entrance, the lioness the interior. They represent the two essential principles of Chinese philosophy and religion—yang (male, sky, round, perfect) and yin (female, earth, square, imperfect), which combine to form tao (supreme law, order, universe).

Right, model of the Temple of the Sky, in the southern suburb of Peking. It was built in 1420, in wood, and rebuilt in 1755, in marble, During the winter solstice, the emperor, standing on the upper platform of the altar (left), would make a sacrifice to his ancestors, i.e. the Sky and former emperors of his dynasty. Contemporaneously, a dignitary on the lower platform would make a sacrifice to the sun, moon, constellations, wind and rain. The last sacrifice took place in 1916. The

plan
⟶

[B]
[D]

summer solstice ceremony was held in the Temple of the Earth (no model here), in the northern suburb of Peking.

1

Left, in *show-case A 1:* objects associated with the cult of the dead, tomb gifts from the time of the Ch'in (221-206 B.C.), Han (206 B.C.-220 A.D.), and Tang (618-906 A.D.) dynasties. There is also a reproduction of a typical funeral procession of the time of the last Ch'in dynasty (1644-1912).

2

Show-case A 2: objects dedicated to the cult of the ancestors (statues of deified ancestors, tablets, household altars, etc.). All the articles except the household altar on the right are from Aberdeen, near Hong Kong. Last dynasty.

In the niche on the right: model of a pagoda from Fukien.

On the right, Taoist painting with finely carved frame; on the left, Taoist altar with emblems, sacrificial vases, etc. Last dynasty.

Following the arrow, we come to a reproduction of the red altar of Confucius in the Pagoda of Confucius, at Küfu (where he was born and buried). This reproduction was made by Chinese artists, in 1934-35, by permission of the descendants of Confucius.

The philosopher (551-479 B.C.) is wearing the imperial insignia of the Chou dynasty (1129-258 B.C.). He holds a tablet of honour, the imperial sceptre of dominion in the reign of thought. In front of the statue, a table for sacrifices, with three sacred vases (11th cent.); above, a gilt tablet with the inscription "Spiritual throne of Confucius, master of holy doctrines", i.e. the place where the soul of Confucius reigns.

3

We now come to a section devoted to Chinese Buddhism. In *show-case A 3* we see Buddha and two of his satellites; in front, three sacred vases from a Buddhist temple in Peking. Outside the show-case, wooden statue of Kwanyin, the most popular Boddhisattva in China. She was an ancient fertility goddess who, thanks to Chinese religious syncretism, occupied an important place in the Buddhist pantheon.

4

Show-case A 4; various representations of Buddha (left) and Kwanyin (right). Outside the show-case, various stone sculptures of Buddha and Kwanyin. Of special interest are the head of a monk, from Lohan, and the statue of a Buddhist monk (Ming dynasty, 1368-1644).

5

Opposite to the right, *show case A 5* (apart): Chinese pottery bearing Arabic inscriptions, a record of the presence of Islam in China. Next to the Islam show-case: copy of the large stone stele erected in 781, China's first Christian document (in Nestorian form). It was unearthed in 1625, near Sianfù, in the province of Shensi. This faithful copy, made in situ was presented to Benedict XV by Fritz Holm in 1916.

Entering the small block of show-cases, we see a Christian altar in the Chinese style (Fu-yen, Peking). Near the altar is the bronze statue of Father Marcellus Sterkendries (ancient bronze vases were melted down to make the statue). This missionary saved the city of King Chow from extermination in 1911-12; to show their gratitude, the Christian converts of the city sacrificed their most valuable vases to have the statue made. Beside it, against a red screen, a Chinese bronze Madonna and Child donated to Paul VI by the diocese of Taiwan.

We now turn back, leaving on our left the Islam show-case; on the right is the documentary section on China, and then the section of Japan.

JAPAN

	plan →
B	
D	

At the entrance, B 1, two lions (Koma-inu), in gilded wood, guardians against evil spirits. — 6

In *show-case B 2*, a model of a Shintoist temple in the ancient capital of Nara. — 7

In *show-case B 3*, against the wall: three small Shintoist garden-temples; in front, sacrificial vases (for wine, water, rice, perfume), a mirror (symbol of the sun goddess, Amaterasu), and foxes (symbols of the god of rice and riches). — 8

In *show-case B 4*, against the wall: several Shintoist-Buddhist masks; worth noting are nos. 10068-69, which are carved in sacred "Sughi-di-Dohi" wood in the ancient manner. — 9

Outside the show-case is a large, metal perfume-burner (the wooden base is a restoration) with scenes and statuettes depicting figures from Shintoist mythology; in the central medallion on the upper part is a scene of Amaterasu, the sun goddess (ancestor of the Japanese imperial family), struggling against the moon and earth. 18th century.

Over the centuries, Shintoism, a religion of Japanese origin, often blended with the Buddhism imported from China (6th cent. A.D.).

In the large show-cases, above: thirteen Kakemono representing the thirteen Buddhas or Boddhisattvas, commemorated on the anniversaries of the dead (from the seventh day after death till the thirty-third year).

In the separate *show-case B 5*: objects pertaining to Japanese Buddhism. Worth noting is the monk (mannequin) in ceremonial dress. Eight prayer scrolls are exhibited on a special support; they are a copy of the book of Hokekyo (Buddhist prayers), written in Kansho in 1289, and preseved in the Temple of Nyohoji. — 10

In the large block of show-cases: two Butsudan (household altars) *show-cases B 6 and B 7*. They contain sacrificial vases, statues of Buddhist and Shintoist deities, ancestral tablets, etc. These Butsudan provide an excellent example of the religious syncretism of Japan. — 11, 12

Show-case B 8, in the same block (proceeding right): paintings by Okayama Shunkyo of Kyoto, of the Japanese martyrs killed in Nagasaki in 1597; wooden tablets bearing persecution edicts. — 13

KOREA
(The entire collection is on display)

Sections C 1, C 2 and C 3 are devoted to domestic objects. There are three models—of the main building of the Imperial Palace (Seoul), a house of the rich, and a house of the poor; lacquered wooden boxes with mother-of-pearl decorations, a wardrobe in the ancient Korean style, and five vases in "crackled" porcelain (from China). Everyday crockery, typical Korean games, and ornaments are exhibited in section C 3. — 14-16

Section C 4 contains examples of Korean dress: traditional costumes, both ceremonial and everyday hats, and a model of a loom. — 17

Section C 5 is devoted to religious life in Korea. Centre: a household altar, sacrificial vases, statue of an ancestor. Left: a shield used in traditional festivals. Above: dies used to print the first Korean catechism, and two tablets with the ten commandments. — 18

141

plan →

⃞B ⃞D TIBET AND MONGOLIA
(Including areas where Lamaism is widespread)

19

Section D 1 contains objects pertaining to Lamaism, and in particular to the original Tibetan Bon-pö religion: representations of spirits, drums made from human skulls, flutes made from human bones (Shamanistic influence).

20

In *section D 2* are two figures of monks representing the main tendencies in Lamaism: yellow (the more orthodox) and red.

21

Section D 3 includes various statues, Lamaistic reliquaries, cult implements and vases. Of special interest are the two brass statues of Kwanyin (or Avalokitesvara) (Chinese, Ming dynasty). In the background we see a tent used by a Mongolian lama on his journeys.

In the centre of the room is a model of the lamasery of Tch'uo-yang-Hien (Eastern Mongolia). The monastery was founded in 1700 by the lama Tchuo-eul-tsi, disciple of the Dalai-Lama of Lhasa, who had sent him to Mongolia. The first temple (from the entrance) is the "Pagoda of the four guardians of the four main parts of the world"; the second the "Pagoda of prayer" (liturgical assemblies were held here on important feast days); and the third the "Pagoda of beneficence", where daily rites were celebrated at dawn and dusk.

22

At the back, in *section D 4*, are Tibetan standards and religious books.

INDOCHINA
(Cambodia, Burma, Laos, Thailand and Vietnam)

23

Left, *show-case E 1*, cult of the dead: rice baskets for tomb offerings, a wooden fence with ancestral figures, and two vases for minor burials (Vietnam).

24

Next comes a model of a Buddhist monastery (Vietnam). In *show-case E 2*, against the wall, a religious book with case (Thailand, 17th cent.), and statuettes of Buddha made from the ashes of Buddhist monks (Tibetan influence, Thailand).

25

In *show-case E 3*: chairs with tablets dedicated to ancestors (Vietnam).

26

Right, *show-case E 4*: statuettes of Buddhas and Boddhisattvas from various Indochinese countries. Note the white marble statuette of the "Sleeping Buddha", found in the ruins of the Temple of Ara, Burma. 16th-17th century.

There follows (outside the show-case) the large Christian sedan chair in gilded wood, built in 1846; it was used in the procession of the Madonna of the Rosary, and needed ten men to carry it (Tonking, Vietnam).

27

Show-case E 5: Christian statues in the Annamite style (Vietnam).

INDIAN SUBCONTINENT
(Bangladesh, Sri Lanka, India, Pakistan)

28

Left, against the wall, *show-case F 1*: three rural deities (central India). Outside the show-case, five funerary stelae carved out of wood (central India).

Hinduism is now the principal religion of India. This museum illustrates the two main currents of the religion, Shivaism (whose supreme god is Shiva) and Vishnuism (whose supreme god is Vishnu).

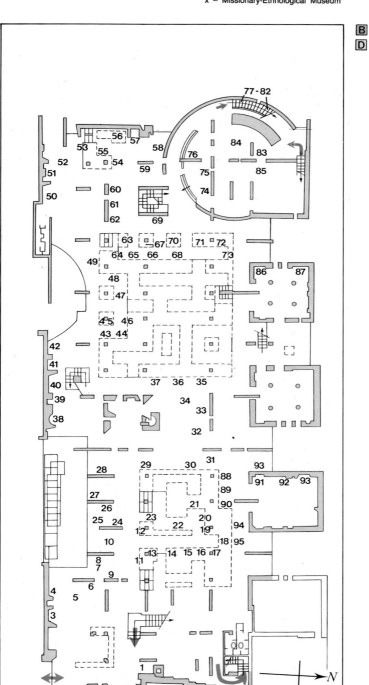

plan
←

B
D
At the entrance to the large Indian room, on the right: votive ox (Nandi), Shiva's legendary means of transport (India, Chamanarayngore, 18th cent.). On the left: small votive temple in honour of Shiva, and wooden door with carved stone.

29   In the large *block of show-cases, F 2,* on the right: painting of Shiva and Kalì, his wife; next to the painting, statuettes of Shiva and Kalì.

30   Further on *show-case F3*, objects pertaining to Vishnuism: a painting of Vishnu, and several statuettes.

31   Close by, *show-case F 4:* two lovely household altars with representations of Vishnu, in the centre, and his various incarnations, at the side. 17th century.

32   *Show-case F 5:* ceremonial masks. Used in ritual dances in various magic rites, these masks combine elements of both Hinduism and primitive religions (Sri Lanka, southern India). Note the triptych mask of Maha Kola, the demon of the eighteen diseases. Below the large portal (Baroda, Shivaistic) is a statue of Bhima, protector against serpents (India, Pulaya).

33   *Show-case F 6* (against the wall), various Hindu cult objects: rattles, knives, vases, altars, etc.

34   In the small *show-case F 7* (apart): model of the Golden Temple at Amritsar (northern India), spiritual centre of the Sikhs.

35   *Show-case F 8* is devoted to Buddhism, widespread in the Indian subcontinent in the last centuries before Christ, but now limited to Sri Lanka.

36   *Show-case F 9* is devoted to Islam, widespread in the Indian subcontinent from the Middle Ages up to the British conquest of India. It is still professed in Pakistan, Bangladesh and some parts of northern India. In the show-case: a Koran (Agra, 19th cent.), jewels with inscriptions from the Koran, alabaster model of the Taj Mahal (Agra).

37   *Show-case F 10* is devoted to Christianity: statues of the Madonna and saints (India, Sri Lanka; Portuguese influence, 17th-18th cent.), several ex votos from the Sanctuary of the Madonna, Verapoly (Syrian-Malabar rite) and several modern paintings.

Turning back, we see on the left a large wooden urn. Scenes from Hindi mythology are carved on the base; inside, about a hundred small statues of Hindu gods.

Going round the urn, we enter, on the right, the section dedicated to Indonesia and the Philippines.

INDONESIA AND THE PHILIPPINES

Left, on the wall, one of the twenty-four bas-reliefs that form part of the Asian collection exhibited outside. These bas-reliefs depict the life of Buddha from his birth to his first sermon. The originals are in Borobudur, Java. 9th century.

38   *Show-case G 1* (along the wall) contains objects pertaining to primitive cults of Indonesia: sacred birds, a basket for offering rice to the dead, a model of a tomb, wooden statuettes of ancestors and heroes.

In the centuries before Christ and up to the arrival of Islam, much of Indonesia was under the influence of Hinduism.

Show-case G 2: iron and bronze statuettes of Hindu-Buddhist deities (Java). *Show-case G 3* contains a shadow theatre (Wayang), common throughout Indonesia, which also bears witness to the Hindu influence.

39
40

Hinduism is still professed on the island of Bali. *Show-case G 3:* painted wooden statues of the chief Hindu deities (Shiva, Vishnu, Kalì, etc.)

41

Islam, now the principal religion of Indonesia, is illustrated in the first section of *show-case G 4* (against the wall). Examples of vases for everyday use are also included (Borneo, Java, Philippines). The end section of *show-case G 5* illustrates Christianity in this cultural zone.

42

On the right, a large Christian altar, the earliest example of Christian monumental art in Indonesia, by the Javanese sculptors Iho and Adi, from a design by Giulio Schmutzer (1926).

POLYNESIA

The objects exhibited in the block of show-cases on the right pertain to the cult of the dead. *Show-case H. 1:* two boats for the conveyance of souls to the hereafter (Marquesas), an ancestral casket (Tuamotu), and various mourning wreaths.

43

Show-case H 2: lovely wooden and stone statues of ancestors and Polynesian gods (Marquesas, Tahiti, etc.). Note the two wooden statues of the god "Tu" and of the god "Rongo" (Mangarewa Islands), true masterpieces of Polynesian sculpture (the four-legged one is the only one of its kind).

44

In the large *show-case H 3* (apart) are various cult implements carved out of wood: axes, oars, clubs, etc.

45

Show-case H 4 bears witness to the presence of Christianity in Indonesia. It contains objects once belonging to Father Damien de Veuster (1840-89) and Father Nicouleau, both of whom dedicated their lives to the care of lepers, and died of leprosy.

46

MELANESIA
(Divided into two parts: Melanesian Islands and New Guinea)

The large sculptures in "talevis" wood (left) represent protective spirits of the home (New Caledonia). On the right are objects pertaining to the cult of the dead and of the ancestors, *show-case I 1*. The small hut on the wooden pillar is used at the cremation of a tribal chief, to offer sacrifices in his honour (Solomon Islands). The statues represent deified ancestors (Solomon Islands, New Caledonia). On the wall are funeral mats (New Hebrides).

47

Show-case I 2: ceremonial masks representing ancestors or protective spirits. Note the fine triptych mask with the carved figures of an ancestor and mythological birds (New Ireland).

48

Turning right, we see various cult implements, *show-case I 3:* ancient stone axes used for human sacrifices (Loyalty Islands); oar-shields with the spirit of death (Solomon Islands); drums, shields, etc.

49

Christianity in Melanesia is represented by·three crucifixes (New Ireland, Solomon Islands, New Guinea) and a painted wooden statue of the Madonna, the earliest Christian sculpture of the Solomon Islands.

The two large masks (left) of the secret society Tubuan (New Britain) bring us to the section dedicated to New Guinea, famous for its wooden sculptures. In the centre of the area is the "tambaran", the Hut of the Spirits, the social and religious centre of New Guinean villages.

plan ←

B
D

Huts dedicated to the cult of the spirits are built with great care by the men of the village. Pillars, supports and architraves are often richly carved. Some tribes build the huts on the ground, others on piles. The hut here was reconstructed from original pieces from central New Guinea. Over the entrance are five skulls (painted) of dead villagers. A shield-shaped mask and a projecting figure complete the architrave. The clay figure at the top of the roof represents the spirit of the house.

Inside the hut, at the back: large wooden statue of the god of war, and a mythological heron decorated with feathers. Left: hand drums, wooden horns, skull mask with boar face, torture instruments (for initiations), stone shields, and rhombs. Right: stools and head-rests, plumed lances, painted human skulls, masks, and sacrificial vessels. To the left of the main supporting post is the hearth, where sacrifices to the spirits are prepared.

Outside the hut, on the left: weapons, flutes, oars, and figures of spirits. Right: funeral shields and figures of spirits. In front of the hut: drums used for communicating at a distance.

These huts are dedicated to the cult of ancestors and spirits. Initiation rites are also performed here. The village women are forbidden to enter.

50
51

52

On the left are two show-cases containing religious sculptures from New Guinea. *Show-case I 4:* figures of ancestors and spirits (Buna, Nor, Kanengara, Korawarì, Tuo, etc.). *Show-case I 5:* various ritual masks also representing ancestors (Ambot Kanengara) and spirits (Nor, Buna, etc.). In the separate *show-case I 6* we see a master dancer with a lovely and very rare head-dress of coloured feathers (New Guinea, Papua).

AUSTRALIA

Ten carved and painted tomb poles (totemic animals). (Northern Territory, Melville Islands).

53

Show-case J 1, front: thirteen paintings on stone, representing mythological motifs (sun, rain, ancestors, totemic animals, etc.) of the Australian aborigines (Drysdale). At the back, various cult implements (funerary wreaths, shields, etc.) (Western Australia, Northern Territory).

We turn back, leaving on our left the show-case with the dancer, and on our right the hut, and enter the African section.

NORTH AFRICA
(Algeria, Morocco, Tunisia, Libya, Egypt)

54

Show-case K 1, front: Egyptian religious statuettes demonstrating various religious influences of the ancient Middle East in North Africa.

55

Show-case K 2: Christian objects including Coptic bracelets (2nd-3rd cent.), terracotta moulds for making the host (Coptic, 9th-12th cent.), and two stamps from the Catholic mission of the Minor Friars. At the back, a throne presented to Pius XI by the King of Egypt.

56

Large *show-case on the right, K 3*: objects illustrating Islam, the chief religion of North Africa. In the first section (left), fragments of coloured terracotta vases of Arab manufacture (Egypt, 9th-16th cent.); typical

Arab manufacture (Egypt, 9th-16th cent.); typical Arab ornaments (Algeria), and vases for everyday use, with inscriptions in Arabic (Algeria, Morocco). At the back, Turkish inscription, in Arabic characters, invoking the protection of Allah (from a fortress in Algeria, 1830).

plan ←

ETHIOPIA

We now come to a *cubical show-case, L 1*, containing ornaments and other objects from southern Sudan and northern Uganda (nomadic peoples). On the right, plaster statue of Cardinal Guglielmo Massaia (1809-89), apostle of Ethiopia.

57

Show-case L 2 (apart) contains Coptic cult objects from Ethiopia: a processional cross (the support is missing), an iron lectern, a cross-shaped altar-stone, censers, etc.

58

Show-case L 3 contains objects pertaining to the animistic cults of the area.

59

Four Ethiopian icons (copies made in ancient Ethiopia) are exhibited in the small, adjoining room.

Going past the elephant tusks, we enter the Madagascar section.

MADAGASCAR

Left (not in a show-case): six tomb stelae carved out of wood; the colour white is a symbol of death (Betsileo).

The small *show-cases M 1, M 2, M 3* (right, against the wall) are dedicated to the cult of ancestors and the dead: two ancestral statuettes of soldiers who died in Europe in World War One; a wooden ancestral head used in magic rites; models of tombs (Betsileo).

60-62

The four lamps (in stone, wood and iron) in front of show-case M 2 reveal the influence of the Orient on the beliefs of this island.

WEST AFRICA
(Senegal, Gambia, Sierra Leone, Guinea, Liberia, Ivory Coast, Burkina Faso, Ghana, Mali, Niger, Togo, Benin, Nigeria, Cameroon)

As we enter the large block of show-cases, we see on the right a group of small statues in painted terracotta (*show-case N 1*); they represent priests, gods and ancestors of the Ashanti tribe, Benin. Turning right, we find a collection of wrought iron objects (*show-case N 2*); these abstract sculptures of ancestors and totemic animals are used for tomb ceremonies (Ewe, Togo). *Show-case N 3* contains a series of vases, wooden objects, and sculptures pertaining to the cult of ancestors (Benin, Nigeria). Next to these are wooden and stone statuettes (*show-case N 4*) representing gods of the various tribes of West Africa (Sierra Leone, Nigeria, Benin, etc.). *Show-case N 5* contains a series of ceremonial masks representing spirits of the dead, gods and sacred animals (secret societies).

63
64
65
66
67

Many of the peoples of western Africa profess the Islamic religion.

CENTRAL AFRICA
(Gabon, Cameroon, Zaire, Congo, Angola, Zambia)

Show-case O 1 (right) contains a series of wooden statuettes ranging in quality from the roughly carved to the finely stylized. These are

68

147

plan
←

B
D

meant to be representation of ancestors of protective spirits, who must be venerated by means of sacrifices and prayers. If they do not receive their due respect, they become vindictive. The mirror on the abdomen of some of the figures appears to be an imitation of statues of saints, imported by the Portuguese in the 17th century, which often had a glass-covered reliquary on the chest.

Many statues known as "fetishes" are used in magic cults.

69

Turning left, we come to *show-case O 2*, against the wall, containing three crucifixes. The two small ones are European in origin, and were introduced by the first missionaries (17th cent.). The large crucifix, made in Africa, is decorated with the figures of four young monkeys. Found in a cave (Lower Congo), these crucifixes were regarded by the natives as representations of protective spirits.

The three metal-plated wooden sculptures represent ancestors (Bakota, Gabon).

70

Turning back, we come to *show-case O 3* (on the left), containing several ceremonial masks from central Africa.

EAST AFRICA
(Ruanda, Burundi, Uganda, Kenya, Tanzania, Malawi)

Small straw huts of the type shown here are found in the forest, and are used as a place of ancestor worship. In times of calamity, sacrifices to appease the spirits of ancestors are performed in the huts, which contain wooden statuettes of ancestors, and various cult implements. At the back of *show-case P 1* is a series of protective and horn amulets. The latter are filled with herbs and other ingredients thought to possess magical powers as a form of lifelong protection against such evils as lightning, enemies, diseases, and even problems arising from the return of the dead.

Islam is widespread in many parts of east Africa.

SOUTHERN AFRICA
(Zambia, Zimbabwe, Botswana, Lesotho, Mozambique, South Africa)

The two pictures are reproductions of prehistoric paintings representing magic rites associated with the hunt (Bushmen, South Africa).

72

Show-case Q 1 includes various wooden statuettes of ancestors and deities. The clay statuettes covered with beads represent ancestors venerated by the women of Basutoland as spirits associated with fertility. On the wall of the show-case are various ceremonial masks (Mozambique) and protective amulets.

73

Show-case Q 2 contains articles from the trousseau of a Zulu bride.

We turn back, leaving this block of show-cases, go down two steps, and enter the section devoted to African Christian art.

AFRICA, CHRISTIANITY

74

In *show-case R 1* are several statuettes, carved out of ebony, forming a nativity scene (the figure of the infant Christ is carved out of ivory).

The figures reveal a strong European influence (Zaire). Two other groups of statuettes, which are also components of a crib are in painted metal (Burkina Faso).

B
D

plan
←

Show-case R 2 contains various statuettes of the Madonna. Those in ivory are simple imitations of European representations. The others show a complete Africanization of Christian sculptural styles.

75

Show-case R 3 contains four groups of brass figures (the Martyrdom, story of the prophet Jonah, the Good Shepherd, the Prayer). Although these groups are clearly interpretations of ancient Roman representations, as we know them from contemporary sarcophagi and frescoes, the style is indigenous (Fon, Benin). In the same show-case are various representations of Christ, especially as the Good Shepherd, a favorite motif of African sculpture.

76

SOUTH AMERICA
(Argentina, Brazil, Chile, Peru, Surinam, Guyana,
Colombia, Ecuador, Venezuela)

On the right is a hut used for initiation rites, once belonging to a now almost extinct tribe (Tierra del Fuego).

As we go up the stairs, we come to a series of six *show-cases, S 2 - S 7,* containing feather ornaments from various South American countries (Argentina, Brazil, Peru, Colombia), used for religious ceremonies and dances. In the room above we find two show-cases devoted to primitive cults of South America. Of special interest in show-case S 8 is the group of five wooden sculptures (two supports, two masks and a statue) from Santa Marta, Colombia. Brought to Rome in 1692, they are the oldest Colombian wooden sculptures in Europe. Show-case S 9 contains various cult objects (flutes, maracas, ceremonial staffs, etc.).

77-82

Going down the stairs on the left, we come to a small room where ceremonial masks are exhibited (Tierra del Fuego and Brazil).

The next, semicircular room contains material pertaining to the higher pre-Colombian religions of South America. At the entrance are four sculptures (plaster copies) representing the goddess Bachue (Chibcha, Colombia) and two Inca gods (Huaraz, Peru).

Show-case S 13 contains representations of Colombian gods, and Colombian articles made of gold (copies).

83

The *central show-case, S 14,* contains material (vases, fragments of sculptures) illustrating the pre-Colombian religions of Peru (Nasca, Tiahuanaco, Trujillo plateau). Of particular interest is the large funerary urn decorated with painted geometrical designs, and a human figure in relief (image of the deceased?).

84

On the wall is a bas-relief (copy) representing the five lunar nights (Chavin de Huantar, Peru).

On the left we enter the room devoted to Central America.

CENTRAL AMERICA
(Mexico, Guatemala, Honduras, Nicaragua, Costa Rica, Panama)

At the entrance: two plaster reliefs; the one on the left represents the destructive god of fire, and a man dancing with a skeleton; the one on the right shows a seated tribal chieftain (Guatemala, Maya). On the

plan
←

B
D

wall: above, relief (copy) portraying Quetzalcoatl, god of the wind (Chichen Itza, Yucatan); below, a representation of the ruins of the Temple of Copan (Honduras). Next, a sculpture in grey stone (palm style), symbol of the sun (Mexican plateau). Next, cast of a richly carved column found in the ruins of Copan (Stele II, Copan, Honduras).

On the right are two plastic models. The first is of the Temple of the Cross; at the top of the cross is a skull; the arms are decorated with serpents and Mayan mythological figures and hieroglyphs. At the sides are the figures of mythological birds, and priests offering sacrifices. At the top, a structure with windows (Yucatan, Mexico). The second model is of the Pyramid of Papantla. The style of the steps recalls that of Indochinese temples (Gulf of Mexico, Totonacos).

85

Show-case T 1 (left) contains minor sculptures of Mexico.

In the centre of the room is a lovely sculpture, in reddish stone, representing Quetzalcoatl (Mexican plateau, classical Aztec style). Next, five fragments of stone statues of gods. Against the wall, four statues (copies) of the main Aztec gods: Tlaloc, god of the rain; Chicomecoatl, goddess of grain; Quetzalcoatl, god of the wind; Chalchiuthlicue, goddess of water.

Right, on the wall, plaster cast of the "Cross of Teotihuacan" (Mexico, Tula). Below, model of the "Temple of the shields and jaguars", dedicated to the goddess Kukulkan (Yucatan, Toltec).

Next, two casts of the corner-stones of the pyramid of Monte Alban (Mexico, Oaxaca), and a model of the Temple of Xochicalco, dedicated to the goddess of rain and fertility (Mexican plateau, Aztec).

At the exit (right) are two casts, one of a stone bearing symbols of the four prehistoric suns, the other of a drum (Teponatztli) (Mexico, Aztec). In the centre is a large cylindrical basin (copy), in the form of an ape bearing a vase on its back, for the sacrificial fire (Guatemala, Maya).

AMERICA, CHRISTIANITY

Material pertaining to Christianity in the Americas (lecterns, sculptures, cult implements) is exhibited at the corner of the large block of show-cases. The following are well worth noting: the wooden lectern, decorated with shell-shaped mounts in mother-of-pearl, once belonging to Fra Bartolomeo de Las Heras, Christopher Columbus's chaplain during his voyages to America (made by the Caribs of Cuba); a metal bell used by the first missionaries to Mexico; two silver ampullae found in the ruins of a Christian temple in Parana.

Proceeding along the corridor, we come to the room dedicated to North America.

NORTH AMERICA
(United States, Canada)

Apart from the contents of the two show-cases along the wall, all the works exhibited in this section were sculpted by Ferdinand Pettrich, a follower of Bertel Thorvaldsen. Acting on the master's advice, Pettrich went to the United States, in 1835, where he made the sketches for his sculptures, which he executed in life-size proportions during his long stay in Brazil. He later donated them to Pius IX.

At the entrance we see a bas-relief representing a war dance of the Sauks-Foxes and Mississippi Sioux tribes. Next, a statue of a young hunter. Left, in *show-case U 1*, Eskimo masks and sculptures (Alaska and Canada).

plan ←
86

Next, a bas-relief representing a battle between the Winnebagos and the Creeks, two hostile tribes. The representation was inspired by stories told by the Indians, though the figures are taken from life. Next to the relief is the statue of the dying Te-cum-seh, the illustrious chief of all the western Indian tribes; when he was wounded during the Battle of Thames, in 1813, he propped himself up on one elbow to encourage his warriors.

Show-case U 2 contains masks and sculptures made by the Indians of British Columbia (Canada). It is followed by a bas-relief depicting a buffalo hunt; the numerous portraits were made from life, at Campden, near the Delaware River. The large statue on the left is of Tahtapesaah (Raging Hurricane), a chief of the Sioux of the Mississippi River Area.

87

The busts along the wall represent various chiefs, counsellors and priests of the Sioux, Sauks-Fox, Winnebago and Creek tribes.

In the centre, a bas-relief from life, representing the council held in Washington in 1837, between United States ministers and the chiefs of the Sauks-Foxes and Mississippi Sioux, for the sale of the lands which by right belonged to the two tribes.

Proceeding through the rest area, we come to the stairway (on the right) leading to the prehistoric section (still being arranged), and enter the Persian section.

PERSIA

Along the wall, Persian and Oriental majolicas from the La Farina Collection, Palermo.

Of special interest is the cross-shaped majolica, with a verse from the Koran around the edges. It reads, "In the name of the clement and merciful god"; the other signs are meaningless arabesques. All the pieces are from Imam zadeh, Veramin (13th cent.). Note the lovely square tile with the image of the mythological bird Simurgh (Persia, 13th-14th cent.).

As we leave the section we find, on the right, a picture composed of small pieces of vitreous enamel, with scenes of travel (Persia, 17th-18th cent.); above, a large arch with fourteen human figures on coloured majolicas (hunting scenes) (Teheran, 17th-18th cent.).

Passing through the arch, we come to the Middle Eastern section.

MIDDLE EAST
(Turkey, Lebanon, Syria, Jordan, Israel, Iraq, Saudi Arabia)

Show-cases W 1 - W 3 include material pertaining to ancient cultures of the Middle East (all the artefacts were found in the Middle East). The collection includes a necklace made of seals representing Oriental gods; a clay tablet with cuneiform writing (2000 B.C.); and fragments of stone bearing Hittite hieroglyphs (1400 B.C.). They are followed by reliefs, statuettes, vases, lamps, crystal bottles, etc., revealing a Hellenistic-Roman influence.

88-90

plan ←

[B] [D] *Turning left, we enter the room dedicated to present religions of the Middle East.*

91 *Show-case W 4* contains material pertaining to the Jewish religion: a scroll (1400) of the Torah, with wooden case (17th cent.); a Hanukija (candle-stick, from a synagogue, early 19th cent.); and two Meghillat Esthers (Story of Esther), one in a silver gilt case (a wedding gift to a bride).

92 *Show-case W 5* contains material pertaining to Christianity: small icons, silver crucifixes, and a representation, in mother-of-pearl, of the Last Supper and the Resurrection. On the wall, a reproduction of a mosaic with a map of the Holy Land (the original is in the ruins of a Christian church in Madaba).

93 Various everyday objects associated with Islam, the predominant religion of the Middle East, are exhibited at the *beginning of the section and in show-case W 6.*

MISSIONARY SYNTHESIS

The last section of the museum contains works of Christian art from mission countries.

In the Middle Eastern room there is a lovely, richly gilded altar carved out of wood (Japan).

94 *Show-case X 1* contains sacred handiwork: enamelled metal decorations for altars; vases; wooden and enamelled candlesticks; crosiers, etc. (China).

95 The *tabernacle, X 2,* in lacquered and gilded wood, was made in Vietnam, after European models.

Noteworthy among the Christian paintings is the lovely representation of the Last Judgement. The anonymous artist has made use of both European and Buddhist elements to create a lifelike vision of the end of the world, of a hell-purgatory (a typically Buddhist hell), and of paradise. Vietnam, 17th century.

The painting of the Last Supper, in Chinese ink on white silk, is a typically Chinese product (Wang-Su-Ta). The two panels representing the Madonna are by the same artist. The last painting of this series depicts the arrival of Christianity in Japan; the arrival of St Francis Xavier; sermon; martyrs of Nagasaki; and the Madonna as Queen of Japan. Japan, Luca Hasegawa.

In the atrium are models of tabernacles (China) and churches (Vietnam), illustrative of Christian architecture. Among these is the model of a pagoda erected in honour of Father Faber S.J. (17th cent.), who for his services was received into the Chinese pantheon (as the venerable Fang, protective deity).

y - Carriage Museum

19th-century carriages

The Carriage Museum, a section of the Historical Museum, was set up by Paul VI in 1973. It is housed in a large room (105 x 14 m) built in 1963-64, below the so-called Square Garden.

In the vestibule we see a bronze bust of Paul VI by Guarino Roscioli. On a table is a small model of the first locomotive that entered the Vatican City on the railway built in accordance with the 1929 Lateran Pacts.

A collection of carriages used by popes and cardinals.

At the sides are exhibited black "*mezza gala*" harnesses, and "*gran gala*" harnesses in red velvet studded with shiny ornaments; saddles, trappings, cushions, travelling-bags, reins and the like.

1, 2

On the walls are representations of the *1912 Eucharistic Congress of Vienna, papal processions before 1870,* and *Clement XIV on horseback*; photographs of popes aboard their vehicles; bronze carriage-lamps, and groups of whips.

3
4, 5

Black landaus, the popes' means of transport on non-ceremonial occasions, used until the early years of the papacy of Pius XI.

6

The sturdier *travelling-carriages*, designed to withstand long journeys on bad roads. Tradition has it that in one of these carriages Pius IX left Rome for Gaeta in November 1849.

7-10

Gala berlin (red and gold) of Cardinal Lucien Louis Bonaparte (1829-95), cousin of Napoleon III; it bears a brass coat-of-arms with the Napoleonic eagle. Two "*terza gala*" *berlins* (red, black and gold, with throne). Two "*mezza gala*" *berlins* (red, black and gold with throne and plumes). Other valuable gala berlins are also exhibited in this section.

11

12, 13
14, 15

16

[B]
[D] The most interesting piece in the collection is the *"gran gala"* berlin built for Leo XII by the famous Roman coach-maker Gaetano Peroni. Used on important occasions, it was also employed by later popes, up to the time of Pius IX.

17,18

This review of papal means of transport also includes the *sedan-chairs*. The one upholstered in red damask was built for Leo XIII, and was also used by his successors. The wooden sedan chair, never used, was presented to Leo XIII by the faithful of Naples in 1887, on the 50th anniversary of his priesthood.

19
20
21

In the final section of the museum there are three cars used by recent popes: a *Graham Page* (1929), a *Citroen* (1930) and a *Mercedes Benz* (1930), which was used by Pius XII on July 19, 1943 when the church of San Lorenzo fuori le Mura was bombed.

The Historical Museum proper was transferred in 1985 to the Lateran, where it is being rearranged.

GUIDE TO THE VATICAN CITY

ST PETER'S SQUARE

St Peter's Square

St Peter's Basilica was completed in 1614 with the construction of the façade. Its grandiose style and theatrical effect are typical of the Baroque period. St

1 Peter's Square, also in Baroque style, is enclosed by two semicircular *colonnades* with 284 columns, built by Gian Lorenzo Bernini from 1656 to 1666,

2 during the papacy of Alexander VII. The colonnade, joined to the *atrium* of the Basilica by two straight and converging wings, appears to physically embrace all who enter the square, and metaphorically, all of mankind.

Along the balustrade overlooking the square there are one hundred and forty statues, each 3.20 m. high, by the school of Bernini.

3 The *Egyptian obelisk* at the center of the square was brought there in 1586 by Domenico Fontana. It previously stood to the left of the Basilica (see p. 159: 8), marking the site of the "spina" in the center of the circus where early Christians were martyred during the reign of Nero (see 1, plan pp. 6-7). The

4 *fountain on the right* is based on a project by Carlo Maderno (1613), while the

5 *fountain on the left* was added by Bernini in 1675, during the papacy of Clement X. Two porphyry disks in the pavement of the square, between the obelisk and the fountains, mark the two centers of the ellipse. Marble decorations surrounding the obelisk indicate the wind rose and the zodiac.

The façade of the Basilica (1607-1614), by Carlo Maderno, comprises the

6 *Loggia of Benedictions*. From the central balcony the Pope imparts the benediction "*urbi et orbi*" after his election and on other solemn occasions. The façade is crowned by thirteen statues, each 5.70 m. high, by the school of Bernini. Christ is at the center and John the Baptist and eleven Apostles (excluding Peter) at the sides.

7 Later, in the 19th century, the *statue of St Paul* on the right (by Adamo

8 Tadolini) and the *statue of St Peter* on the left (by Giuseppe de Fabris) were placed at the base of the façade at either end of Bernini's steps.

9 To the right of the Basilica, behind the colonnade, is the *papal residence*. At the next to the last window of the fourth floor, the Pope appears every Sunday

10 at midday and recites the "Angelus" together with the faithful. The *Bronze Doors (Portone di Bronzo)* are located where the colonnade meets the wing

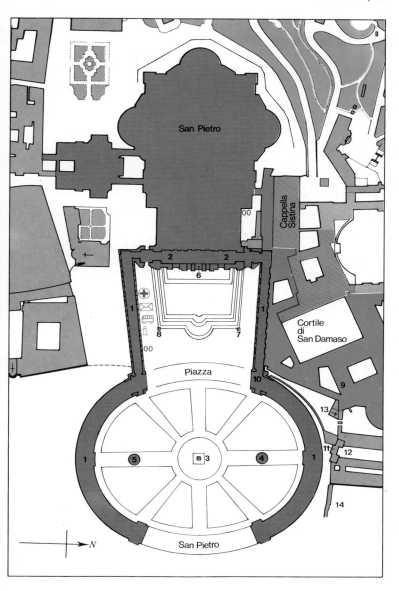

ST PETER'S SQUARE

1 Bernini's colonnade
2 Atrium of St Peter's Basilica
3 Egyptian obelisk
4 Maderno's fountain
5 Bernini's fountain
6 Loggia of Benedictions
7 Statue of St Paul
8 Statue of St Peter
9 Papal residence
10 Bronze Doors (Portone di Bronzo)
11 St Peter's Gate (Porta di San Pietro)
12 Court of the Barracks of the Swiss Guard
13 Chapel of the Swiss Guard
14 Corridor between the Apostolic Palace and
   Castel Sant'Angelo called "il passetto".

◼ Apostolic Palace, buildings not open to the
   public
▨ Apostolic Palace, buildings included in the
   Vatican Museums tour
▨ Vatican Museums
◼ St Peter's Square and Basilica

00 Rest rooms
✚ First aid station (during public audiences)

✉ P.O.
🛈 Information Bureau
🚌 Vatican bus-service

plan
←

The Vatican City from south-east

next to the atrium. This is the main entrance to the Apostolic Palace, defended by the Swiss Guard.

11 Behind the colonnade is *St Peter's Gate (Porta di San Pietro)*, constructed by Alexander VI on the site of the medieval entrance to the Vatican. Beyond the
12 arched gate, which is usually closed, is the *courtyard of the Swiss Guard Barracks* which corresponds to the last stretch of the Via Francigena, the
13 principal medieval road which led from Rome to Northern Europe. The *Chapel of the Swiss Guard*, built by Pius V (1566-1572) and dedicated to St Martin and St Sebastian, is located at the base of the Apostolic Palace, to the left of St Peter's Gate. On either side of the gate is the high medieval wall of the early defense system of the Vatican (see p. 166: 59). Inside the wall, a
14 *corridor* led from the Apostolic Palace to Castel Sant'Angelo, which allowed the popes (as happened in the case of Clement VII - see p. 159) to reach safety swiftly in the great fortress on the edge of the Tiber in moments of danger.

Every morning at 10:00 a.m. except Wednesday and Sunday, in front of the Information Bureau *in St Peter's Square, a tourist bus (licence plate C.V. - Vatican City) departs with visitors wishing to see the Vatican City. The tour described below is one of three tours organized by the information Bureau (see "Useful Information", p. 11). The other tours include, respectively, the Sistine Chapel and St Peter's Basilica. For further information, see the sections in italics on p. 165.*

1

South Area

We begin our visit by crossing the *Arch of the Bells (Arco delle Campane)* at **2** the side of the Basilica, guarded by the Swiss Guard (in uniforms of the early 16th century). This famous military body, constituted by Julius II (1503-1513), is still entrusted with the surveillance of the entrances to the Vatican City and the *Apostolic Palace* (see p. 167). The remaining Vatican territory is guarded **3** by guards of the "Ufficio di Vigilanza". In 1527, when Rome was sacked by the soldiers of Emperor Charles V, the Swiss Guard was decimated in the area that is now the cemetery of the Teutonic College (5). Their sacrifice enabled Pope Clement VII (1523-1534) to flee from his palace in the Vatican and seek refuge in Castel Sant'Angelo. This event occurred on May 6, and every year on this date a memorial service is held in their honour, together with the swearing-in ceremony for new recruits.

At the opposite side of the Arch of the Bells is a sentry-post of the guards of the Ufficio di Vigilanza. Behind the sentry-post is a vast square, called *Piazza* **4** *dei Protomartiri Romani*. To the right is the side of the Basilica and to the left is the Teutonic College of Santa Maria in Campo Santo. A memorial plaque on the wall reminds us that it is the site of Caligula's circus (see 1, plan pp. 6-7), where so many Christians (probably including St Peter) met their death under Nero (64 A.D.). For this reason the square is dedicated to the protomartyrs, the first martyrs of the Church.

The *Teutonic College* (originally a hostel for French pilgrims built by Charle- **5** magne) was formally established by Pius IX in 1876 for priests from the territories of the former Holy Roman Empire. The adjacent cemetery (early 9th century) was the burial place of pilgrims from the northern countries who died in Rome, and is still in use today. The 15th-century church of the cemetery, dedicated to the Virgin Mary, has recently been restored.

Beyond the Teutonic College, on the left at the far side of the square, is *St* **6** *Martha's Hospice*, belonging to the French nuns of St Vincent. It was built in the Holy Year 1900 and is open to all pilgrims.

Facing the Hospice, behind the Teutonic College, rises the great curved white travertine vault of the *Papal Audience Hall*, built by Pier Luigi Nervi and **7** inaugurated by Paul VI on June 30, 1971. Prior to the erection of this building, papal audiences were often held in St Peter's and even now, whenever the number of pilgrims exceeds the capacity of the hall, a second audience is held there or in St Peter's Square. The new hall has 6300 seats and standing room for 4000 people. It has the form of a shell, so that the Pope on his podium may be seen by all. Behind the podium is a large relief sculpture of the Resurrection of Christ by Pericle Fazzini.

Facing the Arch of the Bells (2) is the *Canonical Palace* which includes the **8** Sacristy of St Peter's (on the right with a cupola). The Canonical Palace houses the apartments of the canons (the priests who regularly perform the Divine services in St Peter's). The palace was built between 1776 and 1784 by Carlo Marchionni, at the request of Pius VI, who had been a canon before being elected Pope. Near the palace, set into the paving of the square, is a

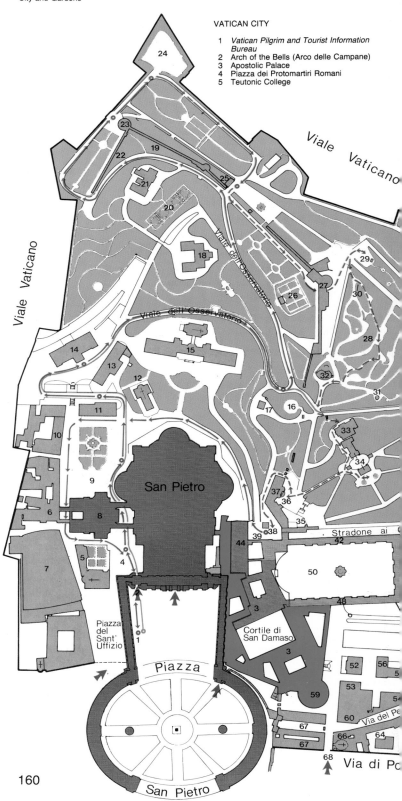

VATICAN CITY

1 *Vatican Pilgrim and Tourist Information Bureau*
2 Arch of the Bells (Arco delle Campane)
3 Apostolic Palace
4 Piazza dei Protomartiri Romani
5 Teutonic College

6 St Martha's Hospice
7 Papal Audience Hall
8 Canonical Palace (Sacristy)
9 Piazza Santa Marta
10 St Charles Palace
11 Courthouse (Palazzo del Tribunale)
12 Church of Santo Stefano degli Abissini
13 Mosaic Studio
14 Railway station
15 Government Palace (Palazzo del Governatorato)
16 Bronze statue of St Peter
17 House of the Gardener
18 Ethiopian College
19 Brick embattlement (walls of Leo IV and Nicholas V)
20 Italian garden
21 First Vatican radio station
22 Small wall (walls of Leo IV and Nicholas V)
23 Tower of St John
24 Heliport
25 Grotto of Lourdes
26 Rose garden
27 Offices of the Vatican radio station
28 English garden
29 Chapel of the "Madonna della Guardia"
30 Statue of St Peter in Chains
31 Chinese pavilion
32 Fountain of the Eagle

33 Pontifical Academy of Sciences
34 "Casina" of Pius IV
35 Building of Paul V and Fountain of the Mirrors
36 Fountain of the Sacrament
37 The Mint (Palazzo della Zecca)
38 Piazza del Forno (Square of the Oven)
39 Arch of the Sentinel
40 Court of the "Pigna"
41 Vatican Pinacoteca
42 Secret Archive of the Vatican, Vatican Library, galleries of Vatican Museums
43 Wind Tower (Torre dei Venti)
44 Sistine Chapel
45 Fountain of the Galley
46 Spiral staircase by Bramante
47 Belvedere Palace, today part of the Vatican Museums
48 Corridor by Bramante, today part of the Vatican Museums
49 Atrium of the Four Gates
50 Court of the "Belvedere"
51 Car-Park
52 Post and Telegraph office
53 Tipografia Poligotta Vaticana and Libreria Editrice Vaticana
54 Grocery stores
55 Pharmacy
56 Health services
57 Mechanical workshop
58 Heating plant
59 Tower of Nicholas V
60 Sentry-post of the guards of the "Ufficio di Vigilanza"
61 Church of San Pellegrino
62 Seat of "L'Osservatore Romano" and "L'Osservatore della Domenica"
63 Living quarters of the guards of the "Ufficio di Vigilanza"
64 Tapestry restoration workshop
65 Refectory
66 Church of St Anne
67 Swiss Guard barracks
68 St Anne's Gate (Cancello di Sant'Anna)

➡ MAIN ENTRANCES
TO THE VATICAN CITY

from left to right:

Gate of the Holy Office (Cancello del Sant'Uffizio)
Arch of the Bells (Arco delle Campane)
(entrances to the Papal Audience Hall and to the City and Gardens)

Entrance to St Peter's Basilica

Bronze Doors (Portone di Bronzo)
(entrance to the Apostolic Palace)

St Anne's Gate (Cancello di Sant'Anna)
(entrance to the north area of the City)

Entrance to the Vatican Museums

▦ Vatican Gardens

tours route:
o——→o
bus route
o– –→o
foot route
o
halts

o——o

Regular bus service connecting St Peter's Square with the Vatican Museums and vice-versa

▨ Buildings in the City and Gardens

▩ Buildings of the Apostolic Palace not open to visitors

▢ Buildings of the Apostolic Palace included in the visit to the Vatican Museums

▦ Vatican Museums

■ St Peter's Square and Basilica

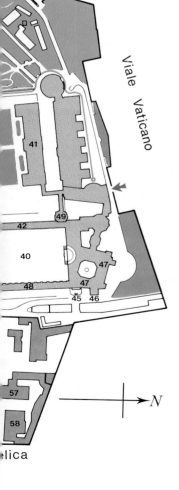

Viale Vaticano

N

lica

161

plan
← granite disk commemorating the original site of the obelisk (in the center of Caligula's circus) now in St Peter's Square (see p. 156: 3). In the small square which unites the Sacristy and the Basilica, there is a plaque that marks the site of a former Hungarian hospice.

9 Passing through the second arch, we come to a vast square called *Piazza Santa Marta* with a pretty garden in the center. Like most of the Vatican territory, the square's present arrangement dates from after 1929, when the
10 Vatican City State was constituted. On the left side is *St Charles Palace*, now
11 used for offices and apartments. Facing it is the *Courthouse (Palazzo del Tribunale)*, which also houses the apartments of the penitentiaries or head confessors (religious officers who hear confession in the Basilica), the Security Office and the court offices of the Vatican, in which the laws of the small State are administered.

12 To the left of the Courthouse is the *Church of Santo Stefano degli Abissini*, originally annexed to a home for Abyssinian pilgrims. The foundations of the church can be traced back to St Leo I (440-461). Ceded in 1479 to Coptic monks, it was extensively rebuilt under Clement XI at the beginning of the 18th century and restored between 1931 and 1933. Worth noting is the 11th-century portal decorated with wreaths of leaves. Fragments of inscriptions and sarcophagi on the outer walls bear witness that the necropolis discovered under St Peter's extended this high (see p. 190).

13 Ascending to the left of the church we come to the building which houses the *Mosaic Studio*, directed by the "Reverenda Fabbrica" of St Peter's. The school teaches the art of mosaics and is responsible for the maintenance of the mosaics in the Basilica. It was founded at the end of the 16th century, but was officially instituted only in 1727 by Benedict XIII.

14 At the end of this brief climb we come to another square. This square faces the *railway station* built by Giuseppe Momo, and inaugurated in 1930. The station's façade has two bas-reliefs by Eduardo Rubino, representing The Miraculous Draught of Fishes and the Prophet Elijah and his Chariot of Fire. The railway is used for the transportation of cargo and is connected to the Italian State railway system. It was from here that John XXIII set out on October 14, 1962 for his first pilgrimage to Assisi and Loreto, on the occasion of the imminent Second Vatican Council. It was the first instance in which the railway was used for passengers. Later it was used also by Pope John Paul II.

15 To the right of the station square is another large square, where the *Government Palace (Palazzo del Governatorato)* is located, which houses the main offices of the State. This is also the work of Giuseppe Momo and it was built in 1930. On the sloping grounds between the square and the apse of St Peter's are flower-beds arranged in the form of the coat of arms of the reigning Pope.

Gardens

Beyond the Government Palace lie the Vatican Gardens, which comprise a third of the Vatican territory. They are made up of lawns and woods, crisscrossed with avenues and adorned by artificial caves, kiosks, monumental statues and fountains.

16 Almost at the center of the Vatican grounds, in the midst of a palm grove, is a *bronze statue of St Peter*. It was once part of the monument erected in the Court of the "Pigna" (40) to commemorate the First Vatican Council (1869-1870).

17 To the right of the statue of St Peter is a small turreted building called the *House of the Gardener* because of its present use. It was probably one of the buildings erected inside the Leonine walls by Innocent III (1198-1216).

18 Towards the left one climbs to the summit of the Vatican Hill. On the left is the *Ethiopian College*, built by G. Momo, where Ethiopian seminarians stay.

Dome of St Peter's from the Vatican Gardens

The German-speaking countries and Ethiopia are the only nations to have colleges inside the Vatican walls.

At the summit of the hill we follow along the *brick embattlement*, part of the first fortified enclosure of the Vatican (see 5, plan pp. 6-7) built by Leo IV (847-855) to protect the ancient Basilica and the Vatican Hill (the early nucleus of the present city) and restored by Nicholas V in the 15th century. **19**

On the left, we come to the *Italian garden* with shrubs and flower-beds symmetrically trimmed and arranged. Only a short distance from here is the **20** building of the *first Vatican Radio transmitting station*, planned by Guglielmo **21** Marconi and inaugurated in 1931.

Proceeding on the left is a *small wall* which, during the papacy of Pius XII, **22** was covered by a transparent roof. This allowed the Pope to take his customary afternoon walks, in all weather conditions.

Past the wall on the right, we reach the highest point of the Vatican Hill (78.50 m.) and the Leonine walls. Here we find the medieval *Tower of St John*, which **23** was used as the summer residence of Pope John XXIII (1958-1963). The tower has lodged many illustrious guests, including Athenagoras, patriarch of Constantinople, who visited the Vatican in 1967. Recently it was inhabited by Pope John Paul II during work on the Pope's private apartment.

Further on, at the extreme western bastion of the perimeter of the Vatican, is the papal *heliport*. **24**

Descending along the ramparts (the boundary of the Vatican territory), built in the 16th century, we come to the Square of the Madonna of Lourdes. There is a cement reproduction of the *Grotto of Lourdes* (Massabielle) where the **25** Madonna appeared before St Bernadette Soubirous in 1858. The grotto was donated to Leo XIII by the Bishop of Tarbes, the diocese which includes the city of Lourdes. Images of the donor and the Pope are represented in mosaic above the grotto. The original altar of the Lourdes grotto, donated to Pope John XXIII, is still used on special occasions.

From here we proceed on foot to a *rose garden* where we have an admirable **26**

plan ← view of the apse and the dome of St Peter's. Behind us is a medieval tower, called the Leonine Tower, rising from another part of the fortified wall built by Leo IV and Nicholas V. This tower and the villa below it were the seat of the Vatican observatory between 1908 and 1936. The observatory was moved there from the Wind Tower (Torre dei Venti) (43) and later transferred to Castel Gandolfo on the Albani Hills, the pope's summer residence. The

27 medieval tower and the villa presently house the *offices of the Vatican radio station*. The villa was once the summer residence of Leo XIII, the Pope who lived the greatest number of years in the Vatican. (Between 1870 and 1929 the popes never left the Vatican because of tense diplomatic relations with the Italian State, which had militarily occupied Rome).

28 Beyond the villa of Leo XIII is the *English garden*, where the vegetation is allowed to grow naturally.

29 In a clearing along the upper border of the garden is the little *Chapel of the "Madonna della Guardia"*, with a reproduction of the statue which overlooks the entry to the port of Genoa, donated by the Genovese to their fellow-citizen, Benedict XV.

30 Visible through the trees of the English garden is a *statue of St Peter in Chains*, sculpted in 1887 by Amalia Dupré (the first woman artist represented in the Vatican). It alludes to the years of virtual captivity of the Pope during the occupation of Rome by the new Italian State at the turn of the century. Like most of the statues in the garden, it is dedicated to Leo XIII.

31 At the lower end of the English garden is a *Chinese pavilion* (donated by Chinese Catholics to Pius XI in 1933 on the nineteenth centenary of the death of Christ). The pavilion was a favorite resting place of John XXIII. From this

41 point we can see part of the Vatican Museums complex, including the *Vatican Pinacoteca*, built in 1930 by Luca Beltrami.

After passing through one of the most attractive and shady areas of the gardens, with little fountains and benches decorated with ancient marble, we descend to

32 the 17th-century *Fountain of the Eagle* by the Dutch artist Jan van Santen. Like all the fountains in the Vatican, the water comes from the Lake of Bracciano, about 40 km from Rome. The eagle and the griffin are the symbols of the Borghese family of Paul V (1605-1621), who commissioned the fountain.

33 Further down on the left is the villa constructed by Pius XI to house the *Pontifical Academy of Sciences*, where scientists from all over the world meet to participate in conventions.

34 Immediately following is one of the finest and best preserved architectural complexes in the Vatican: the *"Casina"* of *Pius IV*, begun in 1558 by Pirro Ligorio and Sallustio Peruzzi, and completed between 1560 and 1562. It is composed of two buildings facing each other across an elliptical courtyard. On the west is the villa with a richly decorated stucco façade, and on the east, the loggia with a fountain and a grotto.

Across the road from the villa rises an impressive building which is part of the
42 Apostolic Palace. The lower floor houses the *Secret Archive of the Vatican*,
42 the middle floor houses the *Vatican Library* and in the upper level are located
42, 43 some of the *galleries of the Vatican Museums*. The *Wind Tower (Torre dei Venti)* rises from this building; until 1908, it served as the seat of the Vatican observatory, instituted by Gregory XIII. Observations made from this tower contributed to the modification of the calendar (in October 1582), now called the Gregorian calendar after this Pope. The observatory was then transferred to the tower of the villa of Leo XIII (see above: 27) and later it was transferred by Pius XI to the papal villa at Castel Gandolfo. Queen Christine of Sweden lived in the Wind Tower in 1655. The Library and the Secret Archive are among the most important cultural institutions of the Holy See. The Library, notwithstanding its ancient origins, was officially founded by Nicholas V (1447-1455) and owes its organization to Sixtus IV (1471-1484), who appointed the first librarian. It has a collection of 800,000 volumes, 80,000 manuscripts, 10,000 incunabula and 100,000 etchings. The Secret Archive keeps various important files of the offices of the Holy See and, since 1660, has also kept the correspondence of the Segreteria di Stato. Both Archive and Library are open to scholars of all nations.

Taverna - Ristorante
"Garden Lino"
Via Tunisi, 18 (angolo) Via Candia, 81

Specialità —
pollo alla griglia
lasagne - ravioli

Proceeding towards the crenelated structure of the Sistine Chapel (44), we see on our left a *building erected by Paul V* (1605-1621) to connect the Apostolic Palace with the gardens. At the foot of the building is the *Fountain of the Mirrors*, probably built by Martino Ferrabosco for Paul V at the beginning of the 17th century. It is an elegant aedicula with side entrances and two small fountains, one inside and one outside, splendidly decorated with blue and gold mosaic. They are inspired by the fountains of Pompeii.

On the tree-lined square is the monumental *Fountain of the Sacrament* (so called because its jets of water resemble a monstrance surrounded by six candles), built on the site of an ancient entrance to the Vatican. This is the work of Jan van Santen (who also designed the Fountain of the Eagle). Two griffins, emblems of the Borghese family, perch on the crenelated towers which flank it (perhaps reflecting the fortified elements of the ancient entrance). The fountain stands to the rear of the *Mint (Palazzo della Zecca)* where the Vatican money was once coined.

From here, visitors whose tour includes the Sistine Chapel (44) will be transported by bus to the Vatican Museums (see text in italics below: 45-48).

The front side of the Mint, founded by Eugene IV in the 15th century and reconstructed by Pius VI at the end of the 18th century, faces *Piazza del Forno (Square of the Oven)*, so called because until recently the Vatican bakery was located there.

Above the square stands an imposing building erected in the second half of the 15th century by Sixtus IV to protect St Peter's and the Apostolic Palace. The middle floor is occupied by the *Sistine Chapel.*

Through the *Arch of the Sentinel (Arco della Sentinella)* at the base of the Sistine Chapel we can see the series of courtyards of the original core of the Apostolic Palace, which has preserved the aspect of a medieval fortress.

For visitors whose tour includes St Peter's Basilica (see p. 171), a bus will take them from Piazza del Forno to the Prayer Door (Porta della Preghiera) in the left arm of the transept (see p. 177:25).

On the return journey in the tour bus, visitors ride by the walls of the apse built by Michelangelo, and reach St Peter's Square passing again under the Arch of the Bells (2). The itinerary ends at the Vatican Pilgrim and Tourist Information Bureau (1).

Before entering the Vatican Museums, visitors whose tour includes the Sistine Chapel are conducted to the Fountain of the Galley *(the cannons of the 17th century lead galley shoot jets of water into the pool), built during the pontificate of Paul V at the foot of the* spiral staircase by Bramante. *From the spiral staircase we ascend to the* Palazzetto del Belvedere, *the summer residence of Innocent VIII (1484-1992) and now part of the Vatican Museums. From this area, dominating the northern part of the City, we can admire the back of the Apostolic Palace (3) and the long powerful walls built by Bramante, which enclose the* corridor *(now part of the Museums) connecting the Apostolic Palace to the Belvedere Palace.*

North Area

This is as far as the organized tour takes us. From Piazza del Forno (38), to the left, the avenue "Stradone ai Giardini" leads to the 18th-century entrance to the Museums (the *Atrium of the Four Gates - Atrio dei Quattro Cancelli*), while through the archway of the Court of the Sentinel (39) we approach the ancient nucleus of the Apostolic Palace.

We shall briefly mention an area normally excluded from the tour offered to visitors, but which constitutes an important part of the Vatican City State. This is the area to the north of the Basilica and palaces, between the *Court of the «Belvedere»,* which gives access to the offices and reading rooms of the plan ← Vatican Library and the Secret Archive of the Vatican (42), and Via di Porta Angelica which leads to St Anne's Gate (Cancello di Sant'Anna) (68).

51
52,53
53
54
55-58
The technical services of the small State are concentrated in this area: the *car-park* (a Roman necropolis was discovered during its construction in 1956), the *Post and Telegraph office*, the *Tipografia Poliglotta Vaticana* (which prints the Vatican's publications, including the official acts of the Pope and the offices of the Holy See, in different languages), the *Libreria Editrice Vaticana* (which distributes cultural and religious publications), the *grocery stores*, the *pharmacy*, the *health services*, the *mechanical workshop*, and the *heating plant*.

59
Before reaching St Anne's Gate (68) we notice the large *tower* belonging to the part of the Apostolic Palace built by Sixtus V at the end of the 16th century. The tower constituted the southeast corner of the fortifications of Nicholas V (1447-1455). The part of Nicholas V's walls to the right of the tower is well preserved.

60

61

62

63,64

65
66
Between the *sentry-post of the guards of the "Ufficio di Vigilanza"* and St Anne's Gate (68) is the Via del Pellegrino. This is the last part of the road (Via Francigena) which in ancient times brought pilgrims from the north to St Peter's. On the east side of the road stands the *Church of San Pellegrino.* Notwithstanding its Baroque façade, it is one of the oldest buildings in the Vatican (it dates from the papacy of Leo III: 795-816) and was the oratory of a pilgrims' hospice. On the Via del Pellegrino are the buildings of *L'Osservatore Romano* (a political and religious daily newspaper of the Holy See, with weekly editions in various languages). Further along the same road are the *living quarters of the guards of the "Ufficio di Vigilanza"*, the *tapestry restoration workshop* (run by French nuns — the Missionaries of Mary — since 1926), and the *refectory* for the employees of the "Ufficio di Vigilanza". At the end of the Via del Pellegrino stands the *Church of St Anne*, by Jacopo Barozzi, called il Vignola, begun in 1572. It is the parish church of the small State and the crypt contains the small cemetery of the Vatican City.

67
68
In front of the Church of St Anne, towards St Peter's Square, are the *barracks of the Swiss Guard*. Between the church and the barracks is *St Anne's Gate (Cancello di Sant'Anna),* one of the principal entrances to the City, guarded by the blue-uniformed Swiss Guard.

THE APOSTOLIC PALACE

plan →

Court of St Damasus (on the left are Loggias of Bramante and Raphael: at the center, the loggias of the wing of Gregory XIII: on the right, the loggias of the building of Sixtus V)

This is the name given to the row of buildings extending from St Peter's Square to the walls of Paul III and Urban VIII at the north end of the City, where the present entrance to the Vatican Museums is located. This part of the Guide describes only the buildings overlooking the Court of St Damasus.

Mention has already been made in the Introduction of the events that led many popes, from Symmachus to Nicholas III, to establish, fortify and embellish a permanent residence near St Peter's. The most ancient part of the palace is the rectangular building planned by Nicholas III (1277-1280) and partially built by him on the southern and eastern sides (see 7, plan pp. 6-7). The most ancient part of the palace is the rectangular building planned by Nicholas III (1277-1280) and partially built by him on the southern and eastern sides (see 7, plan pp. 6-7). The palace grew up around the little Court of the "Pappagallo" over a period of three centuries.

When Nicholas V became Pope (1447-1455), the courtyard was already enclosed by buildings on the south side (which already included the structure containing the present *Sala Regia*), on the east side, and in part on the north **1** side. Under his papacy the northern and western sides were also completed (see 8, plan pp. 6-7). The exterior of the new buildings maintained the sober 13th-century fortress-like aspect of the original nucleus, while the interiors were designed in Tuscan Renaissance style. One of the most important artists who worked for Nicholas V was Fra Angelico. Unfortunately, the only surviving work by this artist in the Vatican is the small *chapel* frescoed with **2** scenes from the lives of St Stephen and St Lawrence. The "Sancti Nicolai" Chapel, also frescoed by Fra Angelico, was destroyed under Paul III (1534-1549).

The work carried out under Nicholas V was resumed with great enthusiasm by Sixtus IV (1471-1484). He set aside four rooms on the ground floor of the building on the north side of the Court of the "Pappagallo" to house the Vatican Library, originally promoted by Nicholas V. (Later, the upper floors of this building were occupied by the *Borgia Apartment* and by the *Raphael* **3,4** *"Stanze"*, which made up the apartment of Julius II.) The rooms of the Vatican Library were frescoed by Domenico and Davide Ghirlandaio, Melozzo da Forlì and Antoniazzo Romano. The name of Sixtus IV is above all associated with the *Sistine Chapel* (see 9, plan pp. 6-7), which he built to the west **5**

167

plan
→

Court of the "Pappagallo" (Apostolic Palace)

of the Sala Regia (1) on the site of an earlier "large chapel" in the Palace of Nicholas III. The Sistine Chapel, decorated by the greatest artists of the time, also served as the third (southwest) corner-tower of the palace planned by Nicholas III.

6 The fourth tower (*Borgia Tower*, see 11, plan pp. 6-7) was built at the northwest corner under Alexander VI Borgia (1492-1503). On the first floor are the first two rooms of the Borgia Apartment (3) and on the second floor is the
7 *Sala dell'Immacolata.*

With the election of Julius II della Rovere (1503-1513), an exceptionally fertile period began both in art and in Christian Humanism.

For most of his architectural projects, Julius II employed Donato Bramante, while for painting and sculpture, he turned to Michelangelo and Raphael. Bramante planned the vast Court of the "Belvedere" (although he only completed part of the east wing — see 12, plan pp. 6-7). He also designed a monumental façade for the east side of the Palace of Nicholas III. It was to be
8 divided into three superimposed *loggias*. After Bramante's death, work on the façade was continued by Raphael, under Leo X (1513-1521).

Artistic activity continued to flourish under the papacy of Paul III (1534-1549). He entrusted Antonio da Sangallo the Younger with the difficult task of reinforcing the foundations of the palace. But Sangallo's major achievement was the almost complete rebuilding of the southwestern wing of the Apostolic Palace, including the Sala Regia (1), where ambassadors were once received,
9 the *Sala Ducale* and the "Sancti Nicolai" Chapel (or Chapel of the Sacra-

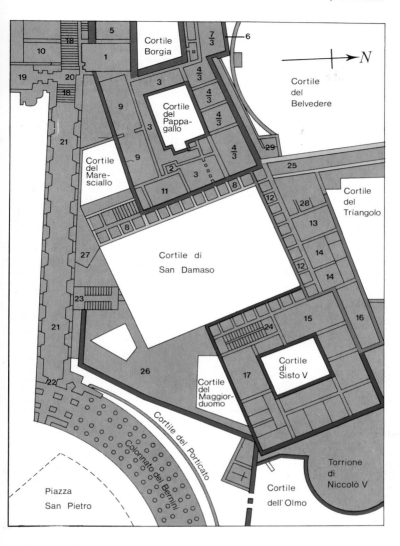

APOSTOLIC PALACE

1 Sala Regia (Royal Hall)
2 Chapel of Nicholas V
3 Borgia Apartment
4 Raphael "Stanze"
5 Sistine Chapel
6 Borgia Tower
7 Sala dell'Immacolata
8 Loggias of Bramante and Raphael
9 Sala Ducale
10 Pauline Chapel
11 Sala dei Paramenti
12 Northern wing with the Loggias of Gregory XIII
13 Cappella Matilde
14 Sale dei Foconi
15 Sala Clementina
16 Sala del Concistoro
17 Private library of the Pope
18 Royal stairway (Scala Regia)
19 Atrium of St Peter's
20 Statue of Constantine by Bernini
21 Portico of Constantine by Bernini

22 Bronze Doors, *entrance to the Apostolic Palace*
23 Stairway of Pius IX
24 Audience Stairway

Buildings not cited in the text of this chapter
25 Corridor by Bramante (today the Galleria Lapidaria of the Vatican Museums)
26 Wing of Julius III
27 Wing of Paul V
28 Building of Urban VIII
29 Building of Benedict XIV

■ Medieval palace

□ 16th century: Loggias of Bramante and Raphael (8); Corridor by Bramante (25)

■ 16th century: Loggias and Palace of Gregory XIII (12, 13, 14, 16)

■ 16th century: Palace of Sixtus V

plan
←
10 ment), as far as the Court of the "Maresciallo". Unfortunately, the Chapel of the Sacrament with its frescoes by Fra Angelico was destroyed. It was replaced by the *Pauline Chapel*, containing Michelangelo's last frescoes.

11 The successors of Paul III generally limited themselves to completing projects already underway. Between the loggias of Bramante and Raphael and the Sala Ducale (9) is the *Sala dei Paramenti,* where the Pope puts on his sacred vestments before entering St Peter's or the Sistine Chapel.

12 During the papacy of Pius IV (1560-1565), Pirro Ligorio built the first part of the *northern wing of the loggias,* overlooking the "secret garden", now the Court of St Damasus. This project was completed under Gregory XIII (1572-1585) by Martino Longhi the Elder, who faithfully imitated the structures and façade of the western wing by Bramante and Raphael. Behind the loggias is
13,14 the apartment of Gregory XIII, with the *Cappella Matilde* and the *Sale dei Foconi.*

Sixtus V (1585-1590) was the last pope to promote building projects worthy of note in the Vatican and in Rome. He chose a new location for the Vatican Library and commissioned Domenico Fontana to begin work. Fontana also began the construction of a new palace — the present residence of the Pope — on the east side of the Court of St Damasus. The building was completed under Clement VIII (1592-1605) by Taddeo Landini, to whom we owe the
15 splendid *Sala Clementina*, decorated by Giovanni and Cherubino Alberti and Paul Bril. This is the first room of the Pontifical "Noble Apartment" (behind it is
16 the *Sala del Concistoro*), a series of rooms along the perimeter of the Court of
17 Sixtus V, terminating in the *private library* where the Pope holds private audiences.

Under the papacy of Alexander VII (1655-1667), the Apostolic Palace was
18 embellished by Bernini's magnificent *Royal Stairway* (*Scala Regia*), connecting
19 the Sala Regia (1) with the *atrium of St. Peter's*. The lower ramp of the stairway is flanked on each side by Ionic columns supporting a barrel vault. The height, diameter and distance of the columns from the wall decrease as we ascend, in proportion to the surrounding structures. (The space really narrows towards the upper part of the stairs). By thus emphasizing perspective effects, the artist creates an impression of monumentality. Bernini's ingenious solution could not have been conceived by any lesser artist. At the foot
20 of the stairway, on the right as we ascend, is the *statue of Constantine* by
21 Bernini. At the end of the *Portico of Constantine* (built by Bernini) are the
22 *Bronze Doors, the main entrance to the Apostolic Palace*, guarded by the Swiss Guard.

23 On the right as we pass the Bronze Doors, we find the *Stairway of Pius IX* which leads to the Court of St Damasus. The building complex which makes up the Apostolic Palace surrounds this courtyard. To the left we see the Loggias by Bramante and Raphael (8) which adorn Julius II's Renaissance façade of the medieval building that constituted the original nucleus of the Apostolic Palace. The offices of the Segreteria di Stato correspond to the third loggia. At the center are the loggias (12) of the wing built by Pius IV and Gregory XIII. To the right is the palace built by Domenico Fontana for Sixtus V.

24 The *Audience Stairway* leads to the Court of St Damasus and the part of the Palace of Sixtus V in which the "Noble Apartment" and the private apartments of the Pope are located.

ST PETER'S BASILICA

plan
→

Façade and dome of St Peter's

In the year 324, the Emperor Constantine ordered the building of a huge Basilica on the site of the tomb of St Peter. It had a nave and four aisles and was preceded by a courtyard with four porticoes (see 3, plan pp. 6-7). The building was not completed until after the Emperor's death in about 349.

Twelve centuries later, during the papacy of Julius II, the Basilica was no longer considered safe and was demolished. On April 18, 1506, the first stone of the new St Peter's was laid on the site of the old transept. The first project for the new Basilica was by Donato Bramante, who planned a centralized structure in the form of a Greek cross. At his death in 1514, the four piers and arches which support the dome had been built.

His successors in the direction of the work were Giuliano da Sangallo, Raphael (who designed a church in the form of a Latin cross, with one arm longer than the others), and Antonio da Sangallo the Younger. But work progressed slowly.

In 1546, when Antonio da Sangallo died, Pope Paul III appointed Michelangelo "commissioner, director of works and architect for life". The seventy-two-year-old artist reverted to Bramante's idea of a central (Greek cross) plan. The apse, the transept (the two transversal arms) and the dome were the first parts to be built. At Michelangelo's death in 1564, the dome had been built as far as the top of the drum.

Pirro Ligorio and Jacopo Barozzi, called il Vignola, succeeded Michelangelo. In 1573, Giacomo della Porta succeeded Barozzi and it is to him that we owe the two minor domes. In 1585, della Porta was joined by Domenico Fontana. During the papacy of Sixtus V, the dome was successfully completed by these two architects between July 1588 and May 1590. In 1591, Fontana completed the lantern of the dome, and in 1593 the cross was placed on the summit at approximately 136 m. from ground level.

In the meantime, part of the five aisles of the old Basilica had remained unchanged.

171

plan
→
In 1602, at the death of Della Porta, Carlo Maderno became Fontana's assistant. Maderno won the competition sponsored by Paul V in 1607 for the work of lengthening the basilica after the original Greek-cross plan had been definitely abandoned.

The façade was completed in 1614 and on Palm Sunday of the following year it was possible to make a complete visit of the new St Peter's (see 4, plan pp. 6-7). Pope Urban VIII supervised the decoration of the Basilica and on November 18, 1626, one hundred and twenty years after the beginning of the work, he solemnly consecrated it, exactly one thousand three hundred years after the consecration of the first Basilica.

In recent centuries many important events in the history of the Church have taken place in St Peter's. In 1869-1870 and from 1962 to 1965, the First and Second Vatican Councils were held there. Ecumenical Councils are meetings in which the Pope and bishops from all over the world deliberate on important questions concerning the life of the Church. (Bishops are nominated by the Pope. They are the heads of local churches, or dioceses, and they presently number about two thousand five hundred.)

In St Peter's, besides performing solemn and public religious rites, the Pope performs the ceremonies of canonization (sanctification) and beatification, in which the Church declares that a person is entitled to public religious honor for the exceptional qualities of Christian virtue demonstrated during his or her lifetime.

Atrium

1   The *atrium of St Peter's*, by Carlo Maderno, measures 71 m. in length, 13.50 m. in width and 20 m. in height.

An inscription commemorating the inauguration of the Second Vatican Council (October 11, 1962), and the coat-of-arms of Pope John XXIII, who convoked it, are located at the center of the floor.

2   Above the central entrance is the heavily restored *mosaic of the "Navicella"*, made by Giotto for the old Basilica on the occasion of the first Jubilee (1300). It represents Jesus and St Peter on the waters of Lake Tiberias and the boat of the Apostles.

The ceiling reliefs represent episodes from the Acts of the Apostles, a text attributed to St Luke the Evangelist, which narrates the early history of the Church.

3   At the left end of the atrium is the 18th-century *equestrian statue of Charlemagne*, the first emperor to be crowned in St Peter's (on Christmas day of the year 800), sculpted by Agostino Cornacchini in 1725. Opposite, to the right, is
3   the *equestrian statue of Constantine* by Gian Lorenzo Bernini (1670) at the foot of the Scala Regia (see 34, plan pp. 6-7) visible behind glass doors.

Five bronze doors lead into the Basilica.

4   In the center is the 15th-century *door of the old St Peter's* by Antonio Averulino, called Filarete. It portrays Christ and the Virgin Mary, and St Peter and St Paul and their martyrdoms. The minor panels portray stories from the papacy of Eugene IV, who commissioned the door. These include the Council of Ferrara and Florence, called in 1438 for the reunification of the Eastern and Western Churches. The borders which frame the panels show decorations inspired by Classical Antiquity (heads of emperors and illustrious men, mythological scenes). It is the first work in the Renaissance style in Rome. On the left side of the door, the sculptor has portrayed himself, fêted upon his return to Florence, his native city, for the completion of his work.

5   The *Door of Death (Porta della Morte)* (1964) by Giacomo Manzù has ten

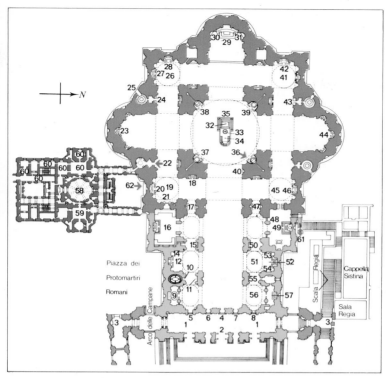

ST PETER'S BASILICA

1 Atrium by Maderno
2 Giotto's mosaic of the "Navicella"
3 Equestrian statue of Charlemagne (left) and Constantine (right)
4 Bronze door by Filarete
5 Door of Death (Porta della Morte)
6 Door of Good and Evil (Porta del Bene e del Male)
7 Door of the Sacraments (Porta dei Sacramenti)
8 Holy Door (Porta Santa)
9 Baptistry Chapel
10 Monument to Maria Clementina Sobieski
11 Monument to the Stuarts
12 Chapel of the Presentation and urn of St. Pius X
13 Monument to Benedict XV
14 Monument to John XXIII
15 Monument to Innocent VIII
16 Chapel of the Choir
17 Monument to Leo XI
18 Altar of the Transfiguration
19 Cappella Clementina
20 Altar of St Gregory the Great
21 Monument to Pius VII
22 Monument to Pius VIII and *entrance to the Sacristy and Treasury*
23 Altar of St Joseph
24 Monument to Alexander VII
25 Prayer Door (Porta della Preghiera)
26 Chapel of the Madonna of the Column
27 Madonna of the Column
28 Marble relief with Leo I the Great
29 Throne of St Peter in Glory, by Bernini
30 Monument to Paul III
31 Monument to Urban VIII
32 Papal altar called of the "Confession"
33 ⊕ Niche of the Palliums
34 Area of the "Confession"
35 Bernini's baldachin
36 Pillar and statue of St Longinus and *entrance to the Vatican Grottoes*

37 Pillar and statue of St Andrew
38 Pillar and statue of St Veronica
39 Pillar and statue of St Helen
40 Bronze statue of St Peter Enthroned
41 Chapel of St Petronilla and the Archangel Michael
42 Altar of St Veronica
43 Monument to Clement XIII
44 Altar of St Processus and St Martinianus
45 Cappella Gregoriana
46 Our Lady of Succor (Madonna del Soccorso)
47 Monument to Gregory XIII
48 Chapel of the Sacrament
49 Tabernacle in the form of a round temple by Bernini, and the Trinity, a canvas by Pietro da Cortona
50 Monument to Matilda of Canossa
51 Mosaics from cartoons by Pietro da Cortona
52 Chapel of St Sebastian with tomb of Innocent XI
53 Monument to Pius XII
54 Monument to Pius XI
55 Monument to Christine of Sweden
56 Mosaics from cartoons by Pietro da Cortona
57 Michelangelo's Pietà
58 Main Sacristy
59 Sacristy of the Canons
60 Treasury
61 *Exit from the Vatican Grottoes and entrance to the dome*
62 *Entrance to the Necropolis*

■ Donato Bramante and Michelangelo Buonarroti

□ Carlo Maderno

▨ Gian Lorenzo Bernini

■ Carlo Marchionni

plan
←

panels illustrating the theme of death. On the back of one of the panels Pope John XXIII is represented receiving the bishops on the first day of the Council on October 11, 1962.

6 The *Door of Good and Evil (Porta del Bene e del Male)* by Luciano Minguzzi, who donated it to Paul VI, portrays the struggle between good and evil on twelve panels.

7 On the *Door of the Sacraments (Porta dei Sacramenti)* (1965), Venanzio Crocetti has represented the seven sacraments of the Catholic Church in eight panels. In the first panel, on the upper left, an angel announces the grace of the sacraments. This door, together with the Door of Death, was made thanks to the bequest of Prince George of Bavaria, canon of St Peter's, who died in 1947.

8 Last on the right is the *Holy Door (Porta Santa)* which is opened by the Pope once every twenty-five years, at the beginning and at the end of every Holy Year or Jubilee. The Holy Year is dedicated to prayer and proselytism. It is an occasion for Catholics throughout the world to meet and share their common faith. In honour of the 1950 Jubilee, two bronze panels, donated by Swiss Catholics, were added to the Holy Door. The sculptor, Vico Consorti, has chosen for 15 of the 16 panels episodes from the Bible that allude to sin, forgiveness (the central theme of the Holy Year) and redemption. In the last panel to the right at the bottom is Pius XII opening the Holy Door, on Christmas day 1949.

Interior

St Peter's has the form of a Latin cross. That is, it has a longitudinal arm (the nave) which is longer than the two transversal arms (the transept) and a fourth arm (the apse) which is the extension of the longitudinal arm. Around the octagonal space of the crossing are the four immense piers (36-39) which support the dome. The papal altar (32) beneath the monumental baldachin, or canopy (35), is situated at the center of the crossing.

In 1962-1965 the Second Vatican Council was held in the nave. On this occasion, special stalls were built to seat the participating bishops.

The first impression one has on entering St Peter's is one of vastness. In fact it is the world's largest church. On the floor along the axis of the nave a metal inscription records the lengths of fifteen of the largest Catholic and non-Catholic churches in the world. None are as long as St Peter's, which (including the walls) measures 192.76 m. The total distance across is 58 m.

The vault with high-relief stucco-work is 44.50 m. high. Between the capitals and above the arches are 17th-century statues in white stucco representing the virtues taught by the Church. At the base of the vault, decorated with rosettes, is a mosaic inscription in Latin and Greek of the words pronounced by Jesus to Peter. According to Catholic doctrine, these words are the foundation of the authority bestowed on the Apostle and on his successors, the Bishops of Rome. The beginning of the sentence "Tu es Petrus..." (Mt. 16, 18-19) appears at the base of the dome.

As we proceed into the interior of the Basilica, we immediately notice the many monuments that adorn both the nave and side aisles: altars, monuments to the popes, statues of the founders of religious Orders and mosaics. (Since the first half of the 17th century, even the paintings and frescoes above the altars, which were beginning to deteriorate, have been replaced by mosaic representations). Since 1727, the execution and maintenance of the mosaics has been entrusted to the Mosaic Studio (see p. 162: 13), founded in order to complete the decoration of St Peter's and still active in the Vatican today. There are thirty-nine niches carved out of the columns in the nave, the transept and the apse. These niches contain statues of the saints who founded religious Orders. (The Catholic clergy includes the members of the Orders as well as the secular priests of the diocese. The members of the Orders

plan
←

St Peter's, view of the naves from the entrance

make vows of poverty, chastity and obedience, and strive to achieve a life of Christian perfection). Most of these statues date from the 18th or 19th centuries; a few date from the 20th century. Many merit attention, although none of them are masterpieces. In the nave there are no representations of popes, except for a bronze statue of St Peter (40). The many papal monuments situated in the side aisles are not tombs but commemorative monuments. The altars of the two second chapels (12 and 52) of the side aisles contain the mortal remains of the last two popes canonized by the Catholic Church: Pope Pius X (1903-1914) and Pope Innocent XI (1678-1689). But most of the tombs of the one hundred and forty-seven popes and other famous people buried in St Peter's are in the Vatican Grottoes, beneath the level of the Basilica (see p. 188).

The oldest monuments, dating from the sumptuous Baroque period, were designed to glorify the Papacy. The Pope is generally represented seated on his throne, dressed in papal vestments and tiara, in the act of blessing the faithful. Often statues representing the virtues for which the Pope was particularly noted stand next to his image. The more recent monuments exalt the piety of the popes, who are usually represented alone and in the act of praying. An exception is the monument to Pope John XXIII (14), which contains many figures other than that of the Pope.

Throughout our visit, we will keep these general criteria in mind. We will pause only before the papal monuments of greatest artistic importance.

Left Aisle

Entering into the left aisle the first chapel we see is the *Baptistry Chapel*. (The **9** sacrament of Baptism, by means of which one becomes a member of the Church, is administered both to adults who choose to become Christian and to children whose parents propose to raise them according to the Christian faith. Baptism is administered with water, which is why the chapel contains a baptismal font rather than an altar.) The font is a red porphyry basin from an ancient Roman tomb which had later been used to cover the sarcophagus of the Emperor Otto II (10th century - see p. 188: 25). The gilt bronze covering is a work of the late 17th century. The mosaic decoration of the chapel alludes to the sacrament of Baptism.

Immediately following the Baptistry Chapel is the 18th-century *monument* **10**

plan
← *to Maria Clementina Sobieski* (d. 1735), niece of John III, King of Poland, and wife of James III Stuart, pretender to the throne of England.

11 Opposite is a highly original work (ca. 1820) by Antonio Canova, the *monument to the Stuarts*, the royal family of Scotland exiled in Rome from 1689. The last of the Stuarts, James III, who died in 1766, and his sons Charles and Henry (who became high-priest and cardinal of the Basilica) are sculpted in profile on the stele.

12,13 Next is the *Chapel of the Presentation*. On the left is the *monument to*
14 *Benedict XV*, sculpted by Pietro Canonica. On the right is the bronze *monument to John XXIII* by Emilio Greco, representing the Pope and the bishops participating in the Second Vatican Council. In the center, under the altar, rests the body of Pope Pius X.

15 At the second column, following the Chapel of the Presentation, is the *monument to Innocent VIII* (1484-1492). It is the only papal monument from the ancient Basilica preserved in the new St Peter's. It is a splendid Renaissance work by Antonio del Pollaiolo. The Pope is represented seated on his throne, holding a model of the spearhead which wounded Christ. This relic, donated to Innocent VIII in 1492 by the Sultan Bayazid II, is preserved in one of the piers of the dome (38).

16 The 17th-century *Chapel of the Choir* is the third in the left aisle. It is enclosed by a rich Baroque bronze gate. The most important Catholic churches are administered by a group of priests called canons. On certain days and hours, the canons recite in chorus the official prayers of the Church. The stalls in this chapel are for this purpose. The chapel is also sometimes used to celebrate Confirmation, the ceremony in which Christians manifest their belief in Christian doctrine and discipline. This ceremony takes place when Christians have matured sufficiently to consciously accept their faith.

This chapel marks the end of the part of the Basilica built by Carlo Maderno between 1606 and 1614.

17 Beyond the Chapel of the Choir, on the left, we find an admirable *monument to Leo XI Medici* by Alessandro Algardi and his assistants (1650). It is a serenely composed marble group. The austerity of the white marble clearly represents a reaction to Bernini's chromatic effects and dramatic style which then prevailed in St Peter's, as we shall see. In the bas-relief, Henry IV, King of France, renounces Protestantism in 1593 in the presence of the Medici cardinal who later became Pope Leo XI.

Transept

18 The left aisle ends with the large mosaic of the Transfiguration, an 18th-century reproduction of the last painting by Raphael, preserved in the Pinacoteca.

We now find ourselves between the structures built by Donato Bramante and those by Michelangelo.

19 Then follows the *Cappella Clementina*, named in honor of Pope Clement VIII
20 who had it richly decorated for the Jubilee in 1600. *The altar of St Gregory the Great* preserves the body of this great Pope of the end of the 6th century in a
21 Roman sarcophagus under the altar. On the left is the *monument to Pius VII* (1800-1823), showing the Pope on his throne. It is by the Protestant Danish sculptor Bertel Thorvaldsen, one of Canova's most talented followers.

22 Next we come to the *entrance to the Sacristy and the Treasury of St Peter's*
22 (see p. 183). Above the door is the *monument to Pius VIII* (1857) by Pietro Tenerani, another of Canova's followers.

In the left arm of the transept we find twelve great confessionals, with signs indicating the various languages spoken by the head-confessors of the Basilica, thus giving pilgrims from all nations the opportunity to receive the sacrament of Penance. The *central altar* is dedicted to St Joseph. **23**

Proceeding towards the apse, we find the *monument to Alexander VII* (1655-1667), the last work of art (1678) by Gian Lorenzo Bernini. The nearly eighty-year-old artist, at the very end of his life, expressed the concept of prayer in all the pomp and splendor of the Baroque style. The exit below the monument, leading out of the Basilica, has recently been adorned by a bronze door called the *Prayer Door (Porta della Preghiera),* by Lello Scorzelli (1972). **24** **25**

On the first altar of the next chapel, the so-called *Chapel of the Madonna of the Column*, is an ancient *image* painted on a column transported from the Constantinian Basilica. Under the altar, in a 4th century sarcophagus, the remains of the canonized Popes Leo II, III, and IV are preserved, and under the floor in the center of the chapel are those of Leo XII. Exhibited on the second altar of the chapel is a large marble relief by Alessandro Algardi, portraying *Leo the Great* (440-461) dissuading Attila, King of the Huns, from invading Italy. This episode occurred near Mantua in 452. The mortal remains of this great Pope are preserved under the altar. **26** **27** **28**

The stupendous altar of the *throne of St Peter in Glory*, a masterpiece by Bernini, dominates the apse. It was executed between 1658 and 1666 during the papacy of Alexander VII. A large bronze throne appears to be supported by four large bronze statues of bishops (two fathers of the Latin Church, St Ambrose and St Augustine; and two fathers of the Greek Church, St Athanasius and St John Chrysostom). An ancient wooden chair is kept inside the bronze throne on which, according to tradition, St Peter supposedly sat when preaching to the Christian population. Actually, it is the chair donated to Pope John VIII in 875 by the Emperor Charles the Bald, and it symbolizes the authority of the Pope (a copy may be seen in the Treasury of St Peter's - see p. 184: II/5). Above the bronze throne, amid flights of angels, billowing clouds and blinding rays, is the Holy Ghost, illuminated by a stained glass window. More than one hundred and twenty-one tons of bronze were used for this enormous decoration. **29**

To the left of the throne of St Peter in Glory is the *monument to Paul III* (1534-1549), completed by Guglielmo della Porta in 1576. To the right is the *monument to Urban VIII* by Bernini, inaugurated in 1647. The statue of this Pope, seated on his throne, clothed in papal vestments and the tiara, represented in the act of blessing, expresses the triumphal character of the Baroque style more than any other work in St Peter's. **30** **31**

In front of the apse, in the center of the transept, we find the *papal altar called of the "Confession".* Since the earliest times of Christianity, this spot is thought to be the burial place of one who has confessed his faith to the point of martyrdom, and, at the same time, a place to which the faithful come to venerate the martyr and profess the same faith. Here, therefore, is the site of the tomb of St Peter. A double ramp of marble stairs can be seen leading to a horseshoe-shaped room, constructed and sumptuously decorated by Carlo Maderno and Martino Ferraboschi after 1615. Seventy gilt oil lamps burn continuously in honor of the Apostle. **32** **34**

At the center of a sumptuous wall and enclosed behind a richly decorated gilded gate, is a small recessed sanctuary. It corresponds to the lower niche of the two-tiered aedicula built in the second half of the 2nd century on the site of St Peter's tomb. Parts of the ancient monument are still in their original position. The walls of the small sanctuary are decorated with mosaics representing Christ (9th century), and Peter and Paul (13th century). The sanctuary is called the *Niche of the Palliums* because the palliums (long and narrow consecrated garments with black woven crosses) are kept there in a small 18th-century casket before being given by the Pope to newly ordained metropolitans. **33**

We now find ourselves below the present *papal altar,* built during the pontificate of Clement VIII (1592-1605). Research conducted under Pius XII (1939-1958) has revealed the existence of two altars beneath it, constructed during **32**

plan
← the papacy of Calixtus II (1119-1124) and Gregory I (590-604). The latter was situated over the monument which the Emperor Constantine had constructed in the 4th century in honor of St Peter. The Constantinian monument in turn contained the small aedicula formerly erected above the first tomb of the Apostle.

35 The papal altar, a bare marble slab found on the site of the Imperial Forum (Forum of Nerva), is situated beneath a gilt bronze *baldachin* (*canopy*) 29 m. high. It was built by Bernini in the third decade of the 17th century, during the reign of Urban VIII. The monumental baldachin exalts the sacred character of the altar without disturbing the harmonious proportions of the Basilica.

In the niches carved at the base of the four colossal piers which support the dome, there are four large statues of saints. These are typical examples of the emphatic taste of the Baroque style. (Facing the apse, in the first column of **36** the right aisle, is the *statue of St Longinus* by Bernini (under the pedestal is the entrance to the Vatican Grottoes - see p. 188). The others, in clockwise **37-39** direction, are: *St Andrew, St Veronica* and *St Helen*. These statues display the symbols of the relics which are or were preserved in one of the recesses (above the statue of St Veronica), which are exhibited during Holy Week. The niches are ornately decorated with spiral columns wreathed with vines (4th century) which originally surrounded the "Confession" of the ancient Constantinian Basilica. These columns inspired the four enormous bronze columns of Bernini's baldachin. The relics are: the spearhead with which the centurion Longinus (who later converted to Christianity) wounded Christ; the head of St Andrew, brother of St Peter (of Eastern origin, it was restored in 1963 to the Orthodox diocese of Patras as a sign of goodwill and to promote Christian unity); the veil with which St Veronica dried the face of Jesus on the way to Calvary; a fragment of the Holy Cross found by St Helen, mother of Constantine.

Above the "Confession" rises the great dome designed by Michelangelo (120 m. high from the floor to the small vault of the lantern, and 42.56 m. wide), supported by huge piers (31 m. high) and arches (45 m. high at the apex) built by Donato Bramante, the first architect of the new St Peter's. The four large mosaic medallions in the spandrels represent the Evangelists Matthew, Mark, Luke and John, whose writings the Church considers to be authentic testimonies of the life of Christ. The mosaics in the dome are based on cartoons by Cavalier d'Arpino. At the base of the dome are images of the canonized popes buried in the Basilica; above are Jesus and the Virgin Mary, St John the Baptist, St Paul and the Apostles. Above these, four rows of angels form a crown around God the Father, who appears in the small cupola of the lantern. Pope Sixtus V is mentioned in an inscription running around the oculus. It was during his papacy (between 1588 and 1590) that Giacomo della Porta and Domenico Fontana built the dome.

At the death of Michelangelo (1564), the drum had been finished and work was interrupted for twenty-four years. The dome was finally completed in only twenty-two months, from July 15, 1588, to May 21, 1590, thanks to a gigantic supporting framework and with the help of eight hundred laborers who worked in shifts, continuing through the night with the use of torchlights.

The mosaics (late 16th century) are among the most valuable and ancient in the church, and are original like those in the four minor domes at the end of the transept. They were made from cartoons especially designed for the decoration of the dome (most of the altar decorations in mosaic are copies of paintings, conceived for other purposes).

40 Under the pillar of St Longinus in the nave is the *bronze statue of St Peter Enthroned.* It is attributed to Arnolfo di Cambio (13th century) and is an object of great veneration. Above we find a mosaic portrait of Pius IX who reigned for thirty-two years (1846-1878). He is the only pope to have reigned longer than St Peter, who is supposed to have reigned for twenty-five years.

41 Behind the pillar of St Helen (to the right towards the apse) is the *Chapel of St Petronilla and the Archangel Michael,* one of the four chapels designed by

178

Michelangelo at the sides of the transept. Above the *altar of St Petronilla* is a **42** mosaic attributed to Pier Paolo Cristofari (first director of the Mosaic Studio of St Peter's). It is a copy of Guercino's painting of the Burial and Glory of St Petronilla, which it substituted in 1730.

Proceeding towards the right arm of the transept, to the left is the *monument* **43** *to Clement XIII*. Inaugurated in 1792, it is Canova's first work for St Peter's and the first monument in the Basilica to be built in the Neoclassical style, after two hundred years of Baroque art. The serene, self-contained forms, inspired by Greek art, replaced the flamboyant manner initiated by the 17th-century masters. Canova's sober style and religious sensitivity, evident in the kneeling figure of the Pope, create a mystical effect. The entire monument is in white marble, in conformity with the principles of the Neoclassical style. The earlier Baroque monuments were mostly made of bronze and polychrome marble.

In 1869-1870, the First Vatican Council took place in the right arm of the transept (the Second Vatican Council was held in the nave). It was here that the dogma of the infallibility of the pope was proclaimed, according to which the pope as Head of the Church cannot err when he declares truths contained in the Divine Revelations, or closely related to these. The *central altar* is **44** dedicated to St Processus and St Martinianus.

The *Cappella Gregoriana* was designed by Michelangelo and built by Giaco- **45** mo della Porta, during the papacy of Gregory XIII, to whom it is dedicated. Above the altar and surrounded by beautiful marble slabs is a 12th-century fresco, transferred from the old Basilica, representing *Our Lady of Succor* **46** (*Madonna del Soccorso*).

Right Aisle

To the left of the Gregorian Chapel is the *monument to Gregory XIII*. The **47** Pope is seated in majesty above an urn. Knowledge, in the guise of Minerva, is uncovering the urn to reveal the relief representing the event which made the Pope famous: the reform of the calendar presently in use (October 1582), which took the name "Gregorian" from this Pope. The two statues (to the left is Religion) are by Camillo Rusconi and the bas-relief is by Carlo Francesco Melloni and Bernardino Cametti.

Proceeding towards the entrance, we leave the central-plan structures of the Basilica planned by Bramante (later re-designed and, to a great extent, executed by Michelangelo) and we re-enter the part built by Carlo Maderno.

Half way along the aisle we find the *Chapel of the Sacrament* enclosed by an **48** elegant Baroque iron gate. It is dedicated to the Eucharist, which according to Catholic doctrine, is based on the words pronounced by Jesus to the Apostles before His death and resurrection. Jesus Himself is present in the bread and wine consecrated by the priest. On the central altar is the precious *tabernacle* **49** *in the form of a round temple* by Bernini. Its design, which reminds us of Bramante's temple in the church of San Pietro in Montorio, is a homage to St Peter's first architect. Behind the altarpiece is the *Trinity*, (the only remaining **49** painting in St Peter's) executed by Pietro da Cortona in 1669. It represents the mystery of the faith, according to Christian doctrine, of the one and only God who is, and manifests himself, in three equal and distinct Persons: the Father, creator of the universe visible and invisible; the Son incarnate, sacrificed for the redemption of sinful humanity, who has risen from death and will come on the Last Day as Supreme Judge of Good and Evil: and the Holy Spirit (here shown as a resplendent white dove) who proceeds from both, inspiration of the prophets and guiding light of the Church. The gilt bronze angels on each side of the ciborium are by Bernini. The vault and walls of the chapel are covered with splendid stucco works by Pietro da Cortona, representing episodes referring to the Eucharist.

In an arch at the foot of the column opposite the chapel is the *monument* **50**

plan
←

Michelangelo's Pietà

to Matilda of Canossa, benefactress of the Roman Papacy in the 11th century, an age of conflict between the Papacy and the Empire. She is represented holding the papal tiara and St Peter's keys in her left hand and the scepter in her right hand. On the sarcophagus which contains the remains of this fiery countess is a representation of Henry IV, Emperor of Germany, in the castle of Canossa on January 28, 1077. He is kneeling at the feet of Gregory VII, who had excommunicated him.

51 The *mosaic decoration of the next bay* (facing the Chapel of St Sebastian), executed between 1654 and 1663 by Fabio Cristofari and his assistants from cartoons by Pietro da Cortona, is among the finest in the Basilica. The vault is decorated with an image of God the Father in Glory, the spandrels with Abel and three martyr prophets (Isaiah, Zechariah and Ezekiel) and the lunettes with six martyrdoms narrated in the Bible: the seven Maccabees and their mother, Mattatia and the apostate, Daniel and the lions, Eleazar, the Hebrew women thrown down from the walls of Jerusalem and the three youths in the fiery furnace.

52 The mosaic altarpiece of the *Chapel of St Sebastian* represents the martyrdom of the saint. It is a copy made by Pier Paolo Cristofari of a famous fresco (1613) by Domenico Zampieri, called Domenichino. The fresco was transferred in 1730 to the church of Santa Maria degli Angeli where it has remained to the present time. Under the altar are the mortal remains of the canonized Pope
53 Innocent XI. To the left is the *monument to Pius XII*, by Francesco Messina. To
54 the right of the altar is the *monument to Pius XI*, by Francesco Nagni.

55 In the next column, above the *monument to Christine of Sweden*, there is a bronze medallion with the queen's portrait. Christine renounced the throne and left the Lutheran Church to convert to the Catholic faith (the incident narrated on the urn occurred at Innsbruck in 1655). She established her residence in

Rome, where she died in 1689. Christine of Sweden is buried in the Vatican Grottoes (see p. 188:17).

plan ←

In the next bay we find more *mosaics* by Fabio Cristofari, based on cartoons by Pietro da Cortona and his school. In the vault is an apocalyptic scene showing the Chosen saved from punishment; in the spandrels are Abraham, Isaac, Moses and Jeremiah, and in the lunettes are the Cumaean and Phrygian sibyls and the prophets Hosea, Isaiah, Amos and Zechariah.

56

The most famous work of art in St Peter's, the *Pietà* by Michelangelo, is in the last chapel. This marble group represents the dead Christ in the arms of the Virgin Mary. It is carved from a single block of marble 174 cm. high. The statue was commissioned in 1498 (when Michelangelo was about twenty-three) by Cardinal Jean Bilhières de Lagraulas, French ambassador to Rome, for the chapel of the kings of France. This chapel was located in the actual left arm of the transept before the construction of the new Basilica. The Pietà is the only signed work by Michelangelo. His name is carved on the ribbon which crosses the left shoulder of the Virgin. In 1962, Pope John XXIII sent the Pietà to the World Fair in New York, where it was admired by millions of people. Ten years later, in 1972, the Pietà was brutally damaged by a vandal. The sculpture has been perfectly restored by the Vatican restorers, and it is now protected by a glass enclosure. In the small dome of the Chapel of the Pietà is the only remaining ceiling fresco in St Peter's. It is by Giovanni Lanfranco (before 1633), and depicts the Triumph of the Cross. This fresco is an excellent example of animated, luminous Baroque decoration.

57

Visit to the Dome

The entrance to the dome is reached from the court on the right side of the Basilica (61, see plan p. 173). The visitor can ascend by lift or on foot to the terrace above the aisles and from there on foot to the interior of the dome.

From the terrace above the side aisles surrounding the sloping roof of the nave rise two larger cupolas and six smaller oval cupolas with lanterns, aligned in two rows, which illuminate the side aisles. The two larger cupolas, 45 m. in height from the terrace, are the work of Giacomo della Porta, director of works from 1573 to 1602, the year of his death. The cupolas are purely decorative, as they do not correspond to any architectural elements in the interior of the Basilica.

Four more large spherical cupolas situated at the corners correspond to the four large chapels at the ends of the transept.

Michelangelo's great dome, built only to the height of the drum by the time of his death in 1564, was completed by Giacomo della Porta and Domenico Fontana between July 1588 and May 1590.

There are two staircases leading to the interior of the base of the dome (diameter 42 m.). From here, the visitor has access to the two walkways that run around the interior of the dome. The upper walkway is 20 m. above the lower one, which is about 53 m. above the floor of the Basilica. The grandiose architecture of the building and its works of art can be admired from here (see pp. 178-179).

The visitor can proceed up the steep passageway between the two shells of the dome to the panoramic terrace at the base of the lantern.

Inscriptions commemorating many illustrious visitors and the Holy Years are on the walls of the downward route.

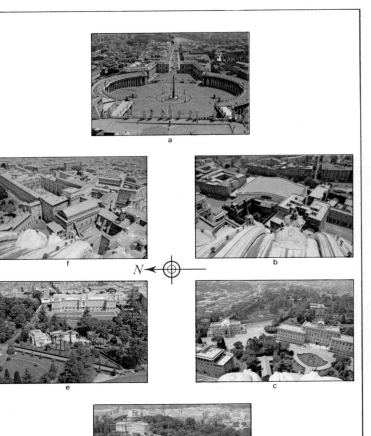

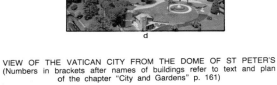

VIEW OF THE VATICAN CITY FROM THE DOME OF ST PETER'S
(Numbers in brackets after names of buildings refer to text and plan
of the chapter "City and Gardens" p. 161)

a St Peter's Square

b
- Palace of the Holy Office
- Papal Audience Hall (7)
- Teutonic College (5)
- Canonical Palace (Sacristy) (8)

c
- Tower of St John (23)
- First Vatican Radio station (21)
- Ethiopian College (18)
- Railway station (14)
- Mosaic Studio (13)
- Government Palace (15)
- Courthouse (11)
- Church of Santo Stefano degli Abissini (12)

d
- Offices of the Vatican radio station (27)
- Fountain of the Eagle (32)
- Bronze statue of St Peter (16)
- House of the Gardener (17)

e
- Vatican Pinacoteca (41)
- Pontifical Academy of Sciences (33)
- and Casina of Pius IV (34)

f
- Vatican Museums (40-50)
- Borgia Tower
- Apostolic Palace (3)
- Sistine Chapel (44)

Sacristy and Treasury

plan ←

The entrance to the Sacristy and Treasury is located at the end of the left aisle of the church (22, see plan p. 173). It is indicated by a sign.

MAIN SACRISTY

The *Main Sacristy*, an octagonal room designed by Carlo Marchionni, was inaugurated in 1784. The fluted columns were brought from Hadrian's villa near Tivoli. From here we proceed to the *Sacristy of the Canons*. The canons are an ecclesiastical body responsible for the administration of the Basilica. On specified days and at certain hours, the canons recite the official prayers of the Church in the Basilica (see p. 176: 16).

58

59

TREASURY
(Historical-Artistic Museum)

plan →

This collection of monuments, vessels and holy objects bears witness to the devotion of Christians throughout the centuries to St Peter and his tomb. Unfortunately, a large number of the objects donated have been dispersed in the various lootings of the Basilica that have occurred throughout its history. The present arrangement of the museum, organized by the Vatican Chapter (college of canons), dates from 1975.

From a small entrance hall we proceed to the

I, ROOM OF THE COLUMN

I

On the left is a *spiral marble column* decorated with vine leaves; it dates from the late imperial period (4th century). It is one of the twelve columns which surrounded the "Confession" in the old Basilica. Eight of these columns were placed in the large recesses in the pillars of the dome of the new St Peter's (see pp. 178: 36-39).

1

Before leaving, it is worth noting high up on the right the *weathercock of old St Peter's*, of gilt metal. During the pontificate of Leo IV (847-855), it stood on the bell tower (demolished in 1608) of the Basilica.

2

II, ROOM OF ST PETER'S THRONE

II

An elevated show-case, which the visitor enters to observe the objects exhibited in the smaller show-case, contains:

The so-called *dalmatic of Charlemagne* (a holy garment worn for important ceremonies), a masterpiece of 11th-century Byzantine embroidery (dark blue cloth embroidered with gold and silver silk). The front portrays Christ the Judge, surrounded by His heavenly court. On the back there are embroidered representations of the Transfiguration (Christ appears above the Apostles Peter, John and James, who are blinded by His splendor), Christ between Moses and Elijah and in the center, Jesus with the Apostles and Jesus with St Peter.

1

A *pectoral reliquary in the form of a cross*, preserved in a gold casket decorated with enamel and pearls. It is a reliquary of the wood of the Holy Cross and is known as the reliquary of Constantine because of the Emperor's image which appears at the lower left. Inside the double doors of the casket are the embossed figures of Jesus and the Virgin Mary with the Apostles and martyrs. These are examples of Byzantine goldsmiths' art of the 6th and 7th centuries. The two supporting angels are in the style of Bernini.

2

The *cross of Emperor Justin II* (called the "Crux Vaticana"), studded with

3

plan
→

II   precious stones. It is a reliquary of the wood of the Holy Cross donated by the Byzantine Emperor to the old Basilica in the second half of the 6th century. The names of the Emperor and his wife and *socia* Sophia are carved on the arms of the cross.

4   Gold *reliquary in the form of a double cross*, containing wood of the Holy Cross. Byzantine art of late 10th - early 11th centuries.

5   *St Peter's throne*. This is a copy of the oak-wood throne donated by the Emperor Charles the Bald to Pope John VIII on December 25, 875 on the occasion of his coronation in St Peter's. The finely pierced ivory bands which decorate the legs and back of the chair are work of the school that flourished at the court of Charles the Bald. The eighteen ivory plaques on the front of the chair were added a little later and may originally have been part of one of Constantine's thrones. They represent the twelve labors of Hercules (the mythical hero of ancient Greece) and six monsters. In the 12th century it was widely believed to be the actual throne of St Peter. Although historical research subsequently established its Carolingian origin, the little throne has always been considered a symbol of the authority of St Peter's successors. The original throne was placed inside the bronze throne created for this purpose by Bernini (see p. 177: 29).

6   *Fragments of an ivory diptych*, Byzantine style (11th-14th centuries?), donated in 1464 by the Greek Cardinal Bessarion, promoter of the Council of Ferrara-Florence (1438-1439-1442) for the unification of the Western and Eastern Churches (see p. 172: 4). On one side are Christ and the Virgin Mary, John the Baptist, Peter and Paul; on the other side are two bishops and St. Demetrius and St. Onofrius, who were particularly venerated by the Eastern Church.

III, CHAPEL OF THE BENEFICIARIES

III

1   Facing the entrance is a *plaster cast of the Pietà* of Michelangelo by Francesco and Luigi Mercatali (1934); thanks to this copy the original was faithfully restored after being damaged in 1972 (see p. 181:57). On the left wall is a
2   *tabernacle*, originally from the ancient Basilica and attributed to Donatello
3   (15th century). The *altarpiece* above the altar is by Girolamo Muziano (16th century). It represents Christ giving the keys to St. Peter. Above the door is a lovely Neoclassical painting of Jesus and St. Peter, called the *Quo vadis?*, by Antonio Cavallucci, a Roman painter of the late 18th century.

IV, ROOM OF SIXTUS IV

IV

1   The splendid *bronze tomb of Sixtus IV*, patron of the arts and founder of the Sistine Chapel and the Vatican Library, can be admired both from floor level and from a balcony. The work is signed by the artist, Antonio del Pollaiolo, and dated 1493. It was commissioned for the old Basilica by Cardinal Giuliano della Rovere, the nephew of the Pope, who later became Pope Julius II. Surrounding the figure of the Pope are the three theological virtues (Hope, Faith and Charity), and the four cardinal virtues (Prudence, Fortitude, Justice and Temperance). The base is decorated with reliefs representing Theology, Philosophy and the liberal arts: the three literary arts (Dialectics, Rhetoric and Grammar), and the four sciences (Arithmetic, Astrology, Music and Geometry), which were the seven disciplines of the medieval scholastic system, to which the artist has added Perspective, a new science.

V, ROOM OF THE RELIQUARIES

V

1   In the large *show-case facing the entrance,* from the right are: large 18-19th century frame in embossed silver, which contained a Slavic icon (see p. 186: VII/2). A wooden frame of the reliquary of St Veronica, perhaps of the 14th century (see p. 178:38). A painting with a gold background of St Peter and St Paul (much restored, 14th century).

2   On the left wall, a *wooden crucifix* (14th century) from the old Basilica.

3-6   The four *show-cases* contain reliquaries of historical and artistical value:

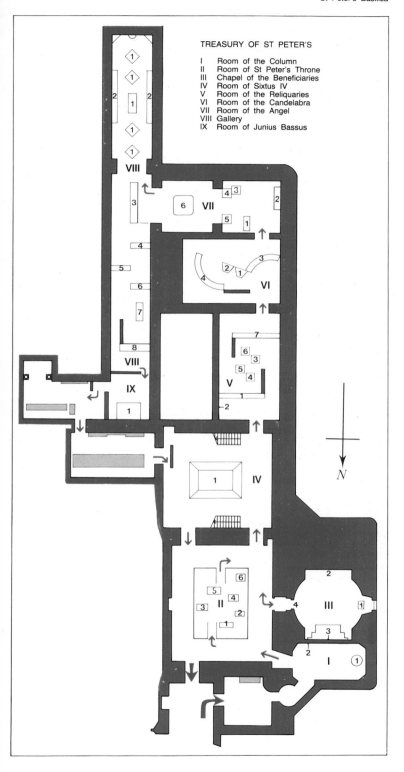

TREASURY OF ST PETER'S

I Room of the Column
II Room of St Peter's Throne
III Chapel of the Beneficiaries
IV Room of Sixtus IV
V Room of the Reliquaries
VI Room of the Candelabra
VII Room of the Angel
VIII Gallery
IX Room of Junius Bassus

St Peter's Basilica

3 *Show-case*: Rock crystal altar cross (18th century). Piscatory ring of Sixtus IV (15th century).

4 *Show-case:* Spheres of copper open-work (12th-16th centuries) which served as hand warmers for the canons. Reliquary of the Holy Cross, Roman gold-smiths' work (15th century). Reliquary of the Holy Spear (Venetian, 14th century), rock crystal and silver, containing the head of the spear which wounded Christ (see p. 176:15).

5 *Show-case*: Reliquary bust of St Luke in embossed silver (13th century). Gothic chalice in silver and enamel (from Viterbo - ca. 1334-1342). Reliquary of the canonized Popes Leo I, II, III, and IV, 18th-century casket of gilt metal with silver ornamentation.

6 *Show-case*: Reliquary of the Childhood of Christ (16th century). *Reliquary of St Blase*: a silver tabernacle made in Naples, 1492. Reliquary of St Sebastian, gold and silver casket in the form of a Renaissance building (15th century).

7 In the large *show-case near the exit* are: two musical manuscripts written in the first half of the 16th century of the Cappella Giulia (a group of singers and musicians), founded by Julius II in 1513 to provide music for the choral services in St Peter's. (This group is still active today.) The first manuscript, to the right, contains thirty-five liturgical compositions by various authors. The second, to the left, contains seventeen motets. In the center of the show-case is a late 17th-century ivory crucifix.

VI ## VI, ROOM OF THE CANDELABRA

1, 2 On pedestals between two large show-cases are two *large candelabra* in gilt bronze, attributed to Antonio and Piero del Pollaiolo (15th century).

3, 4 The two *large show-cases* contain two groups of candelabra. These were used at the high altar of the Basilica for solemn rites until the pontificate of
3 Pius XII. The *first group of candelabra*, gilt bronze with an altar cross, are the work of Sebastiano Torrigiani (ca. 1585). For a long time, this style inspired
4 innumerable altar candelabra. The *second group of candelabra*, of gilt bronze and with an altar cross, are signed (1581) by Antonio Gentile da Faenza. The two candlesticks placed beside it are also attributed to him. The other four candelabra were made by Carlo Spagna (1670-1672), after drawings by Gian Lorenzo Bernini. The scenes of the Passion engraved on medallions of rock crystal set into the pedestals are by Valerio Belli.

VII ## VII, ROOM OF THE ANGEL

1 In the *show-case to the left of the entrance* are the gilt bronze statues of St Peter and St Paul by Sebastiano Torrigiani (1585).

2 In the *show-case* along the wall to the right of the entrance are two manu-scripts from the Cappella Giulia and a Paleoslavic icon representing Saints Peter and Paul; the figures in the lower part of the painting are probably Saints Cyril and Methodius, inventors of the Cyrillic alphabet and translators of the Bible into Slavic; the figure between them, in front of St Nicholas, is probably Queen Helen of Serbia (13th century).

3-5 The following three *show-cases* contain reliquaries:

3 *Show-case*: Two 18th-century Neapolitan reliquaries in gilt metal. A 17th-century amber monstrance.

4 *Show-case*: A reliquary cross known as the "Palace Cross" (15th century). It is made of rock crystal, and has a piece of the wood of the Holy Cross at the center.

5 *Show-case*: Two monstrances, one of rock crystal (17th century) and one of gold filigree (18th century). A silver reliquary of the Lombard and Milanese saints in the form of a Baroque altar.

In the second part of the room is a clay *angel*, modelled by Bernini (ca. 1673). It is the model for one of the two angels of the Tabernacle in the Chapel of the Sacrament in St Peter's (see p. 179:48).

VIII, GALLERY

To the right, the five *show-cases* in the middle of the room contain splendid monumental monstrances, reliquaries, chalices and pyx made of precious metals studded with jewels (18th-19th centuries).   1

In the two *show-cases* facing each other along the walls are holy vestments, tiaras (triple crowns worn during the most important religious services), and hangings embroidered with gold and silver (late 18th century).   2

Halfway down the gallery in a *large show-case* behind the entrance, is an altar-frontal embroidered with gold and silver, representing St Peter and St Paul (late 19th century).   3

Further on in another *show-case*, we find monstrances, reliquaries and chalices of the 17th and 18th centuries. Silver hammer and trowel, with a cast of the hand of Paul VI, used by this Pope for the opening and closing of the Holy Door in the Jubilee of 1975. They are the work of the Hungarian sculptor Amerigo Tot. The *York Chalice*, a large cup of chiselled gold studded with 130 diamonds, by the Roman goldsmith Luigi Valadier, gift of Cardinal Henry Stuart, Duke of York (end of the 18th century).   4

In the next *show-case* we find the Triple Crown (papal tiara with three crowns symbolizing the three powers of the Pope: Father of Kings, Ruler of the World, Vicar of Christ), dating from the 18th century. On St Peter's day (June 29th), it is used to crown the bronze statue of St Peter in the Basilica (see p. 178:40) together with the enormous clasp (or *"razionale"*) for a cope, also for the bronze St Peter (19th century). Two crowns of diamonds and pearls, donated by the French Catholics to Pius XII. Reliquary (17th century) of the "Holy Thorns" from the crown of the Passion of Christ. Gold chalice, donated by King Louis of Portugal to Leo XIII (1883), a copy of the one in "manuelino" style from the church of Belem, with carved scenes from the New Testament.   5

Another *show-case* with pectoral crosses of various epochs and provenance, and a "razionale" with an enormous topaz in its center (18th century).   6

In still another *show-case* we find the so-called Crown of the Immaculate Virgin, with twelve stars made of diamonds mounted in gold, donated by French Catholics to Pope Pius IX on the occasion of the 50th anniversary of the proclamation of the dogma of the Immaculate Conception (December 8, 1854). Above the crown is a votive lamp set with pearls of unusual size. This is a Roman work of the second half of the 19th century.   7

In the *show-case* is the chalice donated to Pope John XXIII by Charles de Gaulle (1959). Chinese chalice and paten with fine enamel work, donated by Cardinal Mariano Rampolla, secretary of state of Leo XIII.   8

IX, ROOM OF JUNIUS BASSUS

IX

The *sarcophagus of Junius Bassus* (d. 359), prefect of Rome who was converted to Christianity, is a marble block found in the area of the "Confession" (see p. 177:34) with reliefs representing ten episodes from the Old and the New Testaments. It is one of the most important documents of the art and faith of the early Christians.   1

plan
→

The Vatican Grottoes

The Grottoes can be reached through a passageway in the pillar of St Longinus (36, see plan p. 173).

1 2	The Grottoes are situated in the area between the floor level of the old Constantinian Basilica and the nave of the present Basilica. They extend to approximately half the length of the nave. The oldest part dates from the 6th century, when Gregory the Great raised the level of the presbytery to create a *crypt* around the apse of the Constantinian building to provide access to the tomb of St Peter (see below: 12). The *semicircular ambulatory*, which runs externally and parallel to the 6th-century crypt, as well as the main crypt divided into three aisles, date from the end of the 16th century. During the reign of Pius XII, ten rooms were added to the north and south of the main crypt to house early Christian sarcophagi found under St Peter's, as well as architectural and ornamental fragments and various monuments from the old Basilica.

3-6 Four passages lead from the semicircular ambulatory to four *chapels* cut out of the base of the piers supporting the dome of the Basilica (see 36-39, plan p. 173). Between the chapels in the piers we find other chapels which may be
7 seen through gates. The first on the right is the *Chapel of Saints Benedict,*
8 *Cirillus and Metodius*, compatrons of Europe; next are the *Polish Chapel* and
9 the *Irish Chapel*.

10 At the center of the semicircle, to the right, is the chapel with the *tomb of Pius*
11 *XII* and opposite it, the *Chapel of St Peter*, or Clementine Chapel, enlarged and decorated by Clement VIII, which projects radially into the Constantinian apse and comes nearest to the burial place of the Apostle. Behind the gate above the altar we can see the back (in Phrygian marble and porphyry) of the monument which Constantine built around the early "*aedicula*" on the site of the Saint's burial place (see p. 177:33 and p. 190:5). Near the end of the
12 ambulatory is the *Czech Chapel* with the tomb of Cardinal Beran, Archbishop of Prague (d. 1969) and a fresco of the school of Pietro Cavallini (14th century), representing the so-called "*Madonna della Bocciata*" whose swollen face is popularly attributed to a sacrilegious blow from a bowling ball thrown
13 by a drunken soldier. Next are the *Chapel of the Madonna "delle Partorienti"*
14 (the fresco is attributed to Melozzo da Forlì) and the *Lithuanian Chapel*.

Entering the nave, we can see through a large glass partition, surmounted by an arch decorated with two angels and two marble lions from the old Basilica, the Niche of the Palliums (see p. 177: 32, 33). This place is the historical motivation and the spiritual center of the whole of St Peter's Basilica.

16, 17 In the right aisle we find the *tombs of John XXIII, Christine of Sweden* (see p.
18 180:55) *and Charlotte of Savoy-Lusignan,* Queen of Cyprus (d. 1487). Farther
19, 20 on are the *sarcophagus of Benedict XV* (d. 1922), and the *tomb of John Paul I* (1978), decorated with Renaissance reliefs. Opposite is the early-Christian
21 sarcophagus in which lie the remains of *Marcellus II* (1555) and, in the next
22 space, the bare *tombstone of Paul VI* (d. 1978). Proceeding further along the
23 aisle, on the left is the opening that leads to the *Hungarian Chapel*.

24, 25 In the left aisle (south) are the *tomb of Pius XI* (d. 1939) and the *tomb of the last Stuarts* (see p. 176: 11).

26 At the end of the nave is the *statue of Pius VI kneeling in prayer*, the last work of Canova (1822).

At the end of the side aisles (not open to the public) are sarcophagi of major
27 historical and artistic importance. The *tomb of Emperor Otto II* (d. 983) is a simple early Christian sarcophagus (for a description of the cover, see p. 175:
28 9). His great grandson, the first German Pope, *Gregory V* (d. 999) lies in a 4th-

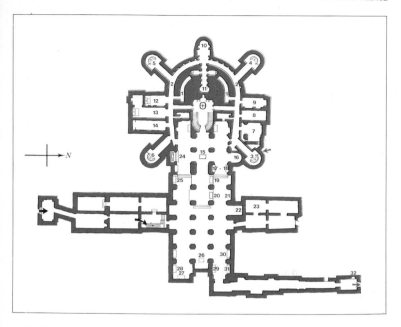

HOLY VATICAN GROTTOES

century sarcophagus decorated with reliefs of episodes from the New Testament. The *tomb of Nicholas III* (d. 1280) is a 4th-century sarcophagus, **29** originally made for the married couple represented at the center, at the feet of Christ. The two final tombs surmounted by reclining statues of the dead Popes are that of *Nicholas V* (d. 1455) from the Renaissance and *Boniface VIII* (d. **30, 31** 1303) by Arnolfo di Cambio.

In the exit corridor, on the left are two column bases of the Constantinian basilica and on the right the sarcophagus with the lying figure of Calixtus III. And, further on, we can admire the imposing *St Peter Enthroned*. It is a statue **32** of a pagan philosopher (3rd century) with head and hands carrying the attributes of Peter substituted for the originals in the 16th century.

plan
→

The Pre-Constantinian Necropolis

In 1940, during work on the tomb of Pius XI (see p. 188: 24) in the Vatican Grottoes, traces of a Roman necropolis were discovered (see 2, plan pp. 6-7). Previous evidence of the existence of this necropolis had been found as early as the rebuilding of the Basilica in the 16th and 17th centuries. Pius XII ordered excavations (1939-1949), which brought to light two rows of chamber tombs with their entrances aligned from east to west (along the axis of the future Basilica). The level of the ground drops noticeably from north to south indicating that the necropolis had been situated on a hillside. The orientation of the mausoleums also shows that the main road around which the necropolis developed had been located further downhill, parallel to the one that visitors follow today.

1 The road must have run close to the circus of Nero and Caligula (see 1, plan pp. 6-7), which is mentioned in the inscription on the façade of *Mausoleum A*, the first to the east, which its owner wanted built "in Vaticano ad circum" (in the Vatican near the circus).

In order to build the foundations for St Peter's Basilica a part of the hill had to be levelled and portions of the burial grounds, which were still in use, had to be filled in and reinforced with supports. This demonstrates the determination of the founders to erect the Basilica on this precise area, which tradition indicated as the site of the tomb of St Peter.

2 The mausoleums, richly decorated with frescoes, stuccoes and mosaics, originally belonged to rich pagan families, but later some became the property of Christians. The beginning of Christian influence can be see in *Mausoleum M*, in the mosaic representations of Christian themes: the Fisherman, Jonah and the whale and Christ-Helios (sun), symbol of the Resurrection. The mosaics date from between the first half of the 2nd century and the period of the construction of the Constantinian Basilica, in the third of fourth decade of the 4th century. There is also evidence that tombs dating from the 1st century had been situated to the east and west of the Basilica, as well as in the area beneath the papal altar (see p. 177: 32), where some simple tombs dug out of the earth have been found.

3
4
5
6,7 This small area was once part of a larger burial ground for people who were too poor to afford walled tombs. At the beginning of the 2nd century, this area (4 m. × 7 m.) was surrounded by rich family tombs built on the site of the earlier cemetery. Evidently this small area (called *"Campo P"* by the archeologists who discovered it) was deliberately kept free. In the middle of the 2nd century, the west side of this area was enclosed by a wall (known as *"Muro Rosso"* because of the colour of the plaster), in which a simple monument was constructed, formed of two superimposed niches, separated by a marble slab and sustained by two small columns. This simple *aedicula* stood on the site of a simple grave dug in the earth. In ancient Rome such aediculae were built in the walls of the mausoleums over individual tombs. In the 3rd century this aedicula was further embellished with marble decorations, and two small walls, called *"Muro g"* to the north and *"Muro s"* to the south, were built next to it. In the 4th century, when the first Basilica was constructed, the sacred character of the small monument was clearly recognized. The Constantinian Basilica was built on this site, even though the sloping terrain, already occupied by the pagan and Christian necropolises, made it

▷ PRE-CONSTANTINIAN NECROPOLIS

(The archeologists have indicated the mausoleums of the necropolis with letters of the Greek and Latin alphabets.)

1 Mausoleum A "in Vaticano ad circum"
2 Mausoleum M, early Christian influence

Site of St Peter's burial place
3 "Campo P"
4 "Muro Rosso"
5 "Aedicula"
6 "Muro g"
7 "Muro s"
⊕ "Confession"

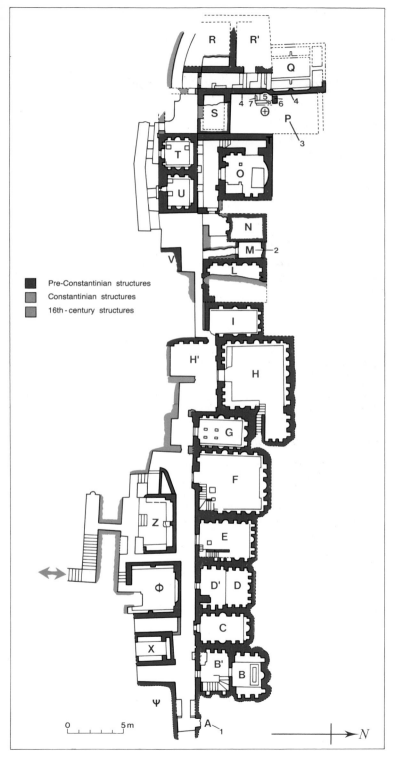

Pre-Constantinian structures
Constantinian structures
16th-century structures

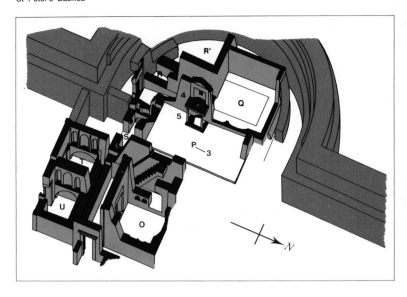

RECONSTRUCTION OF "CAMPO P" AND THE CONSTANTINIAN APSE

Site of St Peter's burial place
3 "Campo P"
4 "Muro Rosso"
5 "Aedicula"

■ Pre-Constantinian structure
■ Constantinian structures

unsuitable. In fact the Basilica was deliberately constructed in such a way that the small monument would remain visible at the center of the presbytery. This was the same monument that had been erected in the 2nd century over the burial place of St Peter, near the circus where the Apostle was probably martyred.

The little monument to St Peter (5) stood alone at the center of the transept of the Constantinian Basilica. The walls which originally surrounded it were demolished (including the "Muro g" (6), in which a locule had been carved out to preserve what were believed to be the remains of St Peter). The monument itself was faced with Phrygian marble on the back (west) and sides (north and south), and a baldachin supported by spiral marble columns was built over it (see p. 178, and p. 183: I/1). Over the centuries, three altars have been built over this shrine: those of Gregory I (590-604), Calixtus II (1119-1124) and Clement VIII (1592-1605). This last is the present papal altar called of the "Confession" (see pp. 177: 32-33), which stands over the tomb of the Apostle.

List of popes mentioned in the text

Adrian I (772-795), 89
Alexander VI, *Rodrigo de Borja* (1492-1503), 85, 86, 89, 90, 158, 168
Alexander VII, *Fabio Chigi* (1665-67), 156, 170, 177
Alexander VIII, *Pietro Ottoboni* (1689-91), 102

Benedict XIII, *Pietro Francesco Orsini* (1724-30), 162
Benedict XIV, *Prospero Lambertini* (1740-58), 2, 14, 34, 101, 110, 112
Benedict XV, *Giacomo della Chiesa* (1914-22), 140, 164, 176, 188
Boniface VIII, *Benedetto Caetani* (1294-1303), 189
Boniface IX, *Pietro Tomacelli* (1389-1404), 89

Calixtus II, *Guy de Bourgogne* (1119-24), 178, 192
Calixtus III, *Alonso de Borja* (1455-58), 189
Celestine V, *Pietro del Morrone* (1294), 105
Clement VII, *Giulio de' Medici* (1523-34), 14, 46, 70, 72, 75, 93, 108, 110, 158, 159
Clement VIII, *Ippolito Aldobrandini* (1592-1605), 170, 176, 177, 188, 192
Clement IX, *Giulio Rospigliosi* (1667-69), 40, 112
Clement X, *Emilio Altieri* (1670-76), 156
Clement XI, *G. Francesco Albani* (1700-21), 14, 34, 38, 162
Clement XII, *Lorenzo Corsini* (1730-40), 14, 102
Clement XIII, *Carlo Rezzonico* (1758-69), 3, 14, 102, 179
Clement XIV, *G. Vincenzo Antonio (Lorenzo) Ganganelli* (1769-74), 3, 14, 37, 39, 41, 43, 153

Eugene III, *Bernardo perhaps of the Paganelli of Montemagno* (1145-53), 2
Eugene IV, *Gabriele Condulmer* (1431-47), 165, 172

Gregory I, *Gregory the Great* (590-604), 76, 84, 176, 178, 188, 192
Gregory V, *Bruno of the Dukes of Carinthia* (996-999), 188
Gregory VII, *Hildebrand* (1073-85), 180
Gregory IX, *Ugolino of the Counts of Segni* (1227-41), 76
Gregory XI, *Pierre Roger de Beaufort* (1370-78), 89
Gregory XIII, *Ugo Boncompagni* (1572-85), 71-74, 79, 82, 89, 93, 164, 169, 170, 179
Gregory XVI, *Bartolomeo Alberto (Mauro) Cappellari* (1831-46), 14-15, 29, 50, 101, 106, 107, 113, 117

Innocent III, *Lotario of the Counts of Segni* (1198-1216), 2, 83, 162
Innocent VIII, *G.B. Cybo* (1484-92), 2, 14, 38, 41, 43, 46, 58, 165, 176
Innocent XI, *Benedetto Odescalchi* (1676-89), 175, 180

John VIII, (872-882), 177, 184
John XXIII, *Angelo Giuseppe Roncalli* (1958-63), 15, 90, 113, 139, 162, 163, 164, 172, 174, 175, 176, 181, 187, 188
John Paul I, *Albino Luciani* (1978), 188
John Paul II, *Karol Wojtyla* (1978 - happily reigning), 15, 162, 163
Julius II, *Giuliano della Rovere* (1503-13), 2, 14, 40-42, 74-79, 82, 83, 84, 86, 93, 97, 107, 159, 167, 168, 171, 184, 186

Leo I, *Leo the Great* (440-461), 75, 84, 162, 177, 186
Leo II (682-683), 177, 186
Leo III (795-816), 78, 89, 166, 177, 186
Leo IV (847-855), 1, 78, 89, 163, 164, 177, 183, 186
Leo X, *Giovanni de' Medici* (1513-21), 2, 36, 70, 75, 76, 79, 80, 82, 89, 92, 110, 168
Leo XI, *Alessandro de' Medici* (1605), 176
Leo XII, *Annibale della Genga* (1823-29), 14, 110, 154, 177
Leo XIII, *Gioacchino Pecci* (1878-1903), 15, 62, 67, 73, 85, 101, 133, 134, 154, 163, 164, 187

Marcellus II, *Marcello Cervini* (1555), 2, 188
Martin V, *Oddone Colonna* (1417-31), 89

List of artists
The artists of the Collection of Modern Religious Art have not been included in this list